All Along the Danube
Expanded Edition

Hippocrene is NUMBER ONE in
International Cookbooks

Africa and Oceania
Best of Regional African Cooking
Egyptian Cooking
Good Food from Australia
Traditional South African Cookery
Taste of Eritrea

Asia and Near East
Afghan Food & Cookery
Best of Goan Cooking
Best of Kashmiri Cooking
The Joy of Chinese Cooking
The Art of South Indian Cooking
The Indian Spice Kitchen
The Art of Persian Cooking
The Art of Israeli Cooking
The Art of Turkish Cooking
The Art of Uzbek Cooking

Mediterranean
Best of Greek Cuisine
Taste of Malta
A Spanish Family Cookbook
Tastes of North Africa

Western Europe
Art of Dutch Cooking
Best of Austrian Cuisine
A Belgian Cookbook
Cooking in the French Fashion (bilingual)
Celtic Cookbook
English Royal Cookbook
The Swiss Cookbook
Traditional Recipes from Old
    England
The Art of Irish Cooking
Traditional Food from Scotland
Traditional Food from Wales
The Scottish-Irish Pub and Hearth
    Cookbook
A Treasury of Italian Cuisine (bilingual)

Scandinavia
Best of Scandinavian Cooking
The Best of Finnish Cooking
The Best of Smorgasbord Cooking
Good Food from Sweden

Central Europe
Best of Albanian Cooking
Best of Croatian Cooking
All Along the Danube
Bavarian Cooking
Traditional Bulgarian Cooking
The Best of Czech Cooking
The Best of Slovak Cooking
The Art of Hungarian Cooking
Art of Lithuanian Cooking
Polish Heritage Cookery
The Best of Polish Cooking
Old Warsaw Cookbook
Old Polish Traditions
Treasury of Polish Cuisine (bilingual)
Poland's Gourmet Cuisine
Taste of Romania
Taste of Latvia

Eastern Europe
The Cuisine of Armenia
The Best of Russian Cooking
Traditional Russian Cuisine (bilingual)
The Best of Ukrainian Cuisine

Americas
Cooking the Caribbean Way
Mayan Cooking
The Honey Cookbook
The Art of Brazilian Cookery
The Art of South American Cookery
Old Havana Cookbook (bilingual)

All Along the Danube

Expanded Edition

MARINA POLVAY

HIPPOCRENE BOOKS, INC.

New York

Second printing, expanded edition, 2002.
Expanded edition ©2000 by Hippocrene Books, Inc.
Hippocrene Books, Inc., paperback edition, 1992.
Copyright© 1979 Marina Polvay.
Originally published by Prentice-Hall, Inc., Englewood Cliffs, NJ.
Cover photograph© Madeline Polss.

For information, address:
Hippocrene Books, Inc.
171 Madison Avenue
New York, NY 10016

ISBN 0-7818-0806-5

Printed in the United States of America.

Acknowledgements

Dedicated to:

Lynne Lumsden, the super editor who gave me the inspiration and incentive, and who never lost faith through all the trials and tribulations of *All Along the Danube.*

With love and gratitude to Joan, without whose drive, research, perseverance, and dedication, this book could not have been written.

To Helena and Roy Choudhry, who unselfishly gave of their time and talents.

And to Brigitta, who loved the Danube, and to Feri who gave me a glimpse of the blue water ...

Executive Researcher and Manuscript Editor (prior to production of the book)—Joan Mittelman
Recipe Editors—Helena and Roy Choudhry

There are so many people who helped to put this book together that inadvertently we may have left someone out; so just accept our thanks with the knowledge that we realize how much you have done, and are a part of the book.

Our sincere thanks go to Mr. Alan Gould of Hilton International for his advice and marvelous help; the Hungarian Tourist Bureau for their many courtesies and help; and Mr. István Fazekas, press attaché of the Hungarian Embassy. We also wish to thank the tourist bureaus of Austria, Germany, Yugoslavia, Rumania, and Bulgaria for their help, cooperation, and inspiration and for providing background material, photographs, and lithographs.

Photography Credits

Black and white photos, artwork, and prints were provided by the following:

German Tourist Office (pages 7, 8, 11, 17, 19, 29, 35, 37, and 45), Austrian Tourist Office (pages 50, 59, 61, 71, 73, 83, 89, 93), Hungarian Tourist Office (pages 3, 172, and 193), Czechoslovakian Tourist Office (pages 107, 113, and 120), Rumanian Tourist Office (pages 245, 247, 249, 251, 253, 257, 260, and 264), Bulgarian Tourist Office (pages 275, 280, 284, 288, 295, 299, and 301), Yugoslavian Tourist Office (pages 213, 219, and 221).

Contents

vii

Preface

THE Danube River is an ageless aquatic phenomenon flowing through the very heart of countries which have the most colorful, turbulent, yet magnificent heritages, and are the cradle of modern civilization.

Countless tribes roamed in the Danube's basin, and nations were spawned on its banks only to vanish later without a trace. All this left an indelible mark on the development and culture of the peoples who remained, and for over two thousand years they have been creating and molding their destinies—those destinies which give such a special fascination to the Danube region.

According to an ancient legend, the Danube "is only blue if one is in love," and couples who meander on the banks of this most romantic of waterways see it as a sparkling azure. Others say dreamily that it is an iridescent marriage of blue and silver blended into a shimmering mosaic of color.

The Danube is a majestic, intriguing river even if its true grayish-brown color does not quite equal the enthusiastic vision of young lovers. Sometimes at sunrise its ripples appear to be bright rose or yellow, and at sunset its waves are brushed with burnished copper—muddy waters bathed in a mystic radiance.

To see the Danube for the first time from the fairytale-like setting of the Royal Castle in Budapest is an unforgettable and deeply moving experience. I was a little girl when my family came to Budapest, and I was led high upon the Castle Hill by the loving, but firm hand of my nurse. I looked down from the ramparts of the Fishermen's Bastion onto the wide expanse of the Danube, spanned by incredibly beautiful bridges. I think that my romance with the river, its people, its cities, and its countries began at that moment.

Growing up in Budapest meant being involved with the river, which bisects the city. Holding fast to my nurse's hand, I would walk along the high embankments, listening enchanted as she told me tales of the river and its people.

Barges with geranium-filled windows, laundry billowing in the breeze, and friendly, waving people would lumber by, while swift pleasure craft, rowboats, and stately passenger steamers would pass us en route to other charming lands.

Kati neni, my nurse, was from Transylvania, the land of many legends and mysteries, and she wove her tales with the natural ability of her people. She spoke of treacherous rapids, great heroes and monsters, and wispy maidens who appeared to the boatmen at night. The seed of interest was planted in my child's mind and as I grew older, so grew my fascination with the Danube. Later, as a teenager, I skimmed the water in a skiff, helped propel a kayak, and sped in motorboats around lovely St. Margaret island in the center of the river at Budapest.

Later I had a chance to take a luxury steamer to Vienna, Linz, and Passau, but my real dream was still unfulfilled: I always wanted to make the long trip from the birth of my river to its Delta and to the Black Sea. Shortly before World War II, part of my dream was realized when on a visit to Belgrade. I climbed up to the Kali-Magdan Fortress, beneath which stretches the wide expanse of the Danube and its mighty tributary, the Sava. The view is breathtaking as the two rivers join majestically and rush together toward the sea.

I left Budapest during the war, and like many of the people from that area, fled to the west. I lived in Austria for a while where to my great delight, while visiting relatives in Linz, we stayed aboard one of the Danube river steamers, docked and used as a hostelery. The water lapped gently at the ship's bow and at night as I would stand at the railing visualizing the "willies" (mythical beings believed to haunt the Danube at that spot), my yearning to travel the length of that river continued.

However, like so many others, instead of going back east, I came to the United States, joining scores of immigrants from Hungary, Rumania, Yugoslavia, Bulgaria, Russia, Poland, and Austria. Soon I found out that the heritage and customs which people brought with them from Eastern Europe had been strongly instilled by loving families into the second and even third generations of Americans. I still hear friends and acquaintances talk nostalgically about the music, the spirited dances, but most of all about the marvelous food and drink of their native countries. Quite often when I speak to audiences about the foods of the Danube lands, eyes light up, and even strangers remark with glee that they do remember a certain dish which grandmother used to make, and that it must be the dish which I spoke about. *Paprikas, Ghivech, Razsnichi, Strudels,* and *Kugelhupf,* are some of the mouthwatering memories cherished by peoples of the Dnaube.

Speaking of, and preparing these marvelous dishes, however, made me homesick for the Danube: I still wanted to travel her length from beginning to end.

Finally, only three years ago, my dream came true. I stood, bewitched, at the well at Donauschingen, where two small brooks unite and give birth to the Danube. I wandered through the lovely Black Forest and, along with the children, gathered mushrooms, finding the same delight as they in the search for the delectable fungi.

At Regensburg where the Danube meets its two tributaries I felt I was really on my way to a great, wondrous adventure. And quite an adventure it turned out to be. I drove from Regensburg to Passau and then to Vienna. In Vienna I boarded the handsome passenger ship which took me back to Budapest, and all the poignant, marvelous memories of childhood and young womanhood returned. I gazed down at the Danube from the Castle Hill—

the very spot from which I first fell in love with the river. I walked on its banks and remembered the gentle hands of my nurse and her soulful tales.

Without much hesitation, I made arrangements, obtained visas, and boarded the *Carpati* for a nine-day journey toward the Black Sea. The *Carpati* is a comfortable, though not a luxurious, ship like the Rhine cruisers, and the food is both international and Rumanian—plentiful and tasty. People are friendly and there is music, singing, and dancing aboard.

My excitement mounted when the ship pulled away from the dock, beginning its long and sentimental journey. I didn't sleep much, preferring to spend most of my hours on deck, not wishing to miss a single hill or embankment or outline of an ancient castle. Though the river steamer travelled quite briskly downstream, there was still time to absorb the beauty of the landscape and wave at the passing barges—seemingly with the same geraniums in the windows, the same laundry hanging on ropes strung on decks. There were fewer pleasure craft, but the fishermens' dugouts were plentiful once we left Budapest and its industrial suburbs.

Past Budapest, the Danube becomes unruly, forks into many arms, skirts innumerable islands, swirls around floating islets and spreads far and wide, creating backwater and swamps. But the cruise ships, barges, and other craft glide easily through regulated and confined channels, while wild birds soar from their momentarily disturbed habitats.

Belgrade is a major stop, with the mighty Kali-Magdan Fortress looming over the river as we approached the city. Here the Sava and the Danube are joined at the foot of the Fortress. Belgrade itself is a mostly modern, bustling metropolis and I could scarcely wait for the ship to continue toward *Djerdap* or the Iron Gate— one of the most beautiful places on earth. It is a gorge where once the rapids ran wild and ships which dared challenge the turbulent waters were shattered. Today the beauty is in the calm waters of the man-made lake and hydroelectric dam, and locks which now let the ships pass safely through. Here Yugoslavia and Rumania are on opposite banks of the Danube which continues serenely through the gorge and toward the Transylvanian wall. As if weary of its torturous course, the Danube slows down after the Iron Gate and skirts Bulgaria—the land that is more eastern and Balkan in flavor than any of her neighbors. On the Bulgarian side, the white banks are chalk configurations. And here the Danube flows through a plain skirting the giant Carpathian Mountains. From Galati to the Black Sea, the Danube proceeds with great dignity. At Tulcea in Rumania it separates into three branches which form the dense marshlands of the Delta, 1600 square miles of swampland and primeval wilderness where swamp people hide among reeds, and several nationalities live side by side. Herons, pelicans, and other aquatic birds inhabit the area, and they fly off in great flocks, often frightened by approaching vessels. One of the branches, the Sulina, is now navigable and a lighthouse marks the end of a 1700-mile kaleidoscopic journey.

For me, it was over far too soon, but I had made my pilgrimage, had travelled the length of the Danube. I had met the people, ate their food and enjoyed their hospitality.

MARINA POLVAY
Miami Shores, Florida

Weight and Volume Equivalents

Common Units of Volume

1 bushel	=	4 pecks
1 peck	=	8 quarts
1 gallon	=	4 quarts
1 quart	=	2 pints
	=	946.4 milliliters
1 pint	=	2 cups
1 cup	=	16 tablespoons
	=	2 gills
	=	8 fluid ounces
	=	236.6 milliliters
1 tablespoon	=	3 teaspoons
	=	½ fluid ounce
	=	14.8 milliliters
1 teaspoon	=	4.9 milliliters
1 liter	=	1000 milliliters
	=	1.06 quarts

Common Units of Weight

1 gram	=	0.035 ounces
1 kilogram	=	2.21 pounds
1 ounce	=	28.35 grams
1 pound	=	453.59 grams

EUROPE'S longest river, the Danube, an enchanting aquatic thoroughfare, has a humble beginning in the Black Forest near the ancient town of Donauschingen, where two bubbling brooks—Brege and Brigach—are united with a crystal clear spring. The spring, surrounded by an ornate wrought iron fence and a decorative balustraded wall, has been designated the origin of the great river, which twists and turns through mountains, valleys, and many countries on its way to the Black Sea.

Donau, Duna, Dunaj, Dunarea, Dunav, or Dunay: The name is old—older than any of the countries it touches—and historians trace the root of the name to the Celts, who lived on the river's shores, and to the earliest Indo-European languages, in which "Danu" means "river of flowing water."

This river, steeped in history, has seen it all: the Etruscans, the Visigoths, the Celts, and the Roman legions, who crossed it on their way to the Rhine. The ancestors of these people, who settled all along the Danube, still consider it their own river, regardless of the country they come from or what name they give to the river.

Today, the "Danubian Cuisine" is a marvelous blend of Austrian, Hungarian, Czechoslovakian, Yugoslavian, and Rumanian cookery. All these countries were once part of the sprawling Austro-Hungarian Empire, ruled for centuries by the House of Hapsburg. The Empire no longer exists, but the gastronomy of the countries that lie in the path of the Danube still reflects its influence.

Before the Hapsburgs conquered Hungary, Czechoslovakia, Yugoslavia, and Rumania, they were domains of the Hungarian Kingdom, and then, along with Hungary, they were absorbed by the Hapsburgs. For a millennium, there was so much migration, upheaval, and mingling of nations along the Danube and the Black Sea that almost every village, hamlet, and town has its own marvelous history, customs, legends, and way of cooking.

The Greeks influenced the development of Rumanian, Bulgarian, and Yugoslavian religion, culture, and cuisine. Greek monks brought Christianity and new dishes to the unsettled lands. The Italian gastronomy spread from Venice along the Adriatic coast to the walled-in cities of Ragusa and Spoleto. From the Asian steppes came the Mongol hordes, who left their own culinary mark on the countries they pillaged, and the Slavs who settled along the Danube wielded their own influence on the cuisine of many nations.

However, the most significant contribution to the Balkan and to the Hungarian gastronomy has been made by the Turks, who brought with them the pepper pods that were called "Turkish Pepper" and that are now known everywhere as "Hungarian Paprika." Turks also introduced coffee to the Western World; the very first coffee houses were opened in Vienna and Budapest during the Turkish occupation.

Nevertheless, there is a native cuisine. Before World War I, the nobility of Bulgaria, Rumania, Hungary, and Yugoslavia customarily employed French chefs, and there are many so-called "native" dishes that may be traced to Provence, Normandy, or Brittany.

The Danube, which flows sometimes serenely, sometimes with turbulence, through that region is a fascinating, moody river which is a seemingly inexhaustible source of food, transportation, poetry, music, and romance to the people who live "all along the Danube."

Old Budapest, circa mid-17th Century

CHAPTER  1

THE BLACK FOREST:
The Land of
Hansel and Gretel
and Cuckoo
Clocks

THE Danube emerges shyly as a bubbling spring in the Black Forest, near the fairy tale-like town of Donaushingen, which is surrounded by 3,200 foot high mountains. Here two crystal-clear brooks, Brege and Brigach, are united with the spring, giving birth to one of the most romantic rivers in the world.

For about thirty kilometers, the Danube remains a brook; then it disappears under the Schwabian Jura hills, which block its way. It emerges a few kilometers further and starts to pick up tributaries, which are fed by Lake Constance, the cradle of the Rhine. The Danube flows alongside doll-like villages, beneath footbridges banked by geraniums so brightly hued that they appear almost unreal.

The Black Forest region of Germany is a cradle of fairy tales and legends. The magnificent forests hide many mysteries and have been irresistible to poets, storytellers, and raconteurs since time immemorial. The gingerbread villages and towns of that region may seem somewhat unreal, but these are ancient, sturdy buildings that have housed generations of Black Forest families. There is a saying here, "A house is forever," and the people think that a house should serve a family until the stones crumble. Atop hills and mountains sit dark reminders of the past: castles and baronial halls that are now only aeries for flocks of birds peering down onto the brook destined to become a mighty river. Small inns and hotels dot the countryside; enchanted moss-covered trails lead into the forests of dark-trunked and heavily limbed fir trees— from which the Black Forest gets its name. The trails often terminate at a tiny inn or a boarding house. Natives and tourists alike revel in walking up these winding trails during the balmy months. Hikers can rest on the sun-drenched terraces of little inns, drink chilled wine, and partake in the hearty fare of the local innkeepers and hausfraus. Out of the kitchens come veal, venison, wild boar, and green salads, along with other delicacies. The venison is provided by local hunters who prowl the nearby mountains, where game is said to be still plentiful. The cooking of the Black Forest is substantial and plentiful.

The Black Forest is also a heaven for mushroom gatherers. Grandmothers educate their grandchildren early in the intricacies of finding just the right fungi. Children probe gently under the moss and needles covering the forest floor for the treasures. The most prized are the "Steinpilze", or yellow boletus, which are eaten sautéed in butter, used as a flavoring for sauces, or dried on long strings for the winter months. The delicate "Pfefferlinge", or chanterelles, add incomparable flavor to veal and fowl dishes and to sourcream sauces. Morels, or "Speisemorchel", are marvelous sautéed in butter and added to omelets and other egg dishes or to delicate veal and chicken creations.

Some of the dishes can be traced to the times of the Nibelungen and the German knights. Pork is prepared with apples, cherries, plums, and a magnificent milk gravy. Sauerbraten is made with gingerbread snaps, and there are as many venison recipes as there are innkeepers and hausfraus. Colorful platters that would do justice to an artist's palette are arranged with stuffed rolled breast of veal, sliced into healthy portions and surrounded by fresh braised vegetables.

The Black Forest is famed for its smoked hams, for bacon, and for partridges cooked in white wine, served with wine-steeped sauerkraut. A wild boar pie is also one of the local delicacies. The succulent plums that ripen in orderly orchards are made into a smooth brandy and into compotes simmered in their own juices. But the crowning culinary achievement of the region is the *Schwarzwälder Kirschtorte*—the famed Black Forest cake made, in many villages, with pumpernickel crumbs and fresh sour cherries.

Leaving the Black Forest, the Danube, now wider and more

Danube tributaries Ilz and Inn, at Passau

Enchanted Forest near Donauschingen in the Black Forest

vigorous, rushes through swamps and green meadowland toward the Alps, skirting them near Donauried and Ulm, where ancient houses line the banks, and where the "Schiefe House," or crooked house, built about 400 years ago, has become a tourist attraction. Until recently, an old cleaning woman sat day by day at the window watching the passing of the river, and who became a legend herself. About twenty kilometers downstream at Regensburg, the Danube becomes navigable and is cluttered with steamers, barges, small craft, and kayaks. The barges haul chemicals for Yugoslavia, fruit for Germany, and steel for the Soviet Union. They fly flags of at least eight nations that use the Danube as a watery highway. The barges dock at quays along the way, the river people exchange news, ideas, and gossip, and the womenfolk trade recipes and the best ways to prepare fish, which is brought by the barges from the Danube Delta all the way upstream to Regensburg.

All along the Danube in Germany the food is hearty and nourishing, and is filled with dishes which have been handed down from mother to daughter for many generations.

OMELET WITH BACON AND POTATOES
serves 2–3

Basic omelet recipe

4 eggs	2 Tbls butter
2 Tbls water	Add herbs to this omelet
½ tsp salt	(see listing below)

Break the eggs into a bowl; add water and salt. Beat gently with a whisk. Heat the butter in a 9 inch omelet pan until slightly brown. Pour the eggs into the skillet; stir briskly with a fork. Let the omelet set for a few seconds. Lift the sides of the omelet with a fork and let some of the egg pour under the omelet. Cook for 1 minute or until the omelet is slightly browned on one side but creamy on the top side. Fill omelet as directed and fold toward the center from both sides or fold over on one side. Slide onto a heated platter.

For the Filling:

5 slices bacon	1 Tbls chopped parsley
½ cup minced shallots or mild onions	1 tsp chopped scallions
2 cups cooked diced potatoes	1 tsp chopped thyme (¼ tsp dry)
½ tsp salt	1 tsp chopped basil (¼ tsp dry)
¼ tsp black pepper	

In a large skillet, cook the bacon until very crisp. Remove bacon from the pan and reserve. Sauté the shallots in the bacon drippings until golden; add the potatoes and cook for 2–3 minutes, stirring occasionally. Sprinkle with salt and pepper. Cover the skillet and set aside. In another skillet or an omelet pan, make the basic omelet, adding the parsley, scallions, thyme, and basil. Prepare the omelet as directed. It should be very creamy and slightly undercooked. Spread the potatoes over the omelet, sprinkle with crumbled bacon, fold over as directed above, and serve immediately.

ASPARAGUS WITH SALMON CROUTONS
serves 8

2 pounds cooked asparagus spears	8 slices white bread
1 ⅓ cups plain bread crumbs	6 Tbls softened butter
4 Tbls butter	1 cup chopped smoked salmon

Sauté the bread crumbs in the butter until golden brown. Set aside and keep warm. Cut out circles of bread, using a 3- or 3½-inch round cookie cutter. Spread bread rounds with softened butter and top each round with chopped salmon. Place asparagus on a heated platter; pour sautéed bread crumbs over the asparagus and arrange salmon-topped rounds around asparagus. Serve immediately.

Note: For variety, chopped smoked ham may be substituted for salmon.

SHRIMP-STUFFED EGGS
serves 4–6

4 hard-cooked eggs	½ tsp curry powder
2 Tbls softened butter	½ tsp salt
1 Tbls mayonnaise	8 medium shrimp, cooked, shelled,
1 tsp Dijon mustard	deveined, and butterflied*
1 tsp minced onion	

Peel and slice the eggs lengthwise. Remove the yolks and press them through a sieve into a bowl. Add butter, mayonnaise, mustard, onion, curry powder, and salt and beat until very smooth. Fill the eggs, using a pastry bag with a star tube, (and place a shrimp over the filling.)

*To Butterfly Shrimp

Cut along the back from top to tail. *Do not* slice through. Place shrimp on top of the filling in whatever way seems most attractive, as a garnish.

HOT SARDINE FRITTERS

serves 6–8

¾ cup seasoned breadcrumbs
⅓ cup water; more if needed
4 tins skinless sardines
1 Tbls minced scallions
2 cloves garlic, mashed
1 Tbls minced parsley
   Salt and pepper to taste

¼ tsp oregano
¼ tsp thyme
1 cup yellow corn meal
2 cups oil; more as needed
3 sliced lemons

In a bowl, combine breadcrumbs and water so that the crumbs are barely moistened. Drain the sardines, reserving ¼ cup of the oil. In another bowl, mash sardines with a fork and combine with the moistened breadcrumbs. Add sardine oil, scallions, garlic, parsley, salt, pepper, oregano, and thyme. Blend thoroughly, forming a smooth mixture. Shape into golf ball-sized croquettes or fritters and roll in the cornmeal. Heat about one inch of oil in a large skillet. (If you drop a small cube of bread in the oil and the bread browns, the oil is hot enough.) Fry fritters until they are golden brown on all sides. Serve hot, with lemon wedges as a garnish.

German pretzel vendor

CHEESE LOG
serves 8–12

1	8-ounce pkg of "Cheddy" cheese or any soft yellow cheese
1	6-ounce pkg of Kraft garlic cheese roll
2	Tbls bleu cheese
2	Tbls butter
12	drops of Tabasco sauce
1	tsp Worcestershire sauce

1	tsp caraway seeds	
4	or 5 Tbls sweet paprika	
5	sprigs parsley	
½	cup olives	
4	halved hard-boiled eggs	for decorations
6	scallions	

Place the cheeses and butter into a bowl and let stand at room temperature for 30 minutes. Mix with your hands until the cheeses and butter are completely blended and very smooth. Add Tabasco sauce, Worcestershire sauce, and caraway seeds and mix again. Place cheese mixture on a sheet of wax paper and roll into a sausage about 12 inches long. Spread paprika on clean wax paper and roll the cheese into the paprika. Be sure that the cheese is completely covered. Decorate with parsley, hard-boiled eggs, scallions, and olives. Serve whole, with crackers or slices of pumpernickel bread. Keep refrigerated until ready to use.

Soups . . . .

LENTIL SOUP
serves 6

¾	pound lentils
6	slices bacon, diced
1	finely chopped onion
1	finely chopped carrot
2	finely chopped stalks of celery
1	medium potato, diced

	Salt and pepper to taste
3	bay leaves
½	tsp thyme
6	cups water
2	Tbls lemon juice
1	thinly sliced lemon (optional)

Place the lentils in a large bowl. Cover the water and soak for 6 hours or overnight. In a large pot, sauté the bacon and onions until both are golden brown. Drain the lentils. Add the lentils, carrot, celery, potato, salt, pepper, bay leaves, thyme, and water. Cover and simmer for 2½–3 hours. Stir in the lemon juice. Garnish with lemon slices.

OYSTER SOUP
serves 6

4	Tbls butter	2	egg yolks
⅓	cup flour	1 ½	cups heavy cream
7	cups fish broth (clam or chicken	24	shucked fresh oysters
	broth may be substituted)	2 ½	cups Rhein wine
1	tsp lemon juice	2	Tbls chives, minced
	Salt and pepper to taste		

In a soup pot melt 4 tablespoons butter, add the flour, and cook, stirring continuously until barely golden brown. Add the fish broth, stirring constantly until the mixture is very smooth. Simmer for 10 minutes. Add the lemon juice, salt, and pepper to taste. Beat the yolks and cream together until well-blended. Add 2 cups of hot broth, beating steadily. Pour the mixture into the soup. Mix well and remove from heat. In a saucepan, cook the oysters in the Rhein wine until the edges begin to curl. Add the cooked oysters and wine to the soup. Heat, but do not boil. Serve with minced chives.

FRANKFURTER BOHNEN SUPPE
Bean Soup with Frankfurters
serves 6–7

1	pound navy beans	2	carrots, scraped and grated
	Water to cover beans	2	stalks of celery, grated
6	cups water		Salt and pepper to taste
5	cups beef broth	7	sliced frankfurters
6	strips of bacon, chopped	2	Tbls chives, minced
1	large onion, chopped		

Wash the beans, then soak them overnight in water. Drain and place in a large pot with 6 cups water and beef broth. Cook over medium heat for 1½ hours. In a skillet, cook the bacon until golden brown. Add the onion and cook for about 5 minutes. Add the grated carrots and the celery and cook 5 minutes longer, stirring occasionally. Add this to the soup. Cook for 15–20 minutes longer or until the beans are tender. Add the frankfurters and salt and pepper to taste. Bring to a boil and simmer for 5 minutes. Serve sprinkled with chives.

GURKEN UND KARTOFFEL SUPPE
Cucumber and Potato Soup
serves 5 or 6

2 cucumbers, peeled
6 medium boiling potatoes, peeled and quartered
5 cups chicken broth (canned may be used)

2 cups heavy cream
  Salt and pepper to taste
1 small onion, minced and sautéed in butter
2 Tbls dill, minced

Cut the cucumbers lengthwise in two. Scoop out the seeds with a spoon. Dice the cucumbers and set aside. In a soup pot, cook the potatoes in chicken broth until they are very tender. Press the potatoes with the liquid into a bowl through a sieve, then return to the soup pot. Add cream, salt and pepper to taste, the onion and the diced cucumber. Simmer for 5–7 minutes or until the cucumbers are tender. Add the dill, stir, bring to boil once, and serve hot.

Tent at the Munich Beer Festival

LEAF LETTUCE SALAD
serves 4

2 large heads lead lettuce—Boston or bibb
1 egg
1 Tbls sugar

3 Tbls vinegar
¼ cup water
2 strips bacon, diced
1 Tbls flour

Wash lettuce, tear it into pieces, drain thoroughly, and chill. In a small bowl, beat the egg, sugar, vinegar, and water together. Set aside. In a small frying pan, sauté the bacon until it is very crisp. Stir in the flour. Slowly stir in the egg mixture and simmer until dressing is slightly thickened. Let cool at room temperature. Arrange leaf lettuce in serving bowls and pour the dressing over it. To store leftover dressing, put it in a jar with a tight lid and refrigerate; it will keep for 3 or 4 days.

CABBAGE SALAD
serves 6

1 head cabbage, shredded
1 small onion, diced
¾ cup sugar
⅔ cup oil
⅔ cup vinegar

1 tsp dry mustard
1 tsp celery seeds
2 tsp brown sugar

In a bowl, mix the cabbage, onion, and sugar and let stand for 1 hour. In a saucepan, combine the remaining ingredients and bring to a boil. Pour over the cabbage. Cool until lukewarm; refrigerate for 2–3 hours.

MUSHROOM POTATO SALAD

serves 6–7

- **1 pound medium-sized fresh mushrooms**
- **¼ cup wine vinegar**
- **½ cup olive oil**
- **¼ cup lemon juice**
- **½ tsp salt**
- **½ tsp tarragon**
- **1 Tbls caraway seed**
- **¼ tsp black pepper**
- **3 cups sliced boiled potatoes**
- **⅓ cup wine vinegar**
- **½ tsp salt**
- **¼ tsp pepper**
- **¼ tsp tarragon**
- **1 cup finely chopped celery**
- **½ cup minced scallions**
- **½ cup minced parsley**
- **2 green peppers, sliced into very thin strips**
- **½ cup of capers**

Cut the stalks off the mushrooms. Do not wash the mushroom caps. Wipe them off well with a damp cloth. Slice the mushroom caps, place them into a bowl, and pour the vinegar, oil, and lemon juice over them. Sprinkle with ½ teaspoon of salt, ½ teaspoon of tarragon, caraway seed, and pepper. Toss with a fork. Marinate for 1 hour.

Toss the sliced potatoes with the wine vinegar, ½ teaspoon salt, ¼ teaspoon pepper, and ¼ teaspoon tarragon. In a salad bowl, combine the mushrooms, potatoes, celery, scallions, and parsley. Toss together lightly. Adjust seasoning. Garnish with the pepper strips and capers.

BRUSSELS SPROUTS SALAD

serves 4–5

- **1 ½ pounds Brussels sprouts or 2 10-ounce packages frozen sprouts**
- **2 cups chicken broth**
- **⅓ cup wine vinegar**
- **⅓ cup olive oil**
- **½ tsp tarragon**
- **½ tsp thyme**
- **1 Tbls salt**
- **¼ tsp pepper**
- **1 dozen cherry tomatoes, halved**
- **1 Tbls minced chives**
- **1 Tbls minced dill**

If using frozen Brussels sprouts, cook as directed on the package, using chicken broth instead of water. If using fresh sprouts, wash well and trim all outer leaves. Bring chicken broth to a boil and add sprouts. Bring to a boil again and cook, uncovered, for 5–7 minutes. Cover and cook on low heat for 15 minutes or until tender. Drain and place into a bowl. Pour vinegar and oil over the hot sprouts and sprinkle with spices, salt, and pepper. Chill for 2–3 hours or overnight. Halve the tomatoes. Add to the sprouts and taste for seasoning. Sprinkle with chives and dill; serve with meat or fowl.

Brussels Sprouts with Brown Butter and Bread Crumbs

Cook the sprouts in the same way as for Brussels Sprouts Salad. Melt ½ cup butter. Add ½ cup bread crumbs. Brown butter and crumbs. Pour over Brussels sprouts and toss well. Serve immediately.

. . . . *Vegetables*

SAUTÉED MUSHROOMS
serves 6

¼ pound butter	¾ tsp caraway seeds
⅔ cup diced onions	Salt and pepper to taste
1½ pounds mushrooms, thinly sliced	

In a skillet, heat butter and sauté onions until just limp. Add mushrooms and caraway seeds and sauté until the juice from the mushrooms is released. Stirring constantly, bring the liquid to a boil and cook until the juice has almost evaporated (5 minutes). Add salt and pepper and serve immediately.

Castle between the Danube and the Rhine

ULMER ALLERLEI
Ulm Style Vegetables
serves 6–8

2 cups cauliflower flowerettes, cooked	½ pound sliced mushrooms
½ pound sliced green beans, cooked	6 Tbls butter
3 carrots, peeled, diced, and cooked	Salt and pepper to taste
1 10-ounce package frozen peas, cooked	3 Tbls parsley, minced

Place hot cooked vegetables onto a platter. Sauté the mushrooms until just limp. Add salt and pepper. Spread mushrooms with their own sauce over the vegetables. Sprinkle with parsley and serve immediately.

SPICED PURPLE CABBAGE
serves 4

1 head purple cabbage, finely shredded	⅛ tsp ground cloves
1 onion, diced	¼ tsp nutmeg
1 apple, peeled and diced	¼ tsp cinnamon
½ cup water	Salt and pepper to taste
2 Tbls wine vinegar, or more to taste	1 onion, very thinly sliced } garnish
2 Tbls bacon drippings	2 Tbls minced parsley }
2 Tbls brown sugar	

In a pot, place the cabbage, onion, apple, and water. Cover and cook until cabbage is just tender. Add the rest of the ingredients. Simmer, stirring occasionally, for 10–15 minutes or until cabbage is very tender. Serve hot, garnished with sliced onion and parsley.

MUSHROOM TIMBALES
serves 5–6

1 rib of celery	2 cups minced mushrooms
½ cup chopped parsley	3 Tbls butter
1 small onion	3 Tbls dry sherry
2 Tbls butter	4 Tbls bread crumbs
*1 lb. fresh chestnuts or 1 16-ounce can of whole chestnuts	4 egg yolks
Salt	¼ cup hot chicken stock
Pepper	¼ cup hot heavy cream
Pinch of crushed fennel seed	Salt and pepper to taste
	4 egg whites

Preheat oven to 350°. Mince celery, parsley and the onion. Sauté celery, parsley, and onion in 2 tablespoons butter. Set aside. Cook chestnuts, peel and mince. Add chestnuts to the vegetables, toss well together, and add salt, pepper, and a pinch of crushed fennel seed.

In a separate skillet, sauté mushrooms in 3 tablespoons of butter. Add sherry and cook until the liquid is reduced to about 2 tablespoons. Combine the chestnuts and mushrooms and add the bread crumbs. In a bowl, beat egg yolks for about 10 seconds; add hot chicken stock, beating continuously; add hot heavy cream, beating well. Add salt and pepper to taste. Pour into the top of a double boiler and cook over hot water, stirring continuously, until the mixture is slightly thickened. Combine the yolk mixture with the mushrooms and chestnuts. Beat egg whites until stiff and fold them into the mushroom mixture. Butter well about 10 timbale cups or custard cups. Fill them ⅔ full. Place the cups in a pan of hot water and bake in a preheated 350° oven for 25–30 minutes or until firm to the touch. To unmold, run a knife around the edge of the cup. Unmold onto a platter and garnish with parsley. Serve immediately.

*To cook Chestnuts

Cut an X into the flat side of each chestnut. Boil in water to cover for 15 minutes. Drain and peel while still warm, making sure that you remove the inner skin. Boil again for about 40 minutes or until very tender. Cool the chestnuts and mince them.

Idyllic Lake Konigsee, not far from the Danube

Fish and Seafood . . . .

SEAFOOD SOUFFLÉ
serves 4–6

3	Tbls butter	½	cup grated Gruyère or Swiss Cheese
2 ½	Tbls all-purpose flour	½	cup minced cooked fish fillet (flounder or sole)
1 ½	cups light cream (room temperature)	½	cup minced shrimp or crabmeat, or combine shrimp and crabmeat to make ½ cup
4	egg yolks (room temperature)		
⅛	tsp salt	6	egg whites (room temperature)
⅛	tsp Italian seasoning		Pinch of cream of tartar
⅛	tsp white pepper		

Preheat oven to 375°. Use a 2-quart soufflé dish. Butter well and sprinkle with grated Parmesan cheese or bread crumbs. Set aside. In an enameled or stainless steel pot, melt butter and add flour. Beating steadily with a whisk, cook for 1 or 2 minutes until the mixture is bubbly. Do not brown. Add cream and cook on medium heat, beating constantly with a whisk until thickened. Add egg yolks one at a time, beating well after each addition. Add seasonings, cheese, fish, and seafood and blend well. Up to this point, you may prepare the soufflé mixture in the morning and keep it refrigerated. It can even be left overnight. If you have refrigerated your soufflé, be sure to heat it slightly—just to lukewarm—at a very low temperature. Beat egg whites with cream of tartar until stiff but not dry. Add 3 tablespoons of egg whites to the soufflé sauce and mix well. Then, fold in remaining egg whites. Using a large spoon, cut through egg whites and sauce in the center and then fold in the whites with a circular motion until all the egg whites have disappeared. Do not stir or beat, just fold. Be sure to place the soufflé in the center of the rack in the center of the oven. Bake in a preheated 375° oven for 20 minutes. Reduce heat to 350° and bake for an additional 25 minutes. Serve immediately. Do not open the oven door for the first 20 minutes of baking.

SOLE IN WHITE WINE
serves 4

2 whole sole, or 8 filets, 4 ounces each, or use 2 flounders	* Simple fish stock
Salt and ground white pepper to taste	3 Tbls butter
2 chopped shallots or small white onion	3 Tbls flour
	1 cup hot milk
¾ cup dry white wine	Salt and white pepper to taste
	· 2 Tbls cream

Preheat oven to 325°. Sprinkle the fish with salt and white pepper. If filets are used, fold them in half and beat them lightly with the palm of the hand to flatten them. Put the sole in a buttered, flat baking dish. Add the chopped shallots or onion, the wine, and only enough fish stock to barely cover the sole. Cover the baking dish with foil. Bake in a preheated slow oven (325°) 15–20 minutes, or only until the fish flakes when tested with a fork. Drain the liquid off the fish into a saucepan and boil the liquid until it is reduced to ⅓ cup. Melt the butter in a separate saucepan, remove from heat, and blend in the flour. Return to heat; stir and cook until the mixture foams—1–2 minutes. Remove from heat and beat in the hot milk. Cook until sauce has thickened. Stir in the ⅓ cup of reduced fish stock. Add salt and pepper to taste; add the cream. Spoon over the poached sole; serve immediately.

*Simple Fish Stock

To each quart of cold water, add 1 pound of fish trimmings (heads, tails, fins, bones), tied in a cheesecloth bag, and 1 tablespoon of salt. Bring to boiling point, reduce heat, and simmer for 30 minutes. Strain. Makes 2–3 cups of stock.

BROILED FISH
serves 6

6   whole small cleaned trout (frozen trout will do)
    Salt and pepper to taste

6   Tbls vegetable oil
4   Tbls lemon juice
½   cup minced parsley

Sprinkle trout with salt and pepper. Use half the oil to grease 1 or 2 baking pans. In a small bowl, mix the rest of the oil with the lemon juice. Baste trout with this mixture. Broil trout on one side for 10 minutes. Turn broiler off and preheat oven to 350°. Add half of the parsley to the basting mixture. Bake fish for 15–20 minutes, basting often. Fish is done when it flakes easily when tested with a fork. Place fish on a hot serving dish or on individual platters. Garnish with remaining parsley.

CRABMEAT PUDDING
serves 6–8

2   Tbls melted butter
12   slices white bread with crusts cut off
10   slices of sharp cheddar cheese
1   16-ounce package defrosted, drained, and shredded king crab meat
5   beaten eggs

2 ½ cups milk
⅓   cup mayonnaise
½   cup finely chopped green pepper
¼   cup finely chopped dill
1   cup finely chopped mushrooms
½   cup finely grated Parmesan cheese

Preheat oven to 375°. Butter a 2-quart baking dish. Line the bottom and sides with bread slices and with the cheese slices. Beat the eggs. Fold crabmeat, eggs, milk, mayonnaise, green peppers, dill, and mushrooms into the eggs. Pour into the baking dish. Sprinkle with Parmesan cheese. Place in a baking pan and pour boiling water into the baking pan half-way up the sides of the baking dish. Bake for 1 ½ hours, or until a knife inserted into the pudding comes out clean. Serve immediately.

BRAISED DUCK
serves 3–4

1	4 or 5-pound duck, cut into serving pieces	1	large onion
			Salt and pepper to taste
¼	tsp salt	½	tsp sweet basil
4	Tbls butter	2	medium-sized apples
1	large cabbage		

Use a large heavy skillet with a cover. Cut duck into serving pieces and sprinkle them with salt. Sauté in butter until golden brown and tender. While duck is cooking, slice the cabbage and dice a large onion. Remove duck and place on a heated platter. Sauté onion in the same skillet where the duck was cooking until it is golden brown. Add cabbage and cook until just tender, but still crisp. Add salt and black pepper to taste, and ½ teaspoon of sweet basil. Pare and slice the apples and add them to cabbage. Add the duck pieces and stir well so the duck is covered with the cabbage. Taste for seasoning, cover, and simmer for 15–20 minutes.

CHICKEN WITH BRATWURST
serves 6

8	boned chicken breasts		Salt
8	Bratwurst, with the skin removed		Pepper
2	slightly beaten eggs		Paprika
2	Tbls water	½	cup margarine
1 ½	cups flour, mixed with	½	cup dry sherry

Preheat oven to 350°. Remove the skin and flatten the chicken breasts with a mallet. Place a sausage on each breast and roll tight. Tie with a string. Dip the breasts into egg beaten with water, then dredge with seasoned flour. In a large skillet, brown the stuffed breasts in margarine. Place into a casserole, or any deep dish, pour drippings from skillet over the stuffed chicken breasts, and add the sherry. Cover and bake at 350° for an hour. Serve immediately.

BREAST OF CHICKEN THERESA
serves 6

6	boned chicken breasts	3	Tbls butter
6	thin slices of ham (boiled or baked)	1	tsp chopped onion
6	slices Swiss cheese	½	lb small mushrooms
	Salt and pepper to taste	½	cup dry white wine
1	beaten egg	1	cup heavy cream
1	cup flour		Salt and pepper

Have the butcher bone the chicken breasts and cut them in half. Pound them with a mallet so that they are even in size. Cut ham and cheese slices the same size as the breast filets. Place ham and cheese slices between 2 filets and sprinkle with salt and pepper. Moisten the edges of the filets with the beaten egg to hold them together. Dredge the breasts in flour and shake off the excess. Melt 3 tablespoons of butter in a skillet. Sauté the filets for 10–12 minutes on one side. Turn them and sauté for 5 minutes on the other side. Remove to a serving platter and keep warm. Place the onion and the mushrooms into the same skillet; add the wine. Cook until liquid is reduced by half. Add the cream, stir, and cook until mixture has thickened. Add salt and pepper to taste. Pour over the chicken and serve.

Meat . . . .

BLACK FOREST PORK ROAST
serves 8–10

6	pounds center-cut pork loin roast	1	tsp turmeric
1	Tbls salt	¼	cup lemon juice
4	cloves finely chopped garlic	6	Tbls melted butter
1	tsp thyme		

Make several cuts near the bones of the roast; place meat onto a double foil. Combine salt, garlic, thyme, turmeric, lemon juice, and butter in a cup and brush the roast on all sides. Wrap in foil and refrigerate for 24 hours. To roast, use a rotisserie over hot coals, or an electric rotisserie. Place pork on a spit. Use meat thermometer; insert it into the end of the roast without touching the bone. Place the spit over hot coals or under the broiler; roast about 4 hours, or until the thermometer registers 185° and the meat is tender. You may also bake the roast in a 350° oven on a rack in a baking dish until the thermometer registers 185°, or about 35–40 minutes per pound. Serve sliced into 1-inch slices.

FLEISH RULADEN
Braised Stuffed Beef Rolls
serves 6

3 pounds top round steak, sliced ½-inch thick, trimmed of all fat and pounded ¼-inch thick	1 cup coarsely chopped celery
	¼ cup thinly sliced leeks, white part only
6 tsp Dusseldorf style prepared mustard, or substitute 6 tsp of some other hot prepared mustard	1 Tbl scraped and finely chopped parsnip
¼ cup finely chopped onions	3 sprigs parsley
3 Tbls lard	1 tsp salt
2 cups beef broth	1 Tbl butter
	2 Tbls flour

Cut the steak into 6 rectangular pieces about 4 inches wide and 8 inches long. Spread each rectangle with a teaspoon of mustard and sprinkle with 2 teaspoons of onions. Spread about 2–3 tablespoons stuffing on the meat. Roll the meat, jelly roll fashion, into a cylinder. Tie the rolls at each end with kitchen cord. In a heavy 10–12-inch skillet, melt the lard over moderate heat until it begins to splutter. Add the beef rolls and brown them on all sides, regulating the heat so that they color quickly and evenly without burning. Transfer the rolls to a plate. Pour the beef broth into the skillet and bring it to a boil, meanwhile scraping in any brown particles clinging to the bottom and sides of the pan. Add the celery, leeks, parsnip, parsley, and salt, and return the beef rolls to the skillet. Cover, reduce the heat to low, and simmer for 1 hour, or until the meat shows no resistence when pierced with a fork. Turn the rolls once or twice during the cooking period. Transfer the rolls to a heated platter and keep them warm while you make the sauce.
Strain pan juices into a blender and purée. Melt the butter in a small saucepan over moderate heat, and when the foam subsides, sprinkle in the flour. Lower the heat and cook, stirring constantly,

until the flour turns a golden brown. Be careful not to let it burn. Gradually add the purée, beating vigorously with a whisk until the sauce is smooth and thick. Taste for seasoning and return the sauce and the ruladen to the skillet. Simmer over low heat only long enough to heat the rolls through. Serve the rolls on a heated platter and pour the sauce over them. Ruladen are often accompanied by purple cabbage (see page 18) and dumplings or boiled potatoes.

Chestnut Stuffing

1 large minced onion	1 can of whole chestnuts*
3 Tbls butter	1 tsp salt
1 stalk minced celery	¼ tsp pepper
5 strips diced bacon	¼ tsp thyme
2 cups bread croutons or prepared bread stuffing	¼ tsp basil
	1 cup chicken broth (approximately)

Sauté the onions and the celery in butter until both are just limp. Cook bacon in a separate skillet until golden brown. Drain off ½ of the fat. Add the croutons, the whole chestnuts, the onion mixture, and the seasonings. Toss together and add the chicken broth, using just enough to moisten the stuffing.

STUFFED BREAST OF VEAL

serves 6

5–6 -pound breast of veal	2 cloves garlic, minced
8 slices of white bread, with crusts cut off	1 tsp paprika
2 cups water	½ tsp salt
2 slightly beaten eggs	½ tsp pepper
1 medium onion, chopped and sautéed in butter	2 medium onions, diced
¼ tsp poultry seasoning	4 carrots, diced
¼ cup vegetable oil	4 stalks celery, diced
	2 cups water

Preheat oven to 350°. Have the butcher cut a pocket in the breast of veal. Soak bread slices in water, squeeze the water out, place

*This will not work with purée, and do not use water chestnuts. Drain the chestnuts before using. Use 1 lb. fresh chestnuts if you wish. For cooking instructions, see page 19.

them in a bowl, and add eggs, sautéed onion, salt, pepper, and poultry seasoning. Fill the pocket in the veal breast with the mixture and skewer or sew together. Mix oil, garlic, paprika, salt, and pepper and rub the meat on all sides with this mixture. Place vegetables in a baking pan and place the veal breast on top. Bake in a 350° preheated oven for 1 hour. Pour 2 cups of water over the meat and bake for 3–3 ½ hours, turning the roast once or twice. Keep basting with the pan juices until the roast is brown and crisp. Serve immediately sliced into thick slices.

GLAZED PORK ROAST

serves 8–10

4–5 -pound pork loin roast
 ½ tsp salt
 ½ tsp white pepper
 ½ tsp thyme
 ½ tsp basil
2–3 Tbls Cointreau (or any other orange liqueur)

Basting mixture

½ cup orange juice
2 Tbls orange liqueur

Sauce

1 Tbls cornstarch
1 ½ cups orange juice
1 Tbls soy sauce
¼ tsp salt
¼ cup Cointreau
1 cup sliced canned kumquats

Preheat oven to 350°. Rub roast with salt, white pepper, thyme, basil, and Cointreau. Place on a rack in a pan and roast 35–45 minutes per pound, or until a meat thermometer registers 170°. Baste the roast frequently with mixture of orange juice and orange liqueur. For the sauce, mix cornstarch with orange juice in a saucepan, add the soy sauce and salt, and bring to a boil. Simmer until sauce thickens slightly. Add Cointreau and kumquats. Heat the sauce but do not let it boil. Place the baked pork on a heated platter and pour the sauce over it. Serve immediately.

KASSLER RIPPCHEN
Smoked Pork Chops
serves 6

6 thick smoked pork chops (1 ½–2"
   thick)
1 large sliced onion
1 chopped tomato
2 cups boiling water

2 Tbls butter
2 Tbls flour
   Salt and pepper to taste
½ cup sour cream

Preheat oven to 375°. Make a deep incision in each chop. Fill with stuffing and secure with a toothpick. In a baking pan, spread onion and the tomato and place the chops over them. Cover pan and bake ½ hour in a 375° oven. Uncover and add 1 cup boiling water. Add more water as needed. Bake an additional 40–50 minutes. Strain the liquid from the pan and purée it in a blender. In a small pan, melt the butter, add the flour, and cook for 1 minute. Add the purée, the sour cream, and salt and pepper to taste. Pour the sauce over the chops. Serve with sauerkraut (see page 32).

Stuffing

1 cup finely chopped apples
4 Tbls bread crumbs
½ cup finely chopped walnuts

2 Tbls melted butter
¼ cup seedless raisins
¼ tsp allspice

Place the apples in a bowl. Add bread crumbs, nuts, 2 tablespoons of melted butter, raisins, and allspice. Blend well.

SAUSAGES AND APPLES
serves 3–4

1 pound country sausage links
¼ cup water
4 red Delicious apples, peeled and
   cored
1 cup sugar

4 Tbls flour
⅛ tsp cinnamon
⅛ tsp nutmeg
   Salt to taste
¼ cup apple brandy or brandy

In a large skillet, cook the sausage links in water until water has evaporated and the sausages are browned on all sides. Remove from the skillet and keep warm. Pour off most of the sausage drippings, reserving about ⅓ cup. Cut the prepared apples into 16 slices. Mix sugar, flour, cinnamon, nutmeg, and salt together in a bowl. Dip apples in this mixture to coat them. Sauté the apple slices in the sausage drippings until delicately browned. Place on the platter with the sausages. In a small pot or ladle, heat the apple brandy until lukewarm. Ignite the brandy and pour it over the sausages and apples. When the flames die down, serve immediately.

The Danube at Regensburg—landmark of this 2000-year-old city is St. Peter's Cathedral and the stone bridge, still on the old foundation

NÜRNBERG SAUSAGE ROLLS
makes about 20 sausage rolls

2 pounds lean, spicy, fresh pork sausage meat	2 garlic cloves, minced
	3 Tbls minced parsley
½ pound lean ground beef	¼ tsp each basil, thyme, mace, sage
½ tsp salt	1 egg
1 large onion, minced	½ cup bread crumbs
1 green pepper, minced	¼ cup milk

Preheat oven to 375°. Place pork sausage, ground beef, onion, green pepper, garlic, and parsley in a large bowl. Add all the seasonings, egg, bread crumbs, and milk. Taste for seasoning, and add more salt or pepper if desired. Preferably with your hands, mix the ingredients until they are well blended and very smooth. Make 2-inch sausages about 1-inch wide from the mixture. Roll out the pastry to about ¼-inch thickness on a lightly floured board and cut into squares that are a little larger than the sausages. Place a sausage in the center of each square, wrap the pastry around the sausage, and seal very well by pinching along the seam. Place about 1 ½ inches apart on an ungreased jelly roll pan and prick each pastry with a fork. Brush with the beaten egg, and bake in a preheated 375° oven for 15–20 minutes or until golden brown. Serve for cocktails or as a luncheon dish with a green tossed salad and vegetables.

Pastry

2 cups unbleached flour	6 Tbls shortening—ice cold
Pinch of cream of tartar	Pinch of salt
1 stick (¼ pound) butter or margarine— ice cold	½ cup ice water (approximately)

Place flour on a large wooden board, add cream of tartar, add butter and shortening. Use a very large knife or cleaver and chop the flour, butter, and shortening together until the butter and shortening are in pieces about the size of hazelnuts and are coated with flour. Add water with a pinch of salt slowly until the pastry just sticks together. Use the knife for blending; do not handle too much. Roll out into a strip about 5–6-inches wide and 10–12-inches long. Fold into thirds. Turn, with the open end toward you, and roll out gently again into the same size strip. Fold into thirds. Wrap in wax paper and refrigerate for 1 hour. Roll out and fold twice again, being careful to always square out the edges before folding. Refrigerate for 1 hour. Repeat rolling out and refrigerating twice more. Wrap securely again and refrigerate overnight.

SAUSAGE WITH ONIONS
serves 4–5

3 Tbls butter or margarine
2 pounds pork sausage links
4 large onions, sliced
2 cups dry white wine or dry sherry

In a skillet, melt the butter. Add the sausages and brown on all sides. Remove the sausages to a heated platter and keep warm. Add the onions to the skillet where the sausages were cooking and sauté them until just tender and transparent—do not brown. Add the wine and simmer for 10 minutes. Place a layer of the onions into a well-buttered baking dish, place sausages on top of the onions, and place the remaining onions on top of the sausages. Bake in a 375° oven for 30 minutes. Serve with boiled parslied potatoes.

SCHWEINS KOTELETTEN MIT SAFT
Pork Chops in Milk Gravy
serves 6

12	pork loin chops, ¾–1″ thick	1 large onion, sliced
	Flour	1 crushed garlic clove
4	Tbls butter	1 cup milk
2	tsp salt	4 Tbls chopped parsley
2	Tbls Hungarian paprika	1 Tbls cornstarch
2	Tbls caraway seeds	

Wipe chops with a damp cloth and make several small cuts around the edges. Dredge with flour on one side only. Brown the chops, floured side down, in a skillet in hot butter. Sprinkle with half the salt, the paprika, and the caraway seeds. Cover and cook 10 minutes. Add onion and garlic, cover, and cook 20 minutes longer. Stir in milk gradually. Sprinkle chops with parsley. Cover and simmer 15 minutes, stirring gravy occasionally. Mix ½ cup of gravy with 1–2 tablespoons cornstarch. Add this to the gravy in the skillet, stir well, and cook for 2–3 minutes.

GARNIRTES SAUERKRAUT
Sauerkraut with meat and sausages
serves 6–7

½ pound bacon, cut up into small pieces
1 chopped large onion
2 pounds lean pork cut into 1 ½-inch cubes
2 16-ounce bags of sauerkraut
2 Tbls caraway seeds

1 ½ cups pale dry sherry
1 pound knockwurst, cut into 2-inch pieces
   Salt and coarsely ground black pepper to taste
2 pounds small boiled potatoes
4 Tbls melted butter

In a large skillet, fry the cut up bacon until crisp. Add the onion and sauté until golden. Add the pork, stir well, and sauté for 15 minutes. Drain the sauerkraut, reserving some of the liquid. Rinse the sauerkraut under cold running water. Squeeze out excess water. Add the kraut to the skillet and stir well. Add caraway seeds and simmer for 30 minutes. Add 1 cup sherry, knockwurst, and salt and pepper. Stir and simmer for 25 minutes. Taste, and if the mixture tastes too bland, add a little of the reserved kraut juice. Add the boiled potatoes. Sprinkle with the remaining ½ cup of sherry and the melted butter. Cover and cook another 15–20 minutes. Serve with pumpernickel or rye bread.

SAUERKRAUT BAVARIAN STYLE
serves 6–7

6–7 pieces of bacon
1 16-ounce bag of fresh sauerkraut
1 large onion, diced
3 Tbls bacon drippings
2 Tbls caraway seeds
1 cup dry white wine
1 pound knockwurst
1 ½ pounds small smoked pork sausage links

   Salt and pepper to taste
1 apple, peeled, cored, and sliced
5 Tbls bacon drippings
36 small round peeled potatoes, cooked in water for 6 minutes
½ cup minced parsley

In a large pot, fry bacon, which has been cut into small pieces, until crisp. Drain sauerkraut, reserve the juice, and rinse under cold water. Squeeze out the excess water. Add kraut to the skillet, stir well, and simmer for 20 minutes. Add the onion, which has been sautéed in the bacon drippings. Add caraway seeds, dry white wine, knockwurst—cut in half—and the small smoked links. Add salt and pepper to taste. Simmer for 30 minutes. Add the apple. Taste and add more sauerkraut juice if the taste is too bland. Cover and cook another 15–20 minutes.

Melt the bacon drippings in a large skillet. Dry the peeled and cooked potatoes with a paper towel and put them into the skillet. Sauté, turning them often until golden brown. Sprinkle with salt. To serve, place the sauerkraut and the sausage on a platter and surround them with the sautéed potatoes. Sprinkle with minced parsley.

Note: In many instances, Weisswurst (white sausage) is used instead of knockwurst. Cut the white sausage in half and sauté it in a little butter or bacon drippings until it is slightly brown on both sides. Add to sauerkraut about 10 minutes before you are ready to serve it. Serve sprinkled with parsley.

· · · · · · · · · · · · · · · *Side Dishes*

BROTKNOEDEL
Bread Dumplings
serves 6–8

10 slices Vienna Bread (2 days old)	1½ cups water
¼ pound butter or margarine	½ tsp basil
1 small minced onion	1 tsp salt
3 Tbls minced parsley	2 tsp baking powder
2 eggs	2½ cups flour

Without removing the crusts, cut the bread slices into very small cubes. Melt the butter in a large skillet. Add the bread and the onion. Sauté until the bread cubes are well toasted and crisp. Add the parsley and toss together. Beat the eggs, water, basil, and salt together. Sift the baking powder and flour together. Add to egg mixture and beat well. Add the bread cubes and mix. Cover with plastic wrap and refrigerate for 2–3 hours. Roll with floured hands into golf ball-sized dumplings. Place gently into simmering salted water. Simmer for 10–12 minutes. Serve with any chicken or meat dish with gravy or with stews. If desired, after draining, place the dumplings into the gravy or add them to a stew and simmer for a few minutes. The dumplings may also be served in clear beef or chicken broth.

OVEN CHIPPED POTATOES
serves 6

4	Idaho potatoes, thinly sliced (do not pare)	⅛	tsp pepper
¼	cup butter or margarine	1	Tbls parsley, chopped
1	Tbls onion, grated	½	tsp dried leaf thyme
1	tsp salt	1 ½	cups shredded Cheddar cheese

Layer potato slices in a greased 13 × 9 × 2-inch baking dish. In a small saucepan melt butter, stir in grated onion, salt, and pepper. Brush potato slices with butter mixture. Bake in a 425° oven for 45 minutes or until potatoes are tender when pierced with a fork. Sprinkle with parsley, thyme, and shredded cheese. Bake 15 minutes longer or until cheese is melted.

POTATOES AND BROCCOLI
serves 6

Potatoes

4	large potatoes, thinly sliced (do not pare)
¼	cup butter or margarine
1	tsp salt
¼	tsp paprika
⅛	tsp pepper
1	10-oz. package frozen broccoli spears, thawed

Cheese Sauce

2	Tbls butter or margarine
2	Tbls flour
1 ¼	cups light cream
½	tsp salt
¼	tsp pepper
¼	cup chopped pimiento
1	cup (4 oz.) shredded Cheddar cheese

Place potato slices into a well-buttered 13 × 9 × 2-inch baking dish. In a small saucepan melt butter; stir in salt, paprika, and pepper. Brush potato slices with the butter mixture. Bake uncovered in a 350° oven for 50 minutes, or until potatoes are tender when pierced with a fork. Meanwhile, prepare cheese sauce. Melt butter in a small saucepan, and blend in flour. Add cream and cook over low heat, stirring constantly until mixture thickens. Add salt, pepper, pimiento, and cheese; stir until cheese melts. Arrange broccoli spears over potatoes. Pour cheese sauce over all. Cover and bake 10 minutes longer or until broccoli is tender and sauce bubbles.

NUDEL PUDDING
Noodle Pudding
serves 6

1 pound wide egg noodles, cooked according to directions on the package, and drained
½ cup melted butter
5 eggs, well beaten

2 cups sour cream
Salt and pepper to taste
½ cup grated Swiss cheese
½ cup grated cheddar cheese

Butter a 2-quart casserole well. In a bowl toss noodles with butter. In a bowl beat eggs with sour cream until very smooth. Fold in the cheese. Pour over noodles. Toss with two forks and put into the buttered casserole. Bake in a 350° oven for about 45–50 minutes or until firm and golden brown.

Schwarzwald Bad Rippoldsau, Black Forest

KIRSCH TORTE
serves 8–10

For the genoise (cake batter):

6   eggs
¾   cup granulated sugar
1   tsp lemon juice

1 ⅔   cups sifted all-purpose flour
*⅓   cup clarified butter, cooled

Preheat oven to 350°. Butter well and sprinkle with flour two 9-inch spring form pans. Use a glass double boiler. Place top of double boiler over simmering water. Break the eggs into it, add sugar, and beat with a whisk until the eggs feel hot to the touch. Do not let the water boil or the eggs will overcook. Remove from heat and pour into a glass or stainless steel bowl and beat with an electric hand mixer for 5 minutes or until the eggs have tripled in size and form soft peaks. Add lemon juice and beat for another minute. Add a little sifted flour and a little liquid clarified butter and fold in gently. Continue adding flour and butter and fold in. Gently work in the flour—no flour should be visible. Pour the batter into the two cake pans. Bake the cake in the preheated 350° oven for 30–35 minutes or until a cake tester comes out clean—do not overbake. Cool on a rack and unmold. Cut each cake in half crosswise, forming 4 layers.

Cream Filling

2 ½   pints heavy whipping cream
**½   cup vanilla sugar
3   Tbls kirsch

⅔   cup black cherry preserves
¼   cup kirsch
½   cup maraschino cherries

Whip the cream until it is almost stiff; add the sugar and whip until very stiff. Do not overwhip or you'll have butter. Add 3 tablespoons of kirsch. Fold in the black cherry preserves. Sprinkle the cake layers with the ¼ cup of kirsch. Spread the whipped cream over each layer and assemble the cake by placing layer upon layer. You should have enough cream left for frosting. Decorate with maraschino cherries. Chill for at least 2 hours before serving.

*Clarified Butter

Melt ½ pound of butter in a saucepan. Do not brown. Set aside for a few minutes. Skim the white sediment from the top and pour off the golden liquid into a saucepan or jar. Discard white sediment from the bottom. Clarified butter will keep in a refrigerator for two or three weeks.

**Vanilla Sugar

Place 1 or 2 whole vanilla beans with 2–3 cups powdered or granulated sugar into a jar with a tight lid. Within 3 days, you will have vanilla sugar. Add sugar as needed. The vanilla beans last for 6 months.

Statues in a castle near Donauschingen

CHOCOLATE MOUSSE WITH CHESTNUTS
serves 12

5   ounces unsweetened chocolate
5   ounces semisweet chocolate
6   egg yolks
2   cups sugar
4   cups whipping cream

4   Tbls any coffee liqueur or brandy
3   egg whites
*2   cups chestnut purée
¼–½   cup grated unsweetened chocolate

Place all the chocolate into the top of a double boiler and melt over simmering water. Set aside. Beat the egg yolks until thickened and add sugar. Beat until light in color and very thick. Add the chocolate and blend well. Cool completely, but do not refrigerate. Whip the cream until it is stiff. Reserve 1 cup. Fold the cream into the chocolate mixture and blend well with a whisk or beater. Add liqueur or brandy. Beat the egg whites until stiff but not dry. Fold gently but thoroughly into the mousse. Fold in chestnut purée. Transfer to a serving dish or to individual serving dishes, and refrigerate for at least 3–4 hours or until completely set. Decorate with the reserved whipped cream and grate some chocolate over the cream.

*Chestnut Puree

*1   16-ounce can whole chestnuts, drained, or use fresh chestnuts
2   Tbls brandy
4   Tbls powdered sugar

Press the drained chestnuts through a sieve, add brandy and sugar, and blend lightly. You may use canned chestnut purée. To cook fresh chestnuts, see page 19.

REGENSBURG CHOCOLATE CAKE
serves 8–10

5	ounces semisweet chocolate	¾	cup milk
½	cup boiling water	8	egg whites
2 ½	cups sugar	½	cup bread crumbs
1	cup unsalted butter	6	ounces semisweet chocolate, grated
8	egg yolks	1	pint whipping cream
3	cups sifted flour	½	cup walnut halves
8	tsp baking powder	½	cup whipped cream
½	tsp salt		

Preheat oven to 375°. Place the chocolate into a saucepan. Pour boiling water over it. Now place the saucepan over very low heat and stir until the chocolate is completely dissolved. In a bowl, cream the butter. Add the sugar; beat together until very smooth and light. Add egg yolks, one at a time, beating well after each yolk is added. Add the chocolate and blend well. Add the sifted flour, baking powder, and salt. Add the milk and blend until completely smooth. In another bowl, beat the egg whites until very stiff and fold into the chocolate mixture. Grease and dust with bread crumbs two 9-inch cake pans with removable sides and bottoms. Divide the batter in two parts and place one part in each cake pan. Bake in a 375° preheated oven for approximately 35 minutes, or until a wooden toothpick comes out clean. Cool for ½ hour in the cake pans. Remove cake, but do not refrigerate. Place grated chocolate and whipping cream in a saucepan and cook over low heat, stirring constantly until the chocolate is completely dissolved. Do not boil. Cool and place in the refrigerator for about 1 hour. Take out, place in a bowl, and whip as you would for regular whipped cream, but do not overwhip. The cream is ready when soft peaks form. Using a very sharp knife, cut off the upper crust from one cake and the bottom crust from the other as thinly as possible (about ⅛–¼" each). (This is done so both cakes are even and can be frosted easily.) Spread half of the whipped chocolate cream on the cake with the upper crust removed. Spread half of the walnuts over the cream. Top with the other cake half and frost the cake with the remaining chocolate cream. After the cake is frosted, with a knife swirl the ½ cup of plain whipped cream into the chocolate to create a pattern. Decorate with the rest of the walnut halves.

GRANDMA'S COFFEE CAKE
makes 1 6" × 10" cake; serves 8–10

1 ½	cups all-purpose flour	¾	cup brown sugar
3	tsp baking powder	4	Tbls flour
1	cup sugar	¾	cup finely chopped English walnuts
¼	pound unsalted butter	1	tsp cinnamon
½	tsp salt	¼	tsp nutmeg
2	well-beaten eggs	3	Tbls melted butter
½	cup milk	1	Tbls cocoa
1	tsp vanilla	1	Tbls butter
¼	tsp nutmeg	¼	cup corn flake crumbs

Preheat oven to 400°. In a bowl, mix together 1 ½ cups flour, baking powder, and sugar. Cut in the ¼ pound of butter and blend with your hands until mealy. Add salt. Add beaten eggs, milk, vanilla, and nutmeg to the batter. Divide the batter into 2 equal parts.

In another bowl, mix the brown sugar, flour, nuts, cinnamon, nutmeg, butter, and cocoa together. Grease well a 6" × 10" baking pan. Dust with corn flake crumbs and spread half of the batter in the pan. Spread half of the filling over the batter and cover with the other half of the batter. Spread the remaining filling on top. Bake in a preheated 400° oven for about 25 minutes. Let cool in the pan. Loosen the sides with a blunt knife, and serve the cake hot or cold.

MARBLE CHEESE CAKE
serves 7–8

1 ½	cups fudge chip cookie crumbs	1	tsp grated lemon rind
½	tsp ground cinnamon	2	eggs
¼	cup melted butter	1 ½	cups sour cream
12	ounces softened cream cheese	4	ounces melted dark semisweet chocolate
½	cup sugar		

Preheat oven to 350°. Combine the cookie crumbs, cinnamon, and melted butter and mix well. Butter the sides and bottom of a 9-inch cake pan. With the back of a fork or damp fingers, press the cookie mixture onto bottom and sides of the cake pan. Chill. Meanwhile, combine cheese, sugar, and lemon rind; beat until well blended. Add the eggs and sour cream and beat until smooth.

Melt the chocolate in a pan over hot water. Cool slightly and stir chocolate gently into the mixture with a fork until the batter is marbleized. Pour into the crust.

Bake at 350° for 35–40 minutes, or until set. Chill at least 2 hours.

COFFEE-HONEY CAKE

serves 6–8

3 eggs	1 tsp almond extract
1 cup light brown sugar	½ tsp cinnamon
2 Tbls melted butter	½ tsp ginger
½ cup honey	¼ cup bread crumbs
½ cup strong cold coffee	1 cup shelled almonds
2 cups unsifted all-purpose flour	1 Tbls flour
3 tsp baking powder	

Preheat oven to 350°. Beat eggs and sugar with an electric beater until very thick; add butter and honey and beat for at least 2 minutes. Pour in coffee and add flour; beat with a wooden spoon until the batter is very smooth. Add baking powder, almond extract, cinnamon, and ginger. Beat again for at least 1 minute. Grease well a 10″ × 10″ square baking pan; dust with bread crumbs. Place ½ cup of almonds in the bottom of the baking pan, pour batter over the almonds, and spread the remaining ½ cup of almonds on top of cake. Bake in a preheated 350° oven for 1 hour. Remove from oven and cool in the pan. Loosen sides of cake from pan with a blunt knife, and place it on a platter. With a very sharp long knife, cut the cake lengthwise in two parts.

Filling and Topping

1 cup whipping cream	½ cup granulated sugar
2 Tbls dry instant coffee	½ cup blanched, toasted crushed almonds
2 Tbls cold water	
2 Tbls honey	

Buy sliced, blanched almonds and toast under the broiler for about 3 minutes, or until golden brown; place them in a plastic or paper bag and crush with a mallet.

Use only pure whipping cream. Whip in a chilled bowl with electric hand beater or standing beater until slightly thickened. Dilute coffee in 2 tablespoons cold water and add to whipped cream. Add honey and sugar and beat until very thick. Add the crushed almonds and beat for 3 seconds. Take half of the cream and spread on the lower part of the honey cake, cover with the upper part of the cake, and spread remaining cream on top of cake. Refrigerate for ½ hour and serve.

CHERRY PANCAKE
serves 6

For the Cherry Filling:

1	15-ounce can of dark pitted cherries	½	cup kirsch
1	15-ounce can water-packed sour pitted cherries	¼	cup sugar
		½	tsp cinnamon

Drain cherries thoroughly. Place them into a bowl and pour kirsch over them. Marinate for 2–3 hours. Drain again; sprinkle with sugar and cinnamon.

For the Pancake:

4	eggs	2	tsp sifted baking powder
4	Tbls sugar	2	Tbls melted butter
¼	tsp salt	½	cup powdered vanilla sugar (see recipe on page 37)
1 ½	cups milk		
¾	cup sifted flour		

Preheat oven to 400°. Place eggs, sugar, salt, milk, flour, baking powder, and butter into the blender. Blend until smooth. Butter well an 8-cup soufflé dish or any deep baking dish. Pour about ½-inch of batter into the baking dish. Place into a 400° preheated oven and bake for about 4–5 minutes, until the batter just sets. Place cherry filling on top of the batter and pour the remaining batter over the filling. Reduce heat to 350° and bake for 25–30 minutes or until an inserted knife comes out clean. Sprinkle with sugar and serve immediately.

SOUR CREAM PANCAKES
serves 4–6

4 egg yolks	7 stiffly beaten egg whites
½ cup sugar	½ cup melted butter for baking
1¾ cup sour cream	pancakes
Salt to taste	½ cup granulated or powdered sugar
2⅓ cups sifted flour mixed with	1 cup sour cream
¼ tsp baking powder	

In a bowl, beat together egg yolks, sugar, sour cream, and salt. Add flour with baking powder; mix until smooth. Fold in egg whites. Heat a griddle or heavy skillet and brush it with butter. Pour about ¼ cup of batter into the skillet for each pancake. Make 3-inch pancakes about ¼-inch thick. Turn once to brown both sides. Serve on a hot platter sprinkled with sugar, and serve the sour cream on the side.

APPLE FRITTERS
makes about 16

1 cup sifted all-purpose flour	½ tsp vanilla extract
2 Tbls sugar	1 tsp melted butter
1 tsp baking powder	4–5 large apples, peeled and cored
½ tsp salt	⅔ cup flour
1 egg and 1 egg yolk	2–4 cups oil
½ cup milk	1 cup powdered sugar

Combine flour, sugar, baking powder, and salt. Set aside. In a mixing bowl, beat egg, egg yolk, milk, vanilla extract, and melted butter until well blended. Gradually add flour mixture, beating until smooth after each addition.

Slice apples into ½-inch thick rings. Coat the rings with flour and shake off the excess. Dip into batter, coating apple rings completely. Fry in oil heated to 375° for 2–3 minutes, turning once, until golden brown. Drain on absorbent paper, sprinkle with powdered sugar, and serve hot.

APRICOT ALMOND SOUFFLÉ
serves 4–6

This is a very tender and moist soufflé. Usually, it does not rise as much as regular dessert soufflés. Serve with additional apricot jam on the side, with slightly sweetened whipped cream, or with apricot sauce.

3 Tbls butter	5 Tbls finely ground blanched almonds
2 ½ Tbls all-purpose flour	
1 ½ cups light cream (room temperature)	¼ tsp almond extract
	¼ tsp rum extract
4 egg yolks (room temperature)	2 Tbls dark rum or apricot brandy
Pinch of salt	6 egg whites
2 Tbls sugar	⅛ tsp cream of tartar
4 Tbls apricot preserves	

Preheat oven to 375°. Grind almonds in a blender or food processor, not in a meat grinder.

Use a 2-quart soufflé dish. Butter well and sprinkle with ground almonds or granulated sugar. Melt butter in a heavy enameled or stainless steel pot. Add flour and, beating steadily with a whisk, cook for 1 or 2 minutes until the mixture is bubbly. Do not brown. Add cream and cook on medium heat, beating constantly with a whisk until thickened. Add the egg yolks one at a time, beating well after each addition. Add salt, sugar, apricot preserves, almonds, flavorings, and rum. Blend well. Beat egg whites with cream of tartar until stiff but not dry. Add 3 tablespoons of egg whites to the soufflé sauce and mix well. Then fold the remaining egg whites into the soufflé. Using a large spoon, cut through egg whites and sauce in the center and then fold in with a circular motion until all the egg whites have disappeared. Do not stir or beat, just fold. Bake in a preheated 375° oven for 25 minutes. Reduce heat to 350° and bake for an additional 25 minutes.

Be sure to place the soufflé in the center of the rack in the center of the oven. Do not open the oven door for the first 20 minutes of baking.

Serve immediately.

KRAPFEN
Raised doughnuts
makes about 22–24 doughnuts

2	packages granulated yeast	½	cup sugar
½	cup lukewarm water	1	tsp salt
2	Tbls sugar	6	Tbls butter or margarine
3 ½–4	cups sifted all-purpose flour	2	eggs plus 2 egg yolks
1	cup lukewarm milk		Vegetable oil for frying

In a small bowl, combine yeast, water, and 2 tablespoons sugar. Set aside to rise. Place 2 cups of flour in a large bowl, add the yeast, and beat well with a wooden spoon. Add the lukewarm milk, ½ cup of sugar, salt, and butter. Stir until butter is melted. Add to the flour and yeast mixture. Add eggs and egg yolks, beating well after each addition. If using an electric mixer, beat for 2 minutes; if using a spoon, beat for 4 minutes. Add remaining flour to make a medium-soft dough. Knead by hand or with a breadhook until dough leaves the sides of the bowl and is very smooth and elastic. Place into a lightly greased bowl. Cover and let rise until doubled in bulk, about 1 ½ hours. Turn out onto a floured board and roll out the dough to about 1-inch thickness. Cut with a 2 ½–3-inch cookie cutter. Cover and let rise for about 30–35 minutes. Heat oil to 375° in a stove-top deep-fryer or an electric deep-fryer. For a stove-top fryer, use a thermometer. Fry in hot deep oil for about 1 minute on each side. Drain on paper towels. Serve sprinkled with powdered vanilla sugar (see recipe on page 37).

Hall in an ancient castle near Passau

BAYERISCHE HIMBEERCREME
Raspberry Bavarian Cream
serves 6

2 packages defrosted frozen raspberries in heavy syrup
1 6-ounce package raspberry gelatin
2 cups boiling water
1½ cups cold raspberry purée (add water if needed to make 1½ cups)
3 eggs
⅔ cup sugar
1 cup scalded cream
1 Tbls cornstarch
3 Tbls cold cream
2 cups whipped cream
1–2 packages lady fingers (optional)
2 cups sweetened whipped cream

Empty the raspberries with their liquid into a sieve over a bowl. Press the raspberries through the sieve. Dissolve gelatin in 2 cups of boiling water. Add all the raspberry purée. If you don't have enough to make 1½ cups, add water. Add to the gelatin. Set aside to cool. In a bowl, beat eggs and sugar until thick. Add hot scalded cream, beating steadily. Combine cornstarch and cold cream and add to the egg mixture. Pour the mixture into the top of a double boiler and cook over simmering water until thickened. Add to the gelatin. Cool, then refrigerate until the mixture is just starting to set. Fold in 2 cups of whipped cream.

If you wish, line the sides of a 2-quart soufflé dish with lady fingers. Pour in the cream. Refrigerate until set. Spread 2 cups of sweetened whipped cream on top.

BLACK FOREST CAKE, COUNTRY STYLE
serves 10–12

This is a different version of the classic cake.

⅓ cup Kirsch
*2¼ cups fresh pumpernickel crumbs
6 egg whites
⅛ tsp salt
1¼ cups sugar
6 egg yolks
1 tsp vanilla
½ tsp almond extract
4 tsp baking powder
⅔ cup coarsely grated walnuts
1 cup grated semisweet chocolate
½ cup Kirsch
3 15-oz cans of sour cherries, drained
3 cups heavy whipped cream
½ cup powdered vanilla sugar
4 Tbls Kirsch
½ cup coarsely grated semisweet chocolate

*Some people may not care for the pumpernickel crumbs. Plain finely ground bread crumbs may be substituted.

Preheat oven to 350°. Butter well and sprinkle with flour 2 9-inch cake pans.

Combine ⅓ cup Kirsch and crumbs in a bowl. Set aside. In a glass, pottery, or stainless steel bowl beat the egg whites with salt until they hold soft peaks. Add sugar, ¼ cup at a time, beating well after each addition. Continue beating until egg whites are very stiff. In another bowl stir the egg yolks with a fork to break them up. Add vanilla, almond extract, and baking powder. Fold about ⅓ of the egg whites into the egg yolks. Pour the egg yolk and egg white mixture over the remaining egg whites. Add the soaked bread crumbs, walnuts, and 1 cup grated chocolate. Gently blend all the ingredients together. Pour the batter into the prepared pans. Bake in the preheated 350° oven for about 35–40 minutes or until a cake tester or an inserted toothpick comes out clean. The cake does not rise much and will shrink away from the sides of the pan. Cool in the pans for about 30 minutes.

Remove cake from pans and place on a cutting board. With a sharp knife even out the tops of the cakes by cutting off about ⅛" to ¼" thick piece from the tops. Split each cake in two layers. Sprinkle each cake layer with ½ cup Kirsch. Set aside. Empty the cherries into a sieve and let them drain while whipping cream. In a chilled bowl whip cream until ripples appear on top. Add powdered vanilla sugar and the 4 tablespoons of Kirsch. Beat until stiff.

Place 1 layer of the cake on a serving platter. Spread about 1 cup of the whipped cream over the cake. Gently squeeze out as much juice as possible from the cherries. Reserve a few cherries for decoration. Spread ⅓ of the cherries all over the whipped cream. Cover with second layer of cake, spread 1 cup of whipped cream and the cherries on top of the cake layer. Cover with third layer, spread with 1 cup of whipped cream and ⅓ cup of cherries, cover with the last layer. Frost the sides and top of the cake generously with the remaining whipped cream. Decorate with the remaining cherries and the ½ cup coarsely grated chocolate. Refrigerate.

CHAPTER  2

AUSTRIA:
Mozart, Schnitzels,
and Strudels

ONCE the Danube crosses into Austria, the aquatic thoroughfare seems to undergo a change. It becomes frothy and more frivolous, flowing to the rhythm of waltzes and Gemütlichkeit. At the industrial city of Linz, the Danube is shrouded with mystery and with legends of the Willies and lights that glimmer in the night. It rolls over boulders, creating vortexes and ripples that foam into a fine spray, shrouding the countryside with a mist that may hide mythical beings who lure the fisherman and boatman to their watery abodes. Then it enters the rolling hills of Wachau and Krems, where vines are cultivated on sunny slopes and where the light, crisp Austrian wine is produced.

In spite of all the songs and romance, the Danube only skirts through Vienna, but to the Viennese, *"Die Blaue Donau"*, or "The Blue Danube," is their very own river, immortalized by music and song. In reality, the Danube is rather muddy, but try to convince a Viennese of that fact. They look at the foreigners with great disdain and a bit of sorrow, because only those who live along the river, and who are in love, will perceive the Danube as a glorious azure blue.

Vienna, the enchanting "Queen of the Danube," was founded on the site of a Celtic settlement and Roman ruins, in the path of the "Amber Route," which stretched from the Baltic to the Adriatic Sea.

Austria grew up around Vienna and expanded into a huge empire, but the Viennese remained unique in their thinking, their culture, and even in their language. Wienerisch or Wiener dialect may be as incomprehensible to an Austrian from another city or province as to a foreigner: The idiom is lovingly punctuated by diminutives, which are tagged on to almost everything from buildings to nightingales!

It was in A. D. 1 that Roman legionnaires built the fortress, Vindobona, as their bulwark against savage Germanic tribes. Emperor Probius, a loyal devotee of Bacchus, sent grapevine cuttings as his gift to the primitive natives, and the vines thrived

Vienna Opera House, circa early 18th Century

gloriously on the sunny slopes along the Danube. The Celtic settlement and the Roman garrison became the medieval walled city of Viennis, pillaged by Avars, Huns, Magyars, and Teutons and traversed by the Crusaders on their journey to the Holy Land.

In the late thirteenth century, when Rudolph of Hapsburg defeated Ottocar of Bohemia, Vienna became Wien and the seat of the Hapsburg dynasty. Under Hapsburg rule, it was besieged by Turks and Swedes and briefly occupied by Napoleon, and, it remained the scene of many internal strifes until Austria became a republic after World War I.

Today, Austria, Vienna, and their peoples are the results of this blending of cultures, which is reflected in the architecture, the music, and the food. Despite all the upheavals, changes, and battles, Austria grew and prospered to become a center of learning, culture, music, poetry, love, and gemütlichkeit—enjoyment of the good life.

The Viennese are charming, cynical, and witty; they have a trememdous capacity to laugh at themselves and to mock others. They love to meddle, and they will even interrupt a conversation or join in an altercation between people they do not know.

Natives may not agree, but the cuisine of Vienna is international, and the most important culinary contributions to Viennese gastronomy were made by chefs brought by the nobility from Byzantium, Italy, and France. For centuries, the talented native cooks absorbed the best recipes from visiting foreigners, as well as from the inhabitants of their vast empire. The result is an exciting melange, known to the world as *Wiener Küche* (Viennese cooking).

Although spices were introduced from many places, it was from Hungary that the chefs acquired paprika, the *Goulash* and *Paprikash*, outstanding fruits and vegetables, and the finest flour. Dumplings, a mainstay of Austrian cooking today, originated in Bohemia, as did several sauerkraut dishes. Venison cookery was elevated to exalted heights, but the undisputed favorite was veal. Today, most chefs—and even houswives—have an impressive and varied repertoire of veal dishes par excellence, led by *Wiener Schnitzel*, which may have originated in Milan.

From the remnants of the Ottoman Empire came coffee, and the coffee houses, which have since become purely Viennese institutions, are an anomaly that could not exist elsewhere. The first coffee house was opened in Vienna in the mid-seventeenth century by a rogue named Frantz Kolshitzky.

The authentic Wiener Kaffeehaus has dark wood paneling stained by smoke from many generations, murky crystal chandeliers, banquettes of worn velvet, and small marble tables surrounded by straight-backed wooden chairs. People go to read, write, concentrate, and discuss business and politics. The *Herr Ober* (headwaiter) greets a customer as an habitué after the second visit, ushering him to his *Stammtisch* (favorite table). The revered old establishments patronized by Schubert, Strauss, Mozart, Beethoven, Suppe, and Lehar are still in existence, although they have been upstaged by the whoosh of espresso machines in the new, garish espresso bars.

Stammgäste (regulars) frown on the practice of serving meals at their favorite old-fashioned cafés. But times are changing, and today most of the cafés will serve lunch, *Jause* (the 4 p.m. coffee and pastry ritual), and dinner—and some even go so far as to cover their marble tables with cloths.

The Mozart on Albertiner Platz—there are at least five Mozart cafés in Vienna—draws affluent businessmen, university professors, and opera singers. Café Sacher remains popular with the nobility and the landed gentry, but the most typical coffee house to be patronized almost exclusively by the natives is Landtmann, where friends meet to play bridge and drink endless cups of fragrant coffee.

All Austrians are especially inventive in blending coffee, and the drink is served in many ways and shades, from the palest *Verkehrt* (four parts milk to one part coffee) to *Mocha* (black coffee served in a demitasse). The beverage is also served with hot milk, and, of course, with whipped cream—even double portions of whipped cream—and as Italian espresso or cappuccino, as well as in a myriad of other ways.

A typical Austrian day of eating begins with a light breakfast: coffee with hot milk, *Semmerlin* (rolls) or *Kipferln* (crescent-shaped rolls), butter, and jam. About 10 o'clock, it's time for a *Gabelfrüschtück* or "fork breakfast," which may consist of a few *Würstel* (small sausages) or a bit of meat, or even a small plate of *Frühstückgulasch* (breakfast goulash). At noon comes the *Mittagessen* (midday meal) and at 4 o'clock the *Jause*—that totally Viennese habit dedicated to the appreciation of cakes, pastries, and coffee! Dinner is served rather late and is usually light.

During *Jause* hour, chic matrons—often a bit on the plump side—go to the cafés for coffee and "just a tiny piece of sweet," brought to the tables by a pastry waitress. Tempting delicacies are displayed on a tray suspended from a leather strap around her neck, or they are set out on a pastry wagon. Most pastry shops and cafés serve a lavish assortment of the divine creations, but nowhere in the world does one find a more tempting array of sweets than at Zuckerbackerei Demel in Vienna.

Demel's is still "old world" and splendidly baroque, a marvelous Viennese landmark of mirrors, black marble tables, and chandeliers covered with white milk glass globes. There and at other pastry shops, dozens of different tortes are offered every day— *Annatorte, Neopolitaner Torte, Pralinen Torte, Giselatorte, Sandtorte, Nelsontorte,* and on and on—and these are in addition to cream-filled horns, *Kugelhupfs,* and a fantastic variety of small cakes and pastries!

When men stop in pastry shops on their way home, they often buy a surprise for their families—a few extra sweets, packed in a telltale white box tied with a long string. (They've even been known to buy a sweet for a horse waiting patiently with its owner for passengers to carry in open landaus through the inner city, which is closed to other traffic.)

But not all Austrian food consists of cream and pastry, and there is outstanding solid fare to be had in scores of appetizing stores, which fill their windows with tempting mounds of hams, sausages, baked chickens, salamis, cheeses, and breads of all shapes and kinds.

Sausage is also sold all over Austria at small wooden stands that are rolled onto street corners after dark. The appetizing aroma from the copper cauldrons entices passers-by to stop for a beef frankfurter; a smoked pork *Krainer;* or another type—mild, spicy, or garlicky—of sausage served on a roll or on a slice of peasant rye bread and topped with a healthy dollop of mustard.

Meat is important enought to the Austrian housewife that she has her own personal butcher, a friend with whom she confers often about the simplest cut or about a certain delicate sausage or ham. Also, in the early morning, the hausfraus (some with maids carrying baskets) go to the "greenmarket" to but the freshest, dewiest fruits and vegetables. Food shopping is serious business; it is possibly the only time when the Viennese become a bit grim, so intent are they on buying the very best possible fare.

The enjoyment of food and drink is such an integral part of the lifestyle that it is interwoven with entertainment. In summer, for

Hotel Sacher, Vienna

example, when music is everywhere and when bands play in gardens and outdoor restaurants, the most popular afternoon concert is at the *Stadtpark* (city park). There, people sit on the terrace of the *Kursaal* restaurant and consume immense amounts of pastries and coffee *mit Schlag* (whipped cream) while listening to the maestro direct his orchestra through a range of Strauss waltzes, Kalman, Lehar, and Suppe. To an outsider, the setting may seem unreal, even staged; people stroll by, swaying to the three-quarter beat of the waltzes, while those on the terrace nod contentedly in tempo to the rhythm of familiar tunes.

Just a short distance from the city center in Vienna are the terraced hills of the vineyards and the Vienna Woods. Here, city dwellers come to relax in the fresh air and to stop at a *Heuriger*, a small tavern or a vine-covered arbor where new wine is served. (The word refers to both the place and the drink.) After people had come to the vineyards for centuries to drink the new wine, the vintners began to set out rough-hewn tables and benches; then later, they built small arbors where visitors could sit and drink in comfort. Now the owners hang a green bush over the entrance to their inns to signal that the wine is ready to be poured from the casks—a cherished spring and summer custom.

At first, those who enjoyed the *Heuriger* took their own food, but now the innkeepers serve smoked meats, hard-boiled eggs, radishes, scallions, cold roasted chicken, Liptauer cheese, and dark peasant bread. Friends gather to eat, drink, and sing to the music of a fiddler or a zither player—and to get maudlin and sentimental about everything Viennese.

Vienna is a sophisticated metropolis, and so is its cuisine. It is frothy, light, and *Schlag-*(whipped cream) oriented, and with so many foreign influences, it is a blend of the best from east to west.

Outside of Vienna, the eight provinces of Austria stretch across the Alpine landscape. Most of the cities are a blend of mountain villages—baroque, rococo, and modern. They lie in high valleys, surrounded by the Alps. Although the cuisine of Salzburg and Innsbruck, the two best known cities outside of Vienna, is typically Austrian, the frilly international Hapsburg influence is evident in many dishes, especially in the luscious desserts. Salzburg's culinary claim to fame is *Salzburger Nockerl*, a type of featherlight egg soufflé, golden brown, risen high in a baking dish. The provincial Austrians don't have to take a back seat to cooking expertise with their cakes, sweets, *Wurst* (sausages), and breads. The people who live in the mountains have developed their own hearty fare, based mostly on things they grow themselves. They make marvelous flour dishes, served with golden home-churned butter, cream cheese, and fresh eggs. To keep out the glacial winds, they warm themselves with robust soups filled with meats from "heaven," a pet name for the smoking chimney where home-smoked hams, sausages, and bacon hang. Thrifty housewives use leftover bacon or sausage to make *"Tirolerknödel,"* the Tyrolean dumplings. Or, if combined with diced potatoes, the bacon or sausage leftovers make delectable *"Gröstle."*

Most houses in the country and in the smaller towns are centered around an intricately tiled stove, which is built into the wall between the kitchen and the living room. On the side of the kitchen, the stove is an open hearth for cooking. It is completely tiled on the living room side and provides the room with a warm, intimate ambiance.

Only Burgenland, one of the provinces that stretches east of Vienna, borders the Danube. Here, the high Alps give way to rolling hills and plains and to the reeds that surround the Neusiedler Lake on the Hungarian border. All of Burgenland was once Hungarian, and here, men wear britches stuck into leather boots, and women are pround of their ability to make *Gulyas, Paprikas,* and thin Hungarian strudels.

Men travel miles to reach the Danube and to fish along its shores or from medieval-looking dugouts. Here, the river is a crossroad and a bond among Austrians, Czechoslovakians, and Hungarians, all of whom claim the Danube as their very own.

Appetizers. . . . .

SHRIMP AND CHEESE CRÊPES
serves 6

For the Crêpes:

¾	cup light cream		1	cup cooked and chilled minced shrimp
1 ¼	cups unbleached all-purpose flour		3	egg whites
3	egg yolks plus 1 egg		⅛	tsp cream of tartar
1	Tbls melted butter		¼	cup melted butter
⅓	cup grated Parmesan cheese		1	lb sliced sautéed mushrooms
⅓	cup grated Romano cheese		*2 ½	cups cheese sauce
1	Tbls minced onion			
	salt and pepper to taste			

In a blender, beat cream, flour, egg yolks, egg, butter, cheeses, onion, salt, and pepper at low speed. Refrigerate the batter for 2 hours. Stir in the shrimp. In a bowl, beat the egg whites with the cream of tartar until very stiff but not dry. Fold egg whites into the batter. Brush a crêpe pan with butter. Slowly pour ¼ cup of the batter into the pan, making a small (about 4 or 5 inch, ¼-inch) thick pancake. Turn and brown on the other side. Roll up each pancake when done and place in a buttered baking pan. Spread mushrooms over the pancakes and top with cheese sauce. Bake in a 350° oven for 10 minutes.

*Cheese Sauce

3 Tbls butter	½ cup grated Gruyere cheese
3 Tbls flour	¼ cup grated Parmesan cheese
2 cups light cream	1 tsp Dijon mustard
1 package chicken broth powdered, or crushed chicken broth cubes	salt and white pepper to taste

In a saucepan, melt the butter. Add flour and cook, stirring constantly. When the butter and flour bubble, slowly add the cream and chicken broth, stirring continuously. Cook for 2–3 minutes over low heat until the sauce thickens. Stir in the cheeses, mustard, salt, and pepper. Pour over the crêpes.

SMOKED SALMON CORNUCOPIAS
serves 8–12

1 pound smoked sliced salmon	¼ cup black caviar
3 Tbls hot white horseradish	1 cup sour cream
1 cup whipped cream	

Cut the salmon pieces diagonally to make triangles. Set aside. In a bowl, combine horseradish and whipped cream. In another small bowl, combine caviar and sour cream. Fill half the salmon triangles with a tablespoon of the horseradish filling and the remaining triangles with a tablespoon of the caviar filling. Roll up the triangles to form cornucopias. A frilled toothpick may be used to secure the base of the cornucopia.

Note: For variation, Westphalian ham slices may be used instead of salmon.

EGGS FILLED WITH CAVIAR
serves 4–6

4	hard-cooked eggs	⅛	tsp finely ground white pepper
1	tsp minced shallots	4	Tbls black caviar
2	Tbls mayonnaise	4	slices of pimento (optional)
2	Tbls heavy cream		

Shell and slice the eggs lengthwise. Place the egg yolks in a bowl and mash with a fork. Stir in shallots, mayonnaise, cream, and white pepper and mix until very smooth. Fill the eggs and spread caviar over the filling. Garnish with pimiento slices if desired.

SALMON MOUSSE
serves 6

1	package plain gelain	¼	pound Nova Scotia salmon, cut into pieces
¼	cup cold water		
½	cup boiling water	¼	tsp white pepper
½	cup mayonnaise	½	cup whipped cream
1	Tbls lemon juice	1	Tbls chopped capers
2	Tbls minced scallions	2	stiffly beaten egg whites
½	tsp salt	4	ounces red caviar
1	18-ounce can drained salmon	6	hard-cooked egg whites } gamish

Sprinkle the gelatin on cold water. Add boiling water and mix well. In a large bowl, mix the gelatin, mayonnaise, lemon juice, scallions, and salt. Place in a blender and add drained salmon, white pepper, and Nova Scotia salmon. Purée the mixture and pour it into a bowl. Fold in whipped cream and capers. Gently fold in the beaten egg whites. Oil a fish mold very well. Pour the mousse into the mold. Refrigerate for a least 3 hours. Unmold by inverting the mold onto a platter and holding a hot towel over it. Decorate with red caviar and hard-cooked egg whites cut into shapes with small cutouts.

The mousse may also be made in individual molds and served as an appetizer on lettuce and accompanied by toasted pumpernickel slices.

CHEESE–SPINACH STRUDEL

serves 8

2 10-ounce packages chopped frozen spinach, defrosted	¼ tsp pepper
½ pound Feta cheese, chopped	2 eggs, well beaten
1 pound creamed cottage cheese	2 Tbls melted butter
3 Tbls finely chopped scallions	1 pound strudel or filo dough
Salt to taste	¼ pound melted butter

Preheat oven to 350°. Squeeze spinach almost dry. In a large bowl, mix the cheese, scallions, salt, and pepper. Blend well. Add the spinach and blend again. Fold in the eggs and the butter. Taste, and add salt if necessary. Open the package of strudel or *filo* dough. Spread a damp towel on the table or counter. Take two strudel leaves and place on the towel. Brush the leaves with melted butter. Take two more leaves and place over the buttered ones. Brush again with butter. Place the cheese filling on one end of the leaves, making a strip about 2 inches wide. Roll up jelly roll style, making sure to tuck in the ends. Place the strudel on an ungreased cooked sheet. Brush the strudel generously with butter and bake in a 350° preheated oven for approximately 20 minutes or until golden brown. Slice and serve hot. The strudel may be frozen unbaked: brush strudel with butter, wrap into buttered foil and freeze. Take directly out of freezer without defrosting and bake at 350° for 40 minutes, or until golden brown. Bake unwrapped, but in foil, on a cookie sheet. While making the strudel, be sure that the dough is always covered, because it dries very fast. The remaining dough may be rewrapped and refrozen.

Alpine chalet, near Vienna

MUSHROOMS IN BEER BATTER, VIENNA STYLE
serves 6

The Mushrooms:

36 medium-sized firm mushrooms

Remove stems from mushrooms. Wipe the caps clean with a
damp cloth and set aside. Then prepare batter and filling.

For the Beer Batter:

1	cup light cream	1 ½	cups flour
2	eggs	2	cups vegetable oil or more for deep
1	cup beer		frying
	Salt and pepper to taste		

In a bowl, combine light cream, eggs, and beer. Beat well and add
salt and pepper to taste. Add flour, beating continuously until
smooth. If necessary, add more flour to make a dough the consistency of a thick cream. Set aside for one hour.

For the Filling:

2	cups lump crabmeat		Salt and pepper to taste
4	Tbls mayonnaise	3	Tbls minced parsley
2	Tbls minced chives		

Shred the crabmeat with a fork into a bowl. Add mayonnaise,
chives, salt and pepper to taste, and parsley. Mix well. Stuff the
mushrooms with crab filling. Dip the filled mushrooms into the
beer batter and deep-fry the mushrooms until golden brown, about
3–4 minutes at 375°. Drain and serve immediately.

POTATO SOUP
serves 8

1	small diced onion	2	Tbls flour
5	Tbls butter	7	potatoes, peeled and diced
1 ½	pounds very lean ground beef	3	quarts water
1	Tbls paprika	1	cup sour cream
	Salt and pepper to taste	2	Tbls chives or scallions minced

In a large pot, sauté the onion in butter until limp. Add the ground beef and stir continuously. Do not allow the beef to lump. Remove pot from heat and add paprika. Stir to coat the meat thoroughly and return the pot to the burner. Sprinkle with salt and pepper and simmer for 3–5 minutes. Sprinkle the flour over the meat and mix well. Add potatoes and water. Cover and simmer until the potatoes are tender, about 40 minutes. Add more salt and pepper to taste. Mix sour cream with 1 cup liquid from the soup and add to the soup. Serve sprinkled with chives.

Famed hand-carved wooden Pacher Madonna and child, Salzburg Cathedral

61

CHICKEN SOUP
Serves 6

3-5 quarts water
3 carrots, scraped and cut into 1-2 inch pieces
2 large onions, quartered
2 green peppers, cut in half
1 tomato, cut in half
2-3 sprigs dill, 3-4 sprigs parsley, and 4 scallions, tied together with a string
6 peppercorns, 1 crushed bayleaf, ½ teaspoon rosemary, 3 cloves, tied into a cheesecloth

3 stalks celery, cut into 3 inch pieces
Salt to taste
2 broiling chickens, cut into serving pieces
1 small onion, minced
1 pound thin egg noodles, cooked as directed
2-3 Tbls chives or scallions minced

Bring water to a boil in a large pot and add carrots, onions, peppers, tomato, parsley, scallions, dill, the bundle with spices tied into cheesecloth, celery, and salt to taste. Bring to a boil and simmer for 15 minutes. Add the chickens. Cover tightly and simmer for 1 hour, skimming off the foam periodically. With a slotted spoon, remove the onions, green peppers, parsley, scallions, dill, bundle of spices, and celery and discard. Take out the chicken pieces and remove the bones. Cut boned chicken meat into large chunks. Return to the pot. Adjust the seasoning and add more salt and pepper if desired. Serve in soup plates with chicken and about ¾ cup of noodles to each plate. Sprinkle with chives.

Gothic stove, Salzburg Castle

RINDSUPPE
Beef Soup
serves 7–8

4 quarts water	2 parsnips, scraped and split in two
3 pounds *flanken* (short ribs of beef)	1 turnip, peeled and sliced
2 pounds oxtails	2 celery stalks, sliced
2–3 pounds marrow and knuckle bones	1 green pepper, cored and quartered
2 medium onions, halved	1 tomato, quartered
3 carrots, scraped and cut into ½ inch pieces	1 ½ Tbls salt or more to taste
	6–7 peppercorns

In a large pot, bring water to a boil, and add *flanken*, oxtails, and bones. Cook 5 minutes and skim off the foam. Keep cooking, and about every 5–6 minutes, skim off the foam. This process should take about 20–25 minutes. Add all the vegetables, salt and peppercorns. Cover the pot and simmer soup for 2 ½–3 hours or until the meat is very tender. Serve the meat as boiled beef with a horseradish sauce and serve the soup the next day. Let the soup cool completely and then refrigerate overnight. Remove fat from the top of the soup and clarify the soup (discard the vegetables).

To Clarify Soup:

3 egg whites
3 broken egg shells
3 Tbls cold water
3–3 ½ quarts cold beef broth

In a bowl, beat together egg whites, egg shells, and water. Add to the beef broth and bring broth to boiling point, stirring continuously. Cook for 3 minutes, then reduce heat and barely simmer over very low heat for about 15–20 minutes. Remove from heat and cool slightly. Strain through a double cheesecloth and a sieve, being careful not to disturb the sediment. The soup should now be clear. Serve it hot with noodles, dumplings, or thinly sliced crêpes. Place noodles, dumplings, or crêpes into each soup bowl along with the broth.

GRÜNE ERBSENSUPPE
Green Pea Soup
serves 6

4 10-ounce packages frozen green peas	Salt and white pepper to taste
6 cups chicken broth	1 egg yolk
2 well-washed leeks, chopped	1 cup heavy cream
4 Tbls butter	2 tsp lemon juice
4 Tbls flour	2 Tbls parsley minced

Cook the peas and the leeks in chicken broth until both are very tender. Cool, drain, but reserve the liquid. Purée peas and leeks in a blender, adding a little of the liquid at a time, or purée in a food mill and combine purée with the cooking liquid. In a saucepan melt butter, add flour, and cook, stirring constantly until it just turns pale gold. Add salt and pepper. Beat egg yolk and cream. Add 1 cup of hot soup, beating steadily. Add this to the flour mixture, beating continuously. Add the lemon juice, then add the mixture to the pea soup. Mix well. Heat the soup, but do not boil. Serve sprinkled with a bit of minced parsley.

ERBSENSUPPE MIT SCHWEINHACKSEN
Dried Pea Soup with Pigs' Knuckles
serves 6

2 ½ cups dried green peas	2 scraped carrots, sliced
Water to cover peas	3 quarts water
3 pigs' knuckles	2 sliced celery stalks
4 cups water	Salt and pepper to taste
2 tsp salt	6 small boiled potatoes
1 small onion, stuck with 2 cloves	

Soak peas overnight in the water. Cook the pigs' knuckles in 4 cups water with 2 teaspoons salt for 20 minutes. Drain the peas and the pigs' knuckles. Place both into a large soup pot. Add the onion, carrots, celery, water, salt, and pepper. Bring to a boil, reduce heat, cover pot and simmer for about 2–2 ½ hours or until the peas and the pigs' knuckles are tender. Remove the knuckles, cool them, and remove the meat from the bones. Pour the soup into a bowl through a sieve and press the peas with vegetables through the sieve. Pour the sieved soup back into the pot, add the meat, and adjust seasoning by adding more salt and pepper. Heat and serve with a small boiled potato in each bowl.

KALTE WEINSUPPE
Cold Wine Soup
serves 6

5 cups beef consommé (canned may be used)	1 tsp grated orange peel
2 cups dry white wine	1 cup whipped cream
	3 thin orange slices, cut in half

In a pot combine consommé, white wine, and orange peel. Bring to a fast boil, remove from heat, and pour mixture into a chilled bowl or soup tureen. Refrigerate until thoroughly chilled. Serve in cups with a dollop of whipped cream on top, garnished with half an orange slice.

SPARGELKREMSUPPE
Cream of Asparagus Soup
serves 6

2 ½ quarts chicken broth	¼ cup butter
1 small onion, quartered	¼ cup flour
1 carrot, scraped and sliced	1 cup heavy cream
1 parsnip, scraped and sliced	2 egg yolks
4 sprigs parsley tied together with a string	24 asparagus tips, cooked in salted water
1 pound fresh asparagus, scraped	Salt and pepper to taste

In a large pot, bring broth to a boil and add onion, carrot, parsnip, parsley, and asparagus. Bring broth to a boil, reduce heat, and simmer for about 20–25 minutes, or until vegetables are tender. Strain into a bowl. Remove parsley and press the other vegetables through the sieve. Pour the soup back into the pot. In a saucepan, melt the butter. Add flour, stir well, and cook until just bubbly. Add cream, stirring continuously, and cook until slightly thickened. Beat the egg yolks, add to cream mixture, and beat well. Add cream mixture to the soup and stir well. Add the asparagus tips and more salt and pepper to taste. Simmer for a few minutes until the soup is slightly thickened. Serve immediately.

Salads . . . .

MARINATED CUCUMBER SALAD WITH A CROWN OF SHREDDED CRABMEAT

serves 4

2 thinly sliced cucumbers
1 Tbls salt
1 tsp salt
4 tsp sugar

½ cup white vinegar
1 tsp white wine
⅔ cup shredded crabmeat

Mix sliced cucumbers and 1 tablespoon of salt. Allow the mixture to stand for 10 minutes, then rinse with water. Add 1 teaspoon of salt, sugar, vinegar, and wine. Mix thoroughly. Fill individual small bowls with cucumbers and top with crabmeat. Refrigerate immediately. Serve when well chilled.

ENDIVE CHEESE SALAD

serves 6

3 heads endive lettuce
1½ pounds thinly sliced Gruyere cheese
1 cup mayonnaise
¾ cup unsweetened whipped cream

1 Tbls French mustard
Salt and white pepper to taste
2½ Tbls lemon juice
1 Tbls grated lemon rind

Slice the endives lengthwise in two. On salad plates, arrange half of the endive leaves. Place cheese slices on top of lettuce. In a bowl, blend the mayonnaise, whipped cream, mustard, lemon juice, salt, and white pepper thoroughly. Place a large spoonful of the dressing on top of each salad. Sprinkle with lemon rind.

POTATO SALAD

serves 6

8 large potatoes, cooked and sliced
10 scallions, minced
3 Tbls parsley, minced
3 cloves garlic, minced
½ cup wine vinegar

4 Tbls vegetable oil
3 tsp prepared mustard
1 tsp salt
¼ tsp black pepper

Place sliced potatoes into a bowl, add scallions, parsley, and garlic. In a saucepan combine vinegar, oil, mustard, salt, and pepper. Heat, stirring until well-blended. Bring to a boiling point and immediately remove from heat. Pour mixture over the potatoes. Toss thoroughly, chill and serve.

RADISH SALAD

serves 6

24 white radishes, thinly sliced	½–1 cup sour cream
2 tsp salt	½ tsp paprika
½ cup white wine vinegar	2 Tbls parsley, minced
Black pepper to taste	¼–⅓ cup olive oil to taste
Lettuce leaves	

Place radishes into a bowl and sprinkle them with salt. Let them stand for 1 hour at room temperature. Add vinegar, toss lightly, and refrigerate for 3 hours. Drain the radishes and add oil to taste, starting with ¼ cup. Place lettuce leaves on 6 salad plates. Pile radishes onto the lettuce. Place a few teaspoons of sour cream on top of the radishes; sprinkle with paprika and parsley. Serve immediately.

Vienna woodcut, circa 18th Century

Vegetables . . . .

BRAISED BELGIAN ENDIVES
serves 6

12 Belgian endives
2 quarts water
1 tsp salt
2 Tbls lemon juice
4 Tbls margarine
4 Tbls lemon juice

1 clove garlic, mashed or ¼ tsp garlic powder
½ tsp basil
¼ tsp black pepper
Salt to taste

Wash the endives. Cut off the ends and remove any damaged or brown leaves. Bring water and salt to a boil and add the lemon juice and the endives. Reduce heat and cook for 10 minutes. Drain well. In a large skillet, heat margarine and lemon juice. Add garlic, basil, pepper, salt, and the endives. Cover and simmer for 5–7 minutes on one side over medium heat. Turn very carefully, using a fork and a spoon. Simmer on the other side for 5–7 minutes until the endives are slightly browned. Serve hot with meat, fowl, or fish.

GREEN BEANS
serves 6

2 pounds green beans
4 cups water
1 Tbls salt
4 Tbls butter
4 Tbls breadcrumbs

½ cup parsley, minced
2 cloves garlic, mashed
⅛ tsp black pepper
1 cup sour cream

Place beans in cold, salted water. Bring to a boil and simmer uncovered until just tender. Drain well. Melt butter in a pan and as soon as it becomes golden, add breadcrumbs and brown them evenly. Mix parsley and garlic, black pepper, and breadcrumbs. Remove the pan from heat and add the parsley mixture to the green beans. Put into an ovenproof dish. Add sour cream and bake for 15 minutes in a 350° oven.

BRAISED FENNEL
serves 6

3 **bulbs fennel**	4 **Tbls melted butter**
4 **cups water**	½ **tsp fresh basil (or ¼ tsp dry basil)**
1 **Tbls salt**	⅛ **tsp black pepper**
1 ½ **cups chicken broth**	

Trim the fennel and wash well. Slice each bulb into ½-inch slices. In a saucepan bring salted water to boil, add fennel slices, and cook 6–7 minutes. Drain well. Place the fennel slices into a baking dish; add the broth and the melted butter. Sprinkle with basil and pepper. Cover the baking dish with a lid or foil and bake in a 350° oven for 20–25 minutes, until fennel slices are tender.

CAULIFLOWER WITH GREEN SAUCE
serves 4

1 **large cauliflower**	3 **Tbls scallions, minced**
2 **Tbls lemon juice**	1 **tsp sugar**
water and salt for cooking	2 **Tbls lemon juice**
⅓ **cup unsalted butter**	½ **cup heavy cream**
1 **package frozen peas, cooked as directed on the package**	**salt and pepper to taste**

Sprinkle cauliflower with lemon juice. Cook cauliflower in salted water until tender. Keep warm. (If made ahead, reheat over steam.) In a saucepan melt ⅓ cup butter and pour it over the cauliflower. Set aside.

Drain the peas and put into a blender; add scallions, sugar, lemon juice and cream. Add salt and pepper. Purée until a thick sauce is formed. Pour into a saucepan and heat, but do not boil. Just before serving, place cauliflower into a deep serving dish and cover it with the pea sauce. Serve immediately.

F*ish* . . . .

FISH ROULADE
serves 4–6

6	filets of sole	1	cup shredded crabmeat (use lump crabmeat or Alaskan king crab)
	Salt and pepper to taste		
2	Tbls lemon juice	½	cup fine bread crumbs
2	finely chopped onions	½	tsp salt
3	Tbls butter or margarine	¼	tsp pepper
10	medium mushrooms, finely chopped	2	Tbls finely chopped parsley

Sprinkle fish with salt, pepper, and lemon juice and set aside. Sauté the onions in butter until just transparent. Do not brown. Add the parsley, salt, and pepper. Bring to a boil and set aside to cool slightly. Place about 2–3 tablespoons of the crab mixture on each sole filet. Roll up each filet and place, seam side down, in a well-buttered baking dish.

Sauce

4	Tbls butter or margarine	½	cup pale dry sherry
3	Tbls flour	2	tsp prepared mustard
½	cup clam broth or chicken broth	⅔	cup finely ground Swiss, Gruyere, or cheddar cheese
⅔	cup light cream		
½	tsp salt	⅔	cup finely ground Romano cheese
½	tsp pepper		Paprika to garnish
¼	tsp basil		

In a saucepan, melt butter, add flour, and bring to a boil. Add broth and cream. Bring to a boil again. Add spices, wine, and mustard. Fold in ½ of the Swiss cheese and ½ of the Romano cheese. Pour over the fish. Bake for 30–35 minutes in a 375° oven. Sprinkle with the remaining Swiss and the Romano cheeses and paprika. Bake for another 10 minutes, or until the fish is tender and flakes easily with a fork.

FORELLEN IN RAHM
Trout in Sour Cream Sauce
serves 6

For the Trout:

2–3	small or two large trout, dressed	3	Tbls butter or margarine
	Salt and pepper	2	onions, finely diced
½	cup flour	½	cup dry white wine
1	Tbls paprika		

Wash the fish and pat dry with paper towels. Sprinkle the fish with salt and pepper. Mix flour and paprika and dredge fish in the mixture. In a large skillet, sauté onions in butter until golden and then remove the onions to another dish. If necessary, put a little more butter in the skillet and brown the fish on both sides. Pour wine over the fish and simmer for 5 minutes.

For the Sauce:

½	cup white wine	1	tsp cornstarch dissolved in 1 Tbls water
½	clove garlic, crushed		
¼	tsp salt	⅔	tsp rosemary
¼	tsp pepper	1	cup sour cream

Remove fish from the skillet and place on a heated serving platter. Keep warm. Pour wine into the skillet where the fish was cooking. Add garlic and a little salt and pepper. Add cornstarch, rosemary, and sour cream. Blend well with a whisk until there are no lumps. Add the onions and simmer for 1 minute. Pour the sauce over the trout. Serve with bread dumplings (see page 33).

The Danube near Linz

PIKE, KREMS STYLE
serves 5–6

3–4	-pound cleaned pike (whole)	5	Tbls lemon juice
½	tsp salt	3	thin slices of lemon
2	cups water	1	tsp salt
2	cups white wine	8	eggs
1	sliced carrot	6	Tbls butter
2	ribs of celery	⅔	cup bread crumbs
1	sliced onion		Salt and pepper to taste
10	peppercorns		Parslied boiled potatoes
3	springs parsley		
3	sprigs dill (if available)		
4	whole scallions		

Use a cleaned pike. Leave the head and tail on or cut them off, as you wish. Sprinkle fish with salt. Use a fish poacher or a very large pan. Pour the water and white wine into the poacher or pan. Add carrot, celery, onion, peppercorns, bouquet garni, 2 tablespoons of lemon juice, lemon slices, and salt. Bring to a boil and cook for 5 minutes. Place the fish on top of the vegetables and cook, basting frequently, for 30–35 minutes or until it flakes easily. While fish is cooking, hard boil the eggs. Cool the eggs and chop very fine. Melt butter in a skillet and add the chopped eggs, breadcrumbs, and 3 tablespoons of lemon juice, salt and pepper to taste. Toss together and simmer 2–3 minutes. Place the fish on a heated platter and spread eggs and crumbs over the fish. Served with boiled potatoes sprinkled with parsley.

KALTE FORELLE

Cold Trout
serves 3–4

3–4	lake trout (or brook trout), about 2 pounds each	5	peppercorns
2	sliced carrots	1–2	quarts water
1	medium onion, quartered and stuck with 3 cloves	1	tsp salt
2	bay leaves		Vegetable decorations of your choice—cucumbers, tomatoes, radishes, and lemons, in pretty shapes

Use 3–4 cleaned trout. Leave the heads and tails on. Place carrots, onions, bay leaves, and peppercorns into a large skillet. Add water and salt. Place trout into the skillet. Cover and simmer for 15–20 minutes. Remove trout from the water, place on a platter, and let them cool. Chill for 2–3 hours in the refrigerator. Decorate the platter with cucumbers, radishes, tomatoes, and lemons. Serve with dill mayonnaise on the side.

Dill Mayonnaise

Add 2 Tablespoons of chopped dill and 2 tablespoons of minced chives to 2 cups mayonnaise and mix well.

Main square in Vienna, circa 17th Century

FILETS OF SOLE WITH SHRIMP AND MUSSELS
serves 6

6 filets of sole
1 ½ cups white wine
*1 ½ cups fish stock
Salt and pepper to taste
3 Tbls sweet butter
2 shallots, finely chopped
**3 Tbls béchamel sauce for fish
3 Tbls sweet butter
2 dozen mussels (canned can be used)

2 dozen shrimp, shelled and deveined
4 cups water and fish stock together
2 dozen mushroom caps
2 Tbls butter
Juice of 1 lemon
2 Tbls unsweetened whipped cream

Poach sole for about 10 minutes in wine and fish stock to which have been added salt, pepper, 3 tablespoons of butter, and shallots. Remove the filets to a flame proof serving dish and cook the liquid until it is reduced by two-thirds. Add béchamel sauce and 3 tablespoons of sweet butter. Stir until the butter is melted and strain the sauce through a fine sieve.

Cook mussels and shrimp in equal amounts of water and fish stock; drain. Sauté the mushrooms in butter and lemon juice. Arrange mussels, shrimp, and mushrooms around the fish filets. Fold whipped cream into the sauce, pour it over the filets, and glaze the sauce very briefly under the broiler.

*Fish Stock

To each quart of cold water, add 1 pound of fish trimmings (heads, tails, fin, bones), tied into a cheesecloth bag, and 1 tablespoon of salt. Bring to a boiling point, reduce heat, and simmer for 30 minutes. Strain.

**Béchamel Sauce

3 Tbls butter
2 Tbls flour
1 cup light cream
Salt and pepper to taste

Melt butter in a saucepan. Add flour, stirring continuously. Cook for 1 minute over low heat. Add cream and cook, beating with a whisk, until slightly thickened. Add salt and pepper to taste.

FISH DANUBE STYLE

serves 4

1 large carp, cleaned and cut into 2-inch steaks (or use any other fish steaks)
4 cups water
2 cleaned and sliced carrots
1 large mild onion, sliced
2 stalks celery
12 peppercoms
3 Tbls lemon juice
Salt and white pepper to taste
10 hard-boiled eggs
½ cup butter
3 Tbls lemon juice

Preheat oven to 375°. Pour the water into a baking dish large enough to accommodate the fish steaks. Spread carrots, onion, celery, and peppercorns evenly in the pan. Add the lemon juice. Sprinkle fish with salt and pepper, place the fish into the baking pan, cover the pan with foil, and bake in a 375° oven for about 45 minutes, or until the fish flakes easily. Baste the fish several times with the liquid. Peel the hard-boiled eggs; chop fine. In a large skillet, heat butter, add chopped eggs, lemon juice, salt and pepper to taste, and simmer over low heat, stirring occasionally, until the eggs are thoroughly heated. When the fish is cooked, remove it gently from the saucepan onto a serving platter and pour the eggs over the fish. Serve with boiled buttered potatoes sprinkled with parsley and horseradish.

Exterior of Salzburg Castle

Poultry . . . .

CHICKEN, WACHAU STYLE
serves 6

2	3-pound broiling chickens, cut in half	4	large potatoes, thinly sliced
1	tsp salt	1	pound green beans, sliced
6	strips bacon	½	tsp pepper
2	onions, cut into thin strips	½	cup white wine
1	pound sliced mushrooms	¼	tsp tarragon

Sprinkle chickens with salt and set aside. Cut bacon into small pieces. Place bacon and onions into a large pot. Cook until the onions are slightly browned. Remove onions and pieces of bacon from the pot and set aside. Brown chickens in the pot on all sides. Add bacon, onions, sliced mushrooms, potatoes, beans, pepper, wine, and tarragon. Cover and cook for 1 ½ hours, until the chicken is very tender.

SPINACH ROLL WITH CHICKEN FILLING
serves 8–12

For the Roll:

1	small onion, diced	3	stiffly beaten egg whites
3	Tbls butter	3–4	Tbls butter
⅓	cup unbleached all-purpose flour	2	Tbls very fine bread crumbs
⅓	cup milk	*	Chicken filling
3	slightly beaten egg yolks	½	cup browned butter
⅓	cup grated Parmesan cheese		
3	10-ounce packages frozen chopped spinach, defrosted, drained thoroughly, and puréed in a blender		

Preheat oven to 350°. In a skillet, sauté the onion in 3 tablespoons of butter for 1 minute. Add flour. Lower heat and gradually stir in milk. Simmer for 3–5 minutes. Remove skillet from heat and add egg yolks, cheese, and spinach purée. Fold in egg whites. Butter a jelly roll pan well and sprinkle with breadcrumbs. Spread the mixture evenly over the jelly roll pan and bake in a 350° preheated oven until the spinach mixture shrinks for the sides of the pan and tests done with a cake tester—about 15–20 minutes. When done, immediately spread with chicken filling and roll up as a jelly roll. Pour browned butter over the roll. Heat the spinach roll in the oven for 5 minutes more and serve on a heated platter.

The secret of the success of this recipe is to drain the defrosted spinach thoroughly squeezing it dry between paper towels if necessary.

*Chicken filling

3 cups cooked minced chicken	2 Tbls minced dill
1 cup heavy cream	2 Tbls minced parsley
2 eggs, well beaten	2 Tbls minced scallions
Salt and papper to taste	1 cup toasted bread croutons

Place chicken into a bowl. Add cream and blend well. Add eggs, salt, papper, dill, parsley, and scallions and blend again. Add the croutons and toss lightly. Spread onto the spinach roll.

The Golden Door, Salzburg Castle

CHICKEN MIMOSA
serves 6

3	small broiling chickens, quartered	6	chicken livers
1	quart water	3	Tbls butter
1	tsp salt	3	Tbls dry sherry
2 ½	cups light cream	5	Tbls butter
2	mild onions, cut in half	4	Tbls flour
1	bay leaf		Salt and pepper to taste
4–5	peppercoms	4	hard boiled eggs, chopped fine
1	clove garlic		Cooked rice
2	sprigs parsley		

In a skillet cook chickens in salted water until very tender. Cool. Remove skin and bones from the chickens and place back into the cooking liquid. Bring to a boil and keep warm.

In a saucepan combine light cream, onions, bay leaf, peppercorns, garlic clove, and parsley. Simmer for 15 minutes. While cream is cooking in a small skillet sauté the livers in butter until they are very tender and still slightly pink inside. Add sherry and simmer for 1 minute. Purée in a blender. Strain the cooked cream into a saucepan and add the puréed liver and strained cooking liquid to where the chicken was cooking. Set aside. In another saucepan melt butter, add flour, and cook until pale golden in color. Slowly add this to the cream mixture, beating steadily. Add salt and papper to taste. Simmer sauce, stirring constantly until slightly thickened. Add 3 minced hard boiled eggs. Heat, but do not boil. Place in the center of a heated platter and surround with cooked rice. Pour sauce over rice and chicken. Sprinkle with the remaining minced egg.

KALTE FEINSCHMECKERPLATTE
Cold Gourmet Plate
serves 6

This delectable and beautifully put together platter of cold meats, vegetables, aspic, and salads comes in many forms; each is as different as the housewives and chefs who put them together.

In the center, place 2 pounds of sliced roast beef, surrounded by aspic (optional)*
Boiled parslied potatoes
Tiny pickled beets

Radish roses
Steamed asparagus and carrots with vinaigrette sauce
Steamed cauliflower marinated in vinaigrette sauce

Decorate with raw turnip daisies with carrot centers. (These are just decorations.) If you wish, you may add sliced pickles, sliced tomatoes, smoked salmon, green olives, salami slices, and hard-boiled eggs stuffed with pâté de foie gras.

For the Vinaigrette Sauce:

1 cup apple cider vinegar
1 tsp dry mustard
1 tsp Worcestershire sauce
½ tsp salt

½ tsp black pepper
½ tsp oregano
1 clove of garlic, crushed
1 cup salad oil

In a glass jar with a tight lid, mix vinegar with mustard, Worcester sauce, salt, pepper, oregano, and garlic. Shake well. Add oil and shake well again.

* Aspic should set completely in the refrigerator before being chopped up for decoration.

NOISETTE OF BEEF WITH MUSHROOMS
serves 6

1 pound sliced fresh mushrooms	¼ tsp basil
4 Tbls butter	½ tsp red port wine
6 1 ½-inch thick filets of beef	¼ cup beef stock
½ tsp salt	1 Tbls tomato paste
⅛ tsp black pepper	⅓ cup bread crumbs

Preheat oven to 400°. Slice mushrooms. Melt butter in a large skillet. Brown beef filet quickly in the hot butter, about 1 minute on each side. Remove it and place it in a well-buttered baking dish.

Put sliced mushrooms into the same skillet. Add salt, black pepper, basil, red port, and beef stock mixed with tomato paste. Simmer for 10 minutes, stirring occasionally. Pour mushroom sauce over the meat. Sprinkle with bread crumbs and bake in a 400° preheated oven for 15 minutes.

GEKOCHETES RINDFLEISCH—TAFELSPITZ
Austrian Boiled Beef
serves 6

1 3-pound boneless bottom round or brisket	3 carrots, cut into 1-inch chunks
2 pounds chicken parts (back, wings, giblets, necks)	3 large celery ribs, cut into 2-inch pieces
2 quarts water	1 leek, white part only
1 tsp salt	4 sprigs parsley
4 Tbls butter	1 bay leaf
2 large onions, chopped	6 peppercorns
2 scraped parsnips, cut into 1-inch chunks	⅛ tsp allspice
	* Horseradish-applesauce

In a 6-quart soup kettle, combine beef and chicken parts and cover with water. Add salt. Bring to a boil over high heat. Skim off the surface scum as it rises. Heat the butter in a large heavy skillet. When the foam subsides, add chopped onions, parsnip, carrots, clelery, leek, and parsley. Over high heat, toss vegetables in the hot butter for 4 or 5 minutes, or until they are lightly browned. Place them into the soup kettle and bring the liquid to a boil again. Skim off the surface scum and add bay leaf, peppercorns, and allspice. Turn heat to low, cover the pot, and simmer slowly for about 2 hours, or until beef shows no resistance when pierced with the point of a sharp knife.

Remove the beef to a heated serving platter. Skim the surface fat from the stock and strain it through a large sieve, pressing down hard on the vegetables before discarding them. Taste for seasoning. The stock may be served as a soup before you serve the beef, or it may be reserved for another occasion. Pour about ½ cup of broth over the meat and serve surrounded with boiled parslied potatoes and carrots or with any vegetables of your choice. Serve horse-radish-applesauce on the side.

* Horseradish-Applesauce

2   cups prepared applesauce
½   cup mild prepared (red) horseradish
    with beets
⅓   cup very hot white horseradish (or
    more to taste)
1   tsp prepared mustard
    Pinch of nutmeg
    Salt and white pepper to taste
1   cup whipped cream

In a bowl, mix applesauce and horseradish. Make it as hot or as mild as you wish. Add mustard, nutmeg, salt, and pepper. Fold in the whipped cream. Adjust seasonings to taste. Refrigerate for ½ hour before serving.

POT ROAST AUGSBURG STYLE
serves 6–8

4–5	pounds brisket, top round, or chuck	4	finely chopped tomatoes
½	cup flour	1	cup chopped parsley
	Salt and pepper to taste	3	Tbls capers
¼	cup butter or margarine	½	cup dry red wine
1	large onion, thinly sliced	6–8	slices of Provolone or Fontina
2–3	mashed garlic cloves		cheese
5	carrots, scraped and thinly sliced into circles		Potato dumplings (see recipes on page 91)
1	tsp rosemary		

Dredge the meat thoroughly in flour and sprinkle with salt and pepper. Heat butter in a large iron pot; add meat and brown on both sides. Add onion and garlic and cook for 35 minutes, turning often. Add carrots and seasoning and cook ½ hour longer. Add tomatoes and parsley. Cook over medium heat for 1½–2 hours or until the meat is very tender. Add wine and capers and cook 15 minutes longer. Place the thinly sliced cheese on top of the meat, cover, and simmer until the cheese is melted. Serve the pot roast sliced thinly, with the sauce and dumplings on the side.

TONGUE IN POLISH SAUCE
serves 6

4–5	pounds smoked beef tongue	6	peppercorns
3	quarts water	3	Tbls wine vinegar
1	onion stuck with 3 cloves		Salt to taste
3	bay leaves		

Wash tongue. In a large pot, bring water to a boil, add the onion with cloves, bay leaves, peppercorns, and wine vinegar. Add the tongue and simmer for about 2 hours, or until very tender. Cool in the liquid. Taste for seasoning and add more salt if necessary. Remove the outside skin and roots of the tongue and slice thin. Strain the cooking liquid and set it aside.

Sauce

4	Tbls sugar	2	Tbls lemon juice
3	Tbls water	1	tsp grated lemon rind
2	Tbls butter		Salt to taste
2	Tbls flour	1½	cups raisins
1	cup Marsala	1	cup blanched almonds, coarsely
3	Tbls wine vinegar		chopped

In a saucepan, combine sugar and water and stir until the sugar is melted. Cover and simmer until the mixture turns honey colored. Knead butter together with flour and add to the caramel; also add 2 cups of reserved strained cooking liquid. Bring to a boil, stirring constantly. Add Marsala, wine vinegar, lemon juice, lemon rind, salt to taste, raisins, and almonds. Mix and simmer for 2–3 minutes. For a tarter sauce, add more vinegar; for more sweetness, add additional sugar. Add the sliced tongue and bring to a boil. Simmer for 3 minutes. Remove from heat and serve.

Castle on the Danube, near Passau

KALBSRUCKEN MIT ESTRAGON BUTTER IMPERIAL
Roast Rack of Veal with Tarragon Butter Imperial
serves 7–8

6–7 pound rack of veal	½ cup Madeira
Salt and pepper to taste	More salt or pepper to taste
8 Tbls melted butter	1 cup butter
½ cup dry white wine	¼ cup chopped fresh tarragon or ½
1 cup veal or beef stock	Tbls dry tarragon

Preheat oven to 350°. Sprinkle the roast with salt and pepper. Place on a rack in a baking pan. Brush generously with a mixture of melted butter and wine. Bake in a 350° oven for about 30 minutes per pound, or 170° on a meat thermometer. The veal must be well done, but do not overcook it or it will be stringy. Brush the roast often with the butter mixture. Remove from pan and place on a heated platter. Skim off the fat from the pan juices, then pour the remaining juice into a saucepan. Add veal or beef stock, Madeira, and salt and pepper to taste. Cook until slightly reduced (by about a third). Serve the sauce separately in a sauce boat. While the roast is baking, mix the butter with tarragon (preferably fresh) and chill. Pipe the butter onto the roast, using a pastry bag fitted with a rosette tip. Serve immediately. This roast is traditionally garnished with whole roasted potatoes, peas, and watercress.

GESPICKTE KALBSVÖGERLN
Larded Veal Birds
serves 6

2 pounds fileted veal cutlets ½–¾-inch thick	Rind of 1 lemon
	1 Tbls chopped parsley
5 slices bacon	1 egg yolk
Salt to taste	3 Tbls sour cream
1 Kaiser roll (or any other hard roll)	¼ cup butter or margarine
½ tsp salt	1 large onion, sliced
Pinch of pepper	3 carrots, thinly sliced
1 crushed garlic clove	¼ cup tomato juice
¼ tsp thyme	¼ cup sour cream

Lard the veal with bacon by making incisions in the veal cutlets and placing 1–2-inch long pieces of bacon into the incisions. Pound, larded veal cutlets until each is ½-inch thick. Salt them and cut into pieces about 4 × 2 inches. Soak the roll in milk and squeeze out the liquid. Mix the softened roll with salt, pepper, garlic, thyme, lemon rind, parsley, and egg yolk beaten into 3 tablespoons of sour cream. Spread 1 teaspoon of the mixture in the center of each piece of veal. Roll up each piece and tie with string. Sauté onion in butter until soft. Add veal rolls and brown on all sides. Add carrots and tomato juice. Simmer, covered for ½ hour or until tender, adding more liquid as needed. Blend sour cream into the sauce and simmer 10 minutes longer. Remove veal birds to a warm platter, discard the string and pour the sauce over the veal rolls.

STUFFED BREAST OF VEAL WITH BUTTERED CHESTNUTS

serves 8–10

1	breast of veal, boned and pounded flat	½	tsp black pepper
2½	tsp salt	½	tsp nutmeg

Place the veal fell side down onto a board. Pound it flat with a mallet. Sprinkle with salt, pepper, and nutmeg on both sides. Set aside.

Stuffing

1	pound ground veal	*24–30	whole buttered chestnuts (use fresh chestnuts if available)
1	pound ground pork (ground beef may be subsittuted)	4	Tlbs butter
¼	cup brandy	½	cup wine
⅔	cup bread crumbs	2	minced garlic cloves
1	cup heavy cream	2	carrots, thinly sliced
2	eggs	2	stalks celery, thinly sliced
	Salt and black pepper to taste	6	or more thin slices of Gruyere cheese
¼	cup minced onion		Paprika
¼	tsp nutmeg		
¼	tsp thyme		

Preheat oven to 400°. In a large bowl, blend together the veal, pork, brandy, bread crumbs, cream, eggs, salt, pepper, onion, nutmeg, and thyme. Blend into a very smooth paste. If needed, add a little more cream—the mixture should be moist. Spread ½ of the mixture down the center of the veal breast. Place 2 whole buttered chestnuts side by side on the stuffing all the way down the breast. You may want to use one row of chestnuts; this is optional. Cover the chestnuts with the remaining stuffing. Roll up the breast jelly roll fashion and tie securely in several places with a string. In a large dutch oven, heat the butter and brown the meat on all sides. Add the wine and all the vegetables; reduce heat, cover, and simmer meat for 2½–3 hours adding a little water as needed. Turn veal often. When the veal feels fork-tender, place on an ovenproff serving platter. Put the thinly sliced Gruyere cheese on top of the veal, overlapping each slice about ¼-inch, and place veal in a 400° preheated oven for 6–8 minutes, or until the cheese is completely melted, but not browned. Sprinkle with paprika if desired. Serve garnished with additional buttered chestnuts.

*Buttered Chestnuts

1½ pounds cooked chestnuts or 1 15-ounce can whole chestnuts	Salt and papper to taste
½ cup butter or margarine	⅛ tsp ground fennel seeds

Slash a cross with a very sharp knife on the flat side of each chestnut. Place the chestnuts in a saucepan and add enough water to cover. Cook for 15 minutes, drain, cool slightly, and remove the tough outer skin. Put the peeled chestnuts into the saucepan again, pour clean water over them, and cook for another 10 minutes, or until the chestnuts are almost soft. Cool completely and remove the inner skin without breaking the chestnuts. Then, in a large skillet, melt the butter. Add the cooked or canned chestnuts and seasonings, stir to coat chestnuts with butter, and simmer for just a few minutes, until chestnuts are heated thoroughly. Use for stuffings and also as an accompaniment for duck, goose, or turkey.

WIENER SCHNITZEL
Breaded Veal Cutlets
serves 6

6 Veal cutlets, cut into 3 ½ × 4 ½-inch pieces, about ¼-inch thick	3 eggs, slightly beaten
½ cup flour	2 cups fine bread crumbs
1 tsp salt	Lemon wedges and flat anchovies
¼ tsp black pepper	*½ cup clarified butter (see recipe on page 37)

The cutlets must be evenly thin (about ⅛" thick). Pound with a mallet to flatten the cutlets. Mix flour, salt, and pepper and dust cutlets with the mixture. Then dip into eggs and then into the bread crumbs. Let stand for 5–10 minutes.

Heat butter in a deep skillet and brown the cutlets on both sides. Turn them gently with tongs, then drain on paper towels, and place on a heated platter. Place a slice of lemon and 2 anchovies on each schnitzel. Serve immediately.

PORK KIDNEYS WITH MUSHROOMS AND MADEIRA
serves 6

2 pounds kidneys	½ pound sliced mushrooms
¼ cup vinegar	3 Tbls sautéed minced onion
1 quart water	⅓ cup Madeira
1 Tbls salt	⅓ cup chicken broth
Salt and black pepper to taste	½ tsp thyme
1 cup flour	½ tsp oregano
2 Tbls paprika	½ tsp cornstarch (optional)
¼ cup butter or margarine	

Remove the fat and membrane from the kidneys. Place them into a bowl. Add vinegar, water, and salt. Refrigerate for 2–3 hours. Remove kidneys from water, rinse them, and pat dry with paper towels. Sprinkle kidneys with salt and pepper. Mix flour and paprika; dredge kidneys in the flour mixture. Melt butter or margarine and brown kidneys on both sides. Add mushrooms and cook until mushrooms are just limp. Add sautéed onions, Madeira, chicken broth, thyme, and oregano. Cover and simmer for 15 minutes. If a thicker sauce is desired, add ½ teaspoon of cornstarch. Serve immediately over hot buttered toast.

VIENNESE STUFFED BREAST OF VEAL

serves 6

1 breast of veal with a pocket cut in it, boned or with bones in	¼ tsp or more salt
2-3 Tbls olive oil	4 minced shallots
½ tsp salt	4 Tbls minced parsley
½ tsp basil	3 eggs, well beaten
½ tsp white pepper	1 large or 2 small apples, pared, cored and cut into cubes
1 tsp paprika	½ cup brandy or sherry
3 cups toasted bread cubes, croutons, or prepared bread stuffing	¼ cup orange juice
4 strips of bacon cooked crisp and crumpled (artificial bacon chips may be substituted)	⅔ cup coarsely chopped pistachio nuts (pecans may be used)
3 Tbls bacon drippings or margarine	¼ cup brandy
¼ tsp each basil, thyme, savory, rosemary, white pepper	⅔ cup pale dry sherry

Preheat oven to 425°. If desired, have the butcher bone the thick meaty part of the veal breast, or use the whole breast with bones intact. Have the butcher cut off as much of the outer skin as possible. Also, have him cut a large pocket in the meat. Place the breast onto a sheet of foil. Brush veal with oil on all sides and sprinkle it with salt, basil, white pepper, and paprika. Set aside. In a bowl, combine the remaining ingredients, except for brandy and sherry, and blend very well. Taste for salt and adjust seasoning if necessary. Stuff the breast with the mixture and secure the opening with skewers. Place into a baking pan. Pour the brandy over the roast. Bake for 45 minutes. Reduce heat to 350° and bake for 1 hour and 15 minutes, basting often with the sherry and the pan drippings. Serve with vegetables of your choice and a green salad.

POTATOES WITH WATERCRESS
serves 5–6

8 ounce softened cream cheese	24 small boiled potatoes, peeled
2 Tbls white wine vinegar	½ tsp salt
¼ tsp tarragon	1½ cups chopped watercress
Pinch cayenne pepper	

Soften cream cheese at room temperature. Add vinegar and beat until cream cheese reaches the consistency of sour cream. Blend in tarragon and pepper. Boil the potatoes in salted water until tender. Put them into a well-heated serving dish, pour cream cheese over the potatoes, and sprinkle with watercress.

Note: ¼ cup of chopped dill or ½ cup of chopped parsley may be substituted for the watercress. The cream cheese and watercress may also be served over noodles.

Straw hut and water trough, Austria, near Hungarian border

HERBED POTATOES

serves 6

¼	cup butter or margarine, softened	*¼	tsp dried thyme
1	Tbls parsley, finely chopped	*¼	tsp basil
½	tsp salt	*¼	tsp dill seeds
¼	tsp paprika	⅛	tsp pepper
¼	tsp dried oregano	6	medium Idaho potatoes

In a medium-sized bowl cream butter, parsley, salt, paprika, oregano, thyme, basil, dill, and pepper. Cut potatoes into ¼-inch slices without cutting them all the way through. Cut within ½ an inch of the other side. Place potatoes into a well-greased 1-quart baking dish. Cover and bake in 425° oven for 45 minutes; uncover and spread butter mixture over potatoes. Bake uncovered 15 minutes longer, basting with butter occasionally. Serve with sour cream topping described below.

Topping

In a small bowl mix 2 cups sour cream, ¼ cup chopped pimiento, ¼ cup chopped pitted black olives, 1 tbs chopped parsley and ¼ teaspoon salt. Chill until serving time.

NOODLES AND MUSHROOMS

serves 6

1	pound medium-wide egg noodles	1	cup heavy cream
1	Tbl vegetable oil	1	tsp salt
1 ½	pounds fresh sliced mushrooms	¼	tsp pepper
4	Tlbs butter	1	cup grated Swiss cheese
⅔	cup minced sautéed onion		flavored bread crumbs
2	egg yolks and 3 whole eggs	4	Tbls melted butter

Preheat oven to 350°. Cook noodles as directed on the package, adding oil to the water. Sauté the mushrooms in 4 tablespoons of butter. Fold mushrooms and onions into the noodles. Beat egg yolks and eggs with heavy cream; add salt and pepper. Pour the egg mixture over the noodles and blend. Butter a baking dish or a

---

*If available use 1 teaspoon fresh chopped thyme, 1 teaspoon fresh basil, and 1 teaspoon fresh dill.

casserole. Place ¼ of the noodles into the casserole. Sprinkle with grated cheese. Repeat the layering of noodles and cheese four times in all. Sprinkle the top layer with flavored bread crumbs and dot with butter. Bake in a 350° oven for 40 minutes. Serve hot.

POTATO DUMPLINGS I
makes about 3 dozen dumplings

7 medium potatoes, peeled
1 cup cream of wheat—uncooked
  Salt to taste
1 slightly beaten egg
1 egg yolk

2¼ cups unbleached all-purpose flour
¼ tsp baking powder
2 cups toasted diced bread cubes
4 quarts boiling salted water
⅔ cup melted butter

In a pan, boil the potatoes until very tender and drain. Place potatoes in a large bowl. Immediately add the cream of wheat and salt and mash until smooth. Stir in egg, egg yolk, flour, and baking powder and mix thoroughly. Add bread cubes and knead. The dough will be sticky. Form into 3-inch balls. Drop dumplings into boiling salted water. When the water begins to boil again, cover and simmer for 15 minutes. Remove the dumplings to a heated platter and sprinkle with melted butter.

POTATO DUMPLINGS II
serves 7–8

7 medium potatoes
2 eggs, slightly beaten
  Salt and pepper to taste
3 cups unbleached all-purpose flour

1 tsp baking powder
4–6 quarts boiling water
⅔ cup melted butter

In a pan, boil the potatoes until tender. Drain them and refrigerate for 12–24 hours. Peel and grate potatoes into a large bowl. Add eggs, salt, pepper, flour, and baking powder. Knead the dough until just firm. Form into four 2½-inch-thick rolls. Drop dumplings into boiling water: do not let them stick to the bottom of the pan. Cook uncovered for 15–20 minutes. Remove to a heated platter. Cut into thick slices and sprinkle with melted butter.

ERDÄPFEL BUCHTELN
Potato Biscuits
makes 18–22 biscuits

2 pounds medium potatoes	1 tsp salt
4 Tbls butter or margarine	2 cups flour or a little more, as needed
2 eggs	6 Tbls butter or margarine

Preheat oven to 375°. Boil the potatoes in their jackets until tender. Peel and mash them while still hot. Add butter, blending well until it is absorbed. Beat eggs until thickened and add them to the potatoes. Add salt and flour and blend. The dough should be stiff: Add a little more flour if needed.

Turn the dough out onto a floured board and roll out to about ¾-inch thickness. Flatten the butter into a 3-inch square. Place in the center of the dough. Fold one side and then the other over the butter. With the open end toward you, turn the dough and fold it again into thirds. Roll out again and fold into thirds. Roll the dough out to ¾-inch thickness and cut into rounds with a 2½-inch cookie cutter. Place the rounds on a buttered cookie sheet and bake them in a 375° oven for 20–25 minutes or until slightly browned.

Cool for 5 minutes. Serve with meat or chicken dishes, for snacks, or instead of bread.

MARROW DUMPLINGS
makes about 20–24 small dumplings

2 eggs	¼ tsp mace
3 Tbls milk or cream	⅛ tsp rosemary
Salt and pepper to taste	2 cups bread crumbs or more, as needed
½ pound marrow (from marrow bones, chopped)	

Beat eggs with milk, salt, and pepper. Add the remaining ingredients and mix into a stiff dough. Form into very small walnut-sized balls. Test the dough by boiling one dumpling. If the test dumpling crumbles, add more bread crumbs to the mixture and test another dumpling. Simmer dumplings for approximately 5–7 minutes. Cook uncovered over low heat. Serve with soup or stew.

Note: Marrow bones are available in all supermarkets and

butcher shops. Butcher customarily cuts the bones into 2–2 ½-inch pieces. The marrow can be scooped out with a teaspoon (the butcher does not do that).

POTATO KUGEL

serves 8–10

5 cups mashed potatoes	3 Tbls melted butter
3 eggs, plus 2 egg yolks, well-beaten	2–3 Tbls grated Parmesan cheese
½ cup heavy cream	Salt and pepper to taste
½ cup grated Emmenthaler (Swiss cheese)	

Beat eggs and add to mashed potatoes (instant potatoes may be used. Prepare as directed on package, using milk instead of water). Add cream, salt and pepper, and cheese and butter. Grease well and dust an oven-proof dish with Parmesan cheese. Put potato mixture into the dish and bake for 20–30 minutes in 375° oven or until puffy and brown.

Mozart Well, St. Gilgen, Austria

LINZERTORTE
Linzer Cake
makes 1 nine-inch cake

1½ cups all-purpose flour	1 cup softened unsalted butter
⅛ tsp ground cloves	2 lightly beaten raw egg yolks
¼ tsp cinnamon	1 tsp vanilla extract
1½ cups finely ground blanched almonds	1½ cups thick raspberry jam
	1 lightly beaten egg yolk
½ cup sugar	2 Tbls cream
1 tsp grated lemon peel	Powdered vanilla sugar (see recipe
2 hard-cooked egg yolks, mashed	on page 37)

Preheat oven to 350°. Sift flour, cloves, and cinnamon together into a mixing bowl; add almonds, sugar, lemon peel, and mashed egg yolks. With a wooden spoon, mix in butter, raw egg yolks, and vanilla extract. Continue to beat until the mixture is very smooth. Form the dough into a ball, wrap it in wax paper, and refrigerate it for at least 1 hour, or until firm.

Rove about ¾ of the dough and return the rest to the refrigerator. Lightly butter a round 9" × 2" spring form cake pan. Add the dough (if it is too firm, let it soften). With your fingers, press and push it out so that it covers the bottom and sides of the pan, making a shell about ¼-inch thick. Spread the raspberry jam evenly over the bottom of the pastry shell with a spatula. On a floured surface, roll out the rest of the dough into 6" × 9" pieces ¼-inch thick. With a sharp knife, cut the dough into strips ½-inch wide: 2 of them should be 9 inches long and the rest should be 8 inches long. Lay one of the 9-inch strips across the center of the cake and flank that strip on each side with one of the 8-inch strips. Rotate the pan about one-quarter of the way to your left and repeat the pattern with the other 3 strips to create a lattice-like effect. Run a sharp knife around the top of the pan to loosen the bottom dough that extends above the strips. Press it down into a border about ¼-inch thick. Beat the egg yolk with the cream and brush all the exposed pastry. Refrigerate the cake for ½ hour. Preheat the oven to 350°. Bake the torte for 45 to 50 minutes, or until it is lightly browned. Let the torte cool for 10 minutes, remove the rim of the pan, and sprinkle the cake with powdered vanilla sugar (see page 37).

NUSSTORTE
Walnut Torte
serves 8–10

1 cup sweet butter	1 tsp nutmeg
2 Tbls melted sweet butter	1 tsp cinnamon
2 cups light brown sugar	2 Tbls brandy
2 whole eggs	4 tsp baking powder
2 egg yolks	2 cups ground walnuts
2⅔ cups sifted flour	* Viennese butter cream
1 cup sour cream	** Mocha butter cream

Preheat oven to 350°. Grease well and sprinkle a 9- or 10-inch spring bottom pan with flour. Set aside. Place the butter and melted butter into a large bowl. Cream with an electric beater until fluffy and creamy. Add sugar and continue beating. Add 1 egg at a time, beating after each addition, until eggs and egg yolks are completely absorbed. Add flour and sour cream. Blend well. Add seasonings and brandy. Blend. Add baking powder and beat with a wooden spoon for at least 2 minutes. Fold in the walnuts. Pour the batter into the greased pan. Be sure that the batter is spread evenly. Place the baking pan on a sheet of foil about 4 inches larger all around than the pan. Bake in a preheated 350° oven for 1 hour and 15 minutes, or until a cake tester comes out clean. Be careful when testing or the cake will fold. Cool on a rack and unmold. Cut across to make three equal layers. Fill with two-thirds of the mocha cream. Frost with Viennese butter cream. Decorate the sides and top of the cake with mocha cream and garnish the top with rosettes of the remaining mocha cream piped through a pastry bag fitted with a No.6 star tube. Refrigerate for at least 4 hours before serving.

*Viennese Butter Cream

1½ cups granulated sugar	¾ lb unsalted butter, softened
1¼ cups water	2 tsp vanilla extract
10 well-beaten egg yolks	2 Tbls lemon juice

In a saucepan combine sugar and water and boil until the syrup spins a thread when dropped from a spoon, or a candy thermometer registers 235°. Pour the hot syrup slowly into the well-beaten yolks, beating steadily, until the mixture is almost cold. Cream the butter until very fluffy and light. Beat the vanilla slowly into the yolk mixture until just blended. Do not overbeat or the cream will separate. If this happens, add a little more butter—about 1–2 tablespoons. Chill the cream before using. Divide the butter cream in half and convert one half into mocha cream.

**Mocha Butter Cream

½   of prepared Viennese butter cream
4   Tbls very strong coffee
6   ounces melted semisweet chocolate
2   Tbls brandy

Beat until smooth and refrigerate.

SACHER TORTE
(The Most Famous Viennese Chocolate Cake)
serves 10–12

¼ pound soft, unsalted butter or margarine	½ cup apricot preserves or jam
	2 Tbls cold water
½ cup sugar	6 ounces semisweet chocolate pieces
6 egg yolks	¾ cup heavy cream
6 ounces semisweet chocolate, melted and cooled	½ cup sugar
	2 tsp corn syrup
¾ cup sifted flour	2 Tbls butter
¼ cup ground blanched almonds	½ glazed apricot or ½ of a dried apricot
8 egg whites	½ cup slivered blanched almonds
½ cup sugar	1 cup sweetened whipped cream

Preheat oven to 350°.

Chocolate Cake

Cream butter and sugar until very fluffy. Add egg yolks one at a time, beating well after each addition. Melt chocolate in a small bowl over simmering water, or in the top of a double boiler. Cool the chocolate and add it to the butter mixture. Blend well. Combine flour and almonds. Beat egg whites until soft peaks form (for better results, add a pinch of cream of tartar to the egg whites). Add sugar and beat until very stiff. Fold in ⅓ of flour-almond mixture into the butter-egg yolk mixture; then fold in ⅓ of the egg whites. Follow with flour then with egg whites, then flour and then egg whites. Fold very lightly rather than mix. Butter two 9-inch cake pans well; line them with wax paper, and sprinkle with flour. Pour batter into the pans and bake for 30–35 minutes or until a cake tester comes out clean. Cool completely and take out of the pan. Remove wax paper. Don't refrigerate.

Apricot Glaze

Press the jam through a sieve. Put into a small saucepan. Add water and simmer for 2–3 minutes. Spread the warm glaze over the lower layer of the cake. Place the second layer on top and spread the remaining jam over entire cake.

Chocolate Frosting

Place the chocolate into the top of a double boiler and melt it over barely simmering water. Remove the top of the double boiler and set the pan on a direct flame. Add cream, sugar, and corn syrup and simmer the mixture, stirring occasionally, for about 1 minute. Remove from heat and add butter. Using a wooden spoon, beat the frosting against the side of the pan. Make sure that the frosting is smooth and shiny and still soft enough to spread. Place the cake on a cake rack with a pan underneath the cake. Spread the frosting smoothly over the cake with a knife that has been dipped in cold water.

Decorate the cake by placing half of the glazed apricot or half of a dried apricot in the center, surrounded by slivers of blanched almonds. Refrigerate for 2–3 hours to set the frosting. Remove from the refrigerator for about ½–1 hour before serving. Serve with sweetened whipped cream.

CRUMBLY CRESCENTS
makes 12–14 crescents

1 cup all-purpose unsifted flour	1 cup ground hazelnuts or pecans
¼ pound unsalted butter	1 tsp almond extract
¼ tsp salt	1 tsp vanilla
¾ cup granulated sugar	¾ cup powdered sugar

Preheat oven to 400°. Place flour into a bowl and crumble the butter into it with your hands. When butter and flour are thoroughly crumbled together, add salt, sugar, nuts, almond extract, and vanilla. Mix well. Make 12–14 even balls from the dough and shape the balls into crescents, rolling the dough between your palms. Grease a cookie sheet, dust it with flour and place the crescents on it. Bake them in a 400° oven for about 25 minutes. Spread the powdered sugar on wax paper and roll the crescents in the sugar while still hot. Let them cool. These crescents may be stored for a long time: They taste even better 3 days after baking!

CHOCOLATE TRUFFLES
makes 1 ½ dozen

4 ounces semisweet chocolate	2 lightly beaten egg yolks
3 Tbls sifted powder sugar	1½ tsp rum
2 Tbls butter	1 ounce grated semisweet chocolate

In a double boiler or glass bowl over hot water, melt together the chocolate, sugar, and butter. Remove from heat. Stir the chocolate mixture, one tablespoon at a time, into the egg yolks, beating well after each addition. Blend in rum. Refrigerate for 1 hour. Shape into small balls about 1 inch in diameter. Roll the balls in grated chocolate and refrigerate.

Note: For a variation, roll the balls in ½ cup finely ground nuts.

SALZBURGER NOCKERL
Delicate Baked Omelet Soufflé
serves 2–3

4 egg yolks
3 Tbls flour
½ tsp lemon rind
5 egg whites
¾ cup granulated vanilla sugar (see recipe on page 37)

½ cup milk plus 2 Tbls granulated vanilla sugar
Powdered vanilla sugar for dusting (see recipe on page 37)

Preheat oven to 350°. In a large bowl, beat egg yolks for 1 minute. Add flour and lemon rind and blend well. Beat egg whites until soft peaks form. Do not overbeat. Add the ¾ cup sugar and beat until very, very stiff. The success of this soufflé depends on the stiffness of the egg whites. Fold the yolks into the whites thoroughly but gently. Use a flat, oblong baking dish with sides about 2–2½ inches high. Heat the milk but do not boil it. Dissolve sugar in the hot milk. Pour the milk into the baking dish and scoop out the soufflé over the milk, spreading the mixture evenly. Place the soufflé in the center of the oven on the middle rack and bake for 15 minutes, or until risen high and well browned. Remove the soufflé from the oven, dust with sugar and serve immediately. You may serve raspberry syrup or any other syrup on the side with this soufflé.

Schönbrunn Castle, Vienna

SPANISCHE WIND TORTE
Spanish Wind Cake
to make one 9-inch torte

For the Shell:

- 8 egg whites
- ½ tsp cream of tartar
- 2 cups superfine granulated sugar

For the Decorations:

- 4 egg whites
- ¼ tsp cream of tartar
- 1½ cups superfine granulated sugar
- 10 candied violets and 1 candied rose

For the Filling:

- 2 cups whipping cream
- ⅓ cup granulated sugar
- ¼ cup Cointreau
- 4 cups strawberries or raspberries, washed and hulled and sprinkled with
- ½ cup powdered sugar

The Shell

Preheat oven to 200°. Lightly butter 2 cookie sheets and sprinkle them with flour. Shake to spread the flour evenly, then invert the pans and strike them on the edge of a table to knock out the excess. Invert a 9-inch layer cake pan on the floured surface of the baking sheet and outline 2 circles as guides in making the layers for the shell. Make four rings. These should not touch each other. With a rotary electric beater, beat the 10 egg whites with the cream of tartar until they begin to foam; then slowly beat in 2⅔ cups sugar. Continue beating for at least 6 minutes, or until the whites form stiff peaks when the beater is lifted out of the bowl. Place a wide plain-tipped pastry tube into a large pastry bag and fill the bag with the meringue. Pipe a 1-inch thick circle of the meringue inside one of the rings on the baking sheet. Continue making circles until the circle is covered with meringue. Smooth the top of the meringue with a spatula. Then make plain rings of meringue about ¾-inch thick inside the other 3 circles on the baking sheets. Do not fill the rings. Bake them in the oven for 2 hours and 45 minutes; then gently slide them off on racks to cool. Now make another filled circle layer like the first one and bake it for 45 minutes. Use this layer as the top. Now construct the shell by piping about a teaspoon of meringue onto 5 or 6 spots around the edge of the bottom circle to serve as cement, then fit one of the rings over this. Continue the process with the other rings, one on top of the other. When the shell is completed, set it on a baking sheet and let it dry out in the 200° oven for about 25 minutes, or longer if necessary. Let the shell cool.

The Decorations

Use a spatula to apply the remaining meringue in the pastry bag to the outside of the shell to make it smooth, then return it to the oven to dry for another 20 minutes. Prepare more meringue from the 4 egg whites, following the directions for the first batch. Fit a No. 6 star tube onto the pastry bag, put the meringue into the bag, and make swirls and rosettes on the outside of the shell and on the circle to be used as a top. Return both circles and the circles that have been put together to the oven again to dry for about 25 minutes. If you wish to decorate the shell with candied violets, pipe small dabs of meringue around the center of the shell and one dab in the center of the top spiral circle and place the violets on them.

The Filling

Whip the chilled cream until it begins to thicken. Add the sugar gradually. Continue to beat until the cream is stiff enough to hold its shape softly; then beat in Cointreau and fold in berries. Gently spoon the filling into the shell. Lay the second spiral gently on top, decorate with rosettes, and place a candied rose in the center.

Note: Do not make this cake in very hot or humid weather because the meringue will become sticky in a very short time.

SCHWEINSOHREN
Sweet Palmiers (Literal translation—"Pigs' Ears")

Rough Puff Pastry

 2   **cups flour**
¼   **tsp cream of tartar**
12   **Tbls unsalted butter (1 ½ sticks)**

Preheat oven to 350°. Sift together flour and cream of tartar onto a cutting board. Place butter and shortening on top of the flour. Chop with a large knife or cleaver until the pieces of butter and shortening are well coated with flour and are about the size of hazelnuts. Add ice water a little at a time, pushing the dough together gently to form a loose, coarse ball. Handle the dough as little as possible. As soon as it barely sticks together into a ball, scoop it up and place it on a clean, slightly floured board. Gently press down with a rolling pin, shaping the dough into a 5" × 11" strip about ½-inch thick. Square off the ends and fold the strip into thirds. Turn with an open end toward you, and again roll gently into a similar strip. Always roll only one way—up and down. Fold into thirds, squaring off the ends. Wrap the dough in wax paper and refrigerate for 1 hour. Repeat the rolling out, folding, and refrigerating process 4 more times. Then, refrigerate the dough for at least 5 hours, or overnight, before using.
Roll out half of the pastry to about 1-inch thickness, sprinkle liberally with granulated sugar, and roll out to about ⅛-inch thick on a sugared board to about 12" × 20". Find the center of the strip. Fold each long side inward into thirds. The two folded halves should meet exactly in the center. Then fold the halves on top of each other to make a 6-layered roll. Cut the roll into ¼-inch slices and place the slices on an ungreased baking sheet. Repeat the procedure with the other half of the pastry. Spread the two halves of each slice out a little. Chill for ½ hour. Bake in a preheated 350° oven for about 25–30 minutes. Turn the pastries over and bake 5 minutes longer or until the palmiers are caramelized and golden brown.

KUGELHUPF
(A Rich Austrian Cake)
serves 8–10

½ pound butter or margarine, unsalted	2 Tbls Cointreau or any other orange liqueur
2 cups sugar	6 Tbls milk
6 egg yolks	6 egg whites
1½ cups sifted flour	⅛ tsp cream of tartar
2 tsp baking powder	Powdered vanilla sugar (see recipe
Grated rind of 1 orange	on page 37)

Preheat oven to 350°. Cream butter until light and fluffy. Add sugar, one cup at a time, and cream until well blended. Beat in egg yolks one at a time, beating well after each addition. Sift together flour and baking powder. Add orange rind and liqueur to the butter mixture. Add flour and milk alternately, stirring gently with a wooden spoon. Beat egg whites with cream of tartar until stiff, but not dry, and fold them into the batter until no whites can be seen. Butter well and sprinkle with flour a large bundt pan (Turks head). Place the batter in the pan. Bake in a preheated 350° oven for 1 hour and 15 minutes, or until a cake tester comes out clean. Cool for 15 minutes. Loosen around the edges and the central stem with a knife and turn the cake out onto a platter. Dust with powdered vanilla sugar.

CHAPTER  3

The Land of the Czechs and the Slovaks

BOUT thirty-five miles from Vienna, the Danube becomes the boundary between Czechoslovakia and Hungary. It spreads into many branches along the border, creating low-lying islands, backwaters, and swamps. The river is lined with sprawling ancient willows, and ghost stories and legends proliferate in the area. The willows rustle, hum, and moan, as if resenting the intrusion of men and civilization into their private domain.

The city of Bratislava, which has been in Austrian, Hungarian, and Czech hands with regular frequency, stretches on the banks of the Danube. It is a city of contrasts where modern hotels welcome visitors with fine international fare which may include caviar, champagne, and sturgeon while the Slovak housewives stand in long lines to buy bread and sausages to the accompaniment of American pop music. Bratislava's skyline is bathed in the eerie glow of a refinery, which belches refuse into the nearby river. Fishermen and riverpeople complain bitterly that the fish tastes like crude oil, and the water of the Danube is murky and filled with industrial waste. But once past Bratislavia, the Danube is bordered with rich, fertile fields, and the landscape of wheat and vegetable fields is interrupted only by clumps of ever-present willows.

From the grain fields of Slovakia, the countryside changes imperceivably to the rolling hills of Bohemia and Moravia. The villages and hamlets have a Germanic air about them—not surprisingly—because Slovakia and Bohemia belonged for a few centuries to the Austro-Hungarian Empire. Farmers still drive horse-drawn carts over the fields that nestle beneath the hills. When the season comes to harvest the wheat, it is cut and tied into cone-shaped golden bundles, and the hay is piled high onto wooden trellises. Ancient churches, some with onion-shaped steeples; stone saints with broken arms, and primitive tiny chapels line the country roads. Peasant women sell eggs, chickens, mushrooms, and fruit from hand-woven baskets.

On the horizon loom the towering mountain ranges of the Matra and the High Tatra, covered with dense, dark forests that still hide many a mystery, and where people live as they did in the times past.

The land we now call Czechoslovakia, with its present boundaries, was created in 1919 during the Treaty of Versailles. Several different nationalities live within its borders. In the fertile south, Slovaks till the soil and live close to the land. The heart of Czechoslovakia is Bohemia. It is the industrial center, inhabited by sturdy, talented people known around the world for their glassblowing skills, lead crystal, lace, woodcarvings, and tinware. To the Austrians and Hungarians, Bohemians also represent those talented female cooks who entered the Viennese and Budapest households, bringing with them culinary know-how in preparing meats, and, especially, marvelous desserts. The famed Karlsbad Spa and the golden city of Praha, or Prague, are in Bohemia, but many travelers claim that the most enchanting part of Czechoslovakia is Moravia, especially the round green hills of Brno. In the first light of the summer morning sun, the low rambling moun-

Embroidery from Tatra region, Czechoslovakia

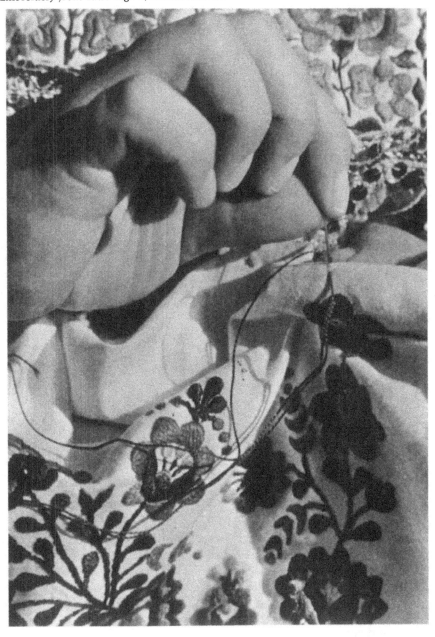

tains of Moravia seem to converge on the city from all directions, looking as though they were tiers of grass-covered terraces. Brno, the capital of Moravia, is an ancient city which has lived through centuries of upheavals.

And there are the Ruthenians, a Ukrainian tribe which settled among the mountains of Tatra. They are mostly Greek Orthodox, and they are a secretive mountain people who still live in semi-isolation.

Czechoslovakia and its provinces is an ancient land, known by many different names through the ages. It was conquered or annexed by Poland, by Germany, and by the Austro-Hungarian Empire. It is a tragic land: Its people have been under almost constant siege for centuries, and the capital city, Prague, has its own violent history. There was upheaval and turbulence during the reformation, and the leader, Jan Hus, was burned at the stake in 1415. The Thirty Years War, which devastated most of Europe, started in Prague as a revolt against the Hapsburgs. But in spite of all the upheavals, the people flourished in their own sturdy way.

The Czechoslovakian cuisine reflects the diversity of its inhabitants. It is a blend of many different ingredients and cooking techniques.

From Poland came the sweet and sour sauces, which the Czech cuisiniers refined and adapted to be served with fish, meat, and fowl. The soups of Czechoslovakia are substantial, made with a meat base, vegetables, and legumes, and flavored with marvelous cured ham and sausages. There are also the so-called "false" soups, prepared without meat from cabbage, sauerkraut, mushrooms, and potatoes, enriched with egg yolks and a thick cream. Stewed and braised meats are liberally sprinkled with caraway seeds and are served with sour cream sauces, but the claims to fame of the Bohemian cooks are their inimitable feather-light dumplings and their scrumptious warm desserts. The beloved dumplings are made from raised or potato dough and filled with cottage cheese, plum or apricot preserves, or fresh fruit. They are simmered in water and served warm with sugar and melted butter. Bohemian *dalken* are small baked buns filled with marmalade, and the *skubanky*—potato dumplings—are baked in loads of butter and served with generous amounts of ground poppy seeds and sugar.

But the most famous are the *Huskove*—bread dumplings. These are made from hard rolls shaped into long sausages, wrapped in clean cloth, and simmered in salted water. These dumplings are never cut with a knife but are sliced with a thin string and served with generous amounts of butter as an accompaniment to meat or fowl.

Pancakes, with apples or berry sauces, and crumbly cakes were all in a Bohemian cook's repertoire. For a long time during the Hapsburg Empire—and even after its demise—Bohemian cooks reigned in Viennese kitchens, performing their own brand of culinary magic, while the Viennese convinced themselves that all the delicacies they were serving were their own original inventions.

The incomparable Czech *uzene*—smoked pork—is cooked until tender with small amounts of water and then served with mounds of potato or bread dumplings and sauerkraut. Mushrooms are plentiful in the vast forests, and it is a national pastime to penetrate the dense greenery to discover the delectable fungi. These mushrooms are fragrant and are akin to the German *Steinpilze*—stone mushrooms. They hide under the moss among the roots of pine trees and are gathered by children and village folk and brought to market to be sold for stews and purées and to be dried for winter.

Today, the Czechs eat substantial but plain fare, and the refinements are left to some of the old women who still remember the good old days and who, once in a while, prepare the "bourgeois" delicacies.

Even in Prague, the refined cooking is giving way to more plebian dishes. In the past, the city was dotted with small restaurants where the cooks were corpulent women and where the food was superb. Today, the dishes taste bland and somehow the same in most of the eateries. Some of the fancy hotel restaurants still offer the fine Czech food, but the locals cannot afford to dine there, and the foreigners who do not know much about Czech dishes do not appreciate the refinements. Even the famed Prague hams are available only for export or for foreign currency, and not many of the hams are seen in the local markets. But the Czechs still have their sausages and beer. The sausages are about the best in the world and are produced in an unbelievable variety. The American frankfurters erroneously called wieners actually originated in Prague. The Czechs, instead of tea or coffee break, take a "*Parky-pause*", or sausage and beer break. There are the *Klobasy*—sturdy leathery sausages, which explode with juice when bitten into, larded *Taliany* (Italian sausages), and thick, short *Vurity*. The sausages are sold steamed in white-tiled *Uzenarsty* sausage shops, served with mustard, sauerkraut, and thick slices of peasant bread. There is nothing more delicious or satisfying than a marvelous *Parky* eaten out of hand on a cold morning in Bratislava, Brno, or Prague.

The national beverage of Czechoslovakia is beer, and, like the sausages, it is supposed to be one of the best in the world. Most beers are Pilsner type, light and frothy, but there is also a robust dark beer.

Czech cities are dotted with ancient somber beer halls. There is no frivolity in these vaulted chambers and no raucous singing; people come here to sit quietly, to meditate, and to ponder. Then they go home to their evening meal, prepared by loving hands.

Appetizers. . . . .

CUCUMBERS STUFFED WITH MEAT
serves 6

3	cups cooked ground veal		2	Tbls butter
1	large onion, diced		2	eggs
	Salt and pepper to taste		¾	cup bread crumbs
4	Tbls butter		6	pared cucumbers
1½	bay leaves		½	cup chopped bacon
4	peppercorns			Parsley and dill for garnish

In a pan, sauté veal and onion in butter until tender. Add seasonings. Add eggs and bread crumbs and blend thoroughly. Halve cucumbers lengthwise and hollow out the centers. Fill the cucumbers with the meat mixture. Place bacon in a skillet and then place the filled cucumbers on top and cook slowly for about 25–30 minutes or until tender. Serve hot, 1 stuffed cucumber per person, garnished with parsley or dill.

ŽELNÉ KARBÉNATKY
Cabbage Patties
serves 6

5 slices bacon, chopped and fried until crisp and drained	1 slightly beaten egg plus 1 egg yolk
3 cups chopped, cooked cabbage	1½–2 cups bread crumbs
3 chopped knockwursts	⅓ cup flour
Salt and pepper to taste	⅓–½ cup oil

In a bowl, mix together bacon, cabbage, knockwurst, salt, pepper, egg, and egg yolk. Add enough bread crumbs to make firm dough. Shape the mixture into small patties and dip them into flour. Heat oil in a skillet and brown the patties on both sides. Serve immediately.

MARINATED FISH
serves 8–12

4 pounds tuna, carp, or pike filets or steaks	⅓ cup butter
	⅓ cup dry sherry
Salt to taste	

Preheat oven to 350°. Place fish in a shallow baking dish with melted butter and sherry. Season with salt and bake for 25 minutes, or until the fish flakes easily when tested with a fork.

Marinade

1¾ cups water	1–2 cloves
⅔ cup vinegar	1 bay leaf
⅔ cup fish or chicken stock or broth	3 tsp chopped capers
1 large onion, thinly sliced	2 medium dill pickles, diced
6 peppercorns	⅓ cup oil
½ tsp allspice	

In a 1½–2 quart saucepan, boil the water, vinegar, stock, onion, and spices together for 25 minutes. Allow to cool and add capers, pickles, and oil. Put the baked fish into a large oven-proof glass dish. Pour marinade over fish. Cover and refrigerate 24 hours before serving. Serve chilled with pumpernickel slices or crackers.

Soups . . . .

BARLEY SOUP
serves 8

⅔ cup barley
3 cups beef broth
½ cup water
3 Tbls butter
1 large onion, chopped
2 carrots, diced
2 ribs of celery, chopped
2 medium potatoes, diced
½ pound sliced mushrooms

Salt and pepper to taste
2 pounds cooked beef, chopped
4 cups beef broth
¼ tsp thyme
2 cups cooked sliced green beans (optional)
3 Tbls sour cream
½ cup chopped parsley or dill

Wash and drain barley. In a large pot, cook the barley in the beef broth until tender, adding the water if necessary. In a skillet, melt butter, add onions, and cook until the onions are limp. Add carrots, celery, and potatoes and stir well. Cook until the potatoes are tender. Add mushrooms and cook 1–2 minutes longer. Sprinkle with salt and pepper. Add vegetables, chopped beef, 4 cups beef broth, and thyme to the barley. Bring to a boil and simmer for 3–4 minutes. If desired, add sliced green beans. In a small bowl, combine the sour cream with ½ cup of the hot broth, mix well, and add to the soup. Bring to a boil. Serve the soup sprinkled with chopped parsley or chopped dill. If the soup seems too thick, add more beef broth.

LUŠTĚNINOVÁ POLÉVKA
Legume Soup
serves 6

1 pound legumes, dried peas, lentils, and/or navy beans
8 cups water
¼ cup flour
6 Tbls butter or margarine
1½ cups finely chopped vegetables (parsnip, carrot, and onion)

Salt and pepper to taste
4 minced garlic cloves
2 Tbls caraway seeds (optional)
⅔ cup heavy cream
Sautéed bread croutons (optional)

Simmer legumes in water in a pot for about 2 hours or longer, until very tender. Drain, reserving the liquid. Press the legumes through a sieve or purée them in a food processor. Return them to the pot with the reserved liquid. Brown flour in butter until just slightly browned. Add it to the soup. Add vegetables and simmer for 20 minutes. Add salt, pepper, garlic, and caraway seeds if desired. Take 1 cup of the hot broth, blend it with the cream, and return the mixture to the soup. Heat the soup but do not boil it. Serve the soup sprinkled with croutons.

POLÉVKA Z OHÁŇKY
Oxtail Soup
serves 6

1½ pounds oxtail	3 Tbls butter
8 cups water	5 peppercorns
2 parsnips, diced	Salt to taste
3 carrots, diced	3 cups chopped cooked cauliflower
1 medium onion, diced	2 Tbls minced parsley

Have the butcher slice the oxtail into pieces. In a large pot, simmer the oxtails in the water for 2 hours or until tender. In a skillet, sauté parsnips, carrots, and onion in butter until limp. Add peppercorns, and add the vegetables to the soup. Bring to a boil and simmer for 10 minutes. Remove meat from the bones and chop it into small pieces. Add salt to taste. Return vegetables and meat to the broth and discard peppercorns. Add cauliflower and parsley and cook for 15 minutes longer. Serve immediately.

Czechoslovakian pottery

POLÉVKA Z DRŮBEZICH DRŮKŮ
Gizzard Soup
serves 6

8 cups cold water	3 carrots, sliced
1 pound gizzard, 10 wings, the backbone, and the neck from a small turkey, chicken, or duck, cleaned and rinsed	2 parsnips, sliced
	2 onions, thinly sliced
	½ cup rice or thin noodles
	⅛ tsp mace
Salt and pepper to taste	2 Tbls minced parsley

Pour water into a large pot. Place gizzard, wings, back, and neck into the water. Add salt, pepper, and all the vegetables. Simmer for 3 hours until tender. Strain the soup, reserving the liquid. Press vegetables through a sieve or use a blender. Remove meat from bones and dice it. Return meat and vegetables to the broth. Add rice or noodles and cook for 20 minutes or until the rice is done. Before serving, add mace and parsley. Serve with rice or noodles.

Salads . . . .

CAULIFLOWER SALAD
serves 6

5 cups flowerettes of cauliflower	1½ bay leaves
6 cups water	4 peppercorns
Salt to taste	

In a two quart saucepan, boil cauliflower in water with the seasonings for 10 minutes, or until tender. Drain and set aside, but keep warm.

Dressing

⅔ cup water	1 tsp sugar, or more to taste
5 Tbls vinegar	Salt and pepper to taste
5 Tbls oil	3 Tbls minced dill
1 medium onion, minced	

Blend all ingredients thoroughly. Place cauliflower in an airtight container and pour dressing over the flowerettes. Refrigerate for at least 4 hours before serving.

MUSHROOM SALAD
serves 6

1   pound mushrooms
1   bunch celery hearts
2   Tbls scallions, minced
4   Tbls olive oil
3   Tbls wine vinegar

Bibb or romaine lettuce leaves
Salt, pepper to taste
Red pepper and sliced hard-cooked eggs to garnish

Wash mushrooms and pat dry. Cut off stems and slice thin. Slice the stalks of the celery. Combine mushrooms and celery with minced scallions and a mixture of olive oil, vinegar, salt, and pepper. Chill for 1 hour. When ready to serve, place mushrooms onto bibb or romaine lettuce leaves. Garnish with red pepper strips and slices of hard-cooked eggs.

PRAGUE SALAD
serves 6

1   cup thin strips of roast pork
1   cup thin strips of roast veal
1   large mild onion, thinly sliced
1   cup thinly sliced pickles
1   cup thin strips of sour apple

Salt and pepper to taste
1   Tbls lemon juice
1   cup mayonnaise
Romaine lettuce leaves

In a bowl, mix together all the ingredients except the mayonnaise and the lettuce. Add mayonnaise and toss until all ingredients are coated with the mayonnaise. Refrigerate for 4 hours before serving. Serve on a bed of lettuce leaves.

Vegetables . . . .

SAUERKRAUT
serves 4–6

2 pounds sauerkraut
2 sliced onions
2 slices diced bacon
2 Tbls butter
¼ tsp pepper

1 Tbl caraway seeds
2 Tbls sugar
½ cup beef bouillon
1 cup white wine

Rinse sauerkraut with warm water and drain well. Cook onion and bacon in butter until onion is soft. Add the drained kraut, pepper, caraway seeds, and sugar. Cover tightly. Cook ¼ hour. Add bouillon and wine. Simmer ½ hour longer. Serve with pork, poultry, or ham.

KVĚTAK SMAŽENÝ
Fried Cauliflower
serves 6

1 head large cauliflower
Salt to taste
2–3 cups boiling water
⅔ cup milk

2 eggs
¾–1 cup flour or more
Salt and pepper to taste
3 cups oil or shortening

Clean cauliflower and break it into small flowerettes. Drop them into boiling salted water and cook for about 8 minutes. Drain thoroughly. In a bowl, beat the milk, eggs, flour, salt, and pepper together to make a fairly thick batter. Dip the cooked flowerettes into the batter. Heat oil in a deep pot or deep-fat fryer. Fry flowerettes until golden brown. Drain on paper towels. Serve immediately.

116

DUŠÉNÉ HŎUBY
Sautéed Mushrooms
serves 6

2 large chopped onions
½ cup butter
1½ pounds sliced mushrooms

Salt and pepper to taste
1 tsp caraway seeds

In a skillet, sauté onions in butter. Add mushrooms, salt, pepper, and caraway seeds and sauté for 10 minutes, till just transparent.

CREAMED CABBAGE
serves 6

1 large head cabbage, finely shredded
1 small onion, minced
5 Tbls butter

Salt and pepper to taste
1 Tbls flour
1 cup heavy cream

In a large skillet, sauté cabbage and onions in butter until limp. Sprinkle them with salt and pepper. Blend flour and cream and pour over the cabbage. Cover and simmer until tender, 10–15 minutes.

BAKED ASPARAGUS
serves 6

⅓ cup butter
¼ cup flour
2 cups light cream
Salt and pepper to taste

¼ tsp nutmeg
2 pounds cooked asparagus
1¼ cups grated Gruyere cheese
⅓ cup butter

Preheat oven to 350°. In a pan, melt butter, add flour, and cook, stirring constantly, until golden brown. Add cream, salt, pepper, and nutmeg. Simmer 5 minutes, stirring continuously. In a greased baking pan, layer the asparagus, sauce, and cheese, alternating the layers. Dot the top layer with butter and bake for 30 minutes.

Fish . . . .

CARP JEWISH STYLE
serves 5–6

5–6	pound carp	8	cups water
4	carrots, diced	8	peppercorns
4	ribs celery, diced	3	bay leaves
2	large onions, diced	1	dozen capers
2	parsnips, diced	2	cloves
6	Tbls chopped parsley	1	tsp marjoram
4	Tbls butter		Salt and white pepper
	Salt and pepper to taste		

Remove head and tail from carp. Set aside. Slice the carp into 2½–3-inch pieces. Prepare a vegetable stock: In a very large skillet or pot, sauté carrots, celery, onions, parsnips, and parsley in butter until the vegetables are just limp. Add salt and pepper to taste and the water. Simmer for 20 minutes. Add peppercorns, bay leaves, capers, cloves, marjoram, and the head and tail of the fish. Place the carp pieces on top of the vegetables and sprinkle them with salt and white pepper. No liquid should cover the fish. Steam the fish, covered, until tender—about 20–25 minutes. Place the fish slices on a serving platter with sloping sides.

To serve hot

Strain the cooking liquid into a saucepan and reduce to about 3 cups. Add 1 lightly beaten egg white and bring to the boiling point, stirring lightly. Strain the liquid twice through a double thickness of cheesecloth. Decorate fish with slices of cooked carrot, sliced lemon, hard-cooked eggs, and capers. Pour the sauce over fish and vegetables.

To serve cold

Place the fish on a platter and decorate with sliced vegetables and hard-cooked eggs. Strain the fish stock twice through cheesecloth into a saucepan and bring it to a boil. Add 1 slightly beaten egg white. Strain the stock again through a double thickness of cheesecloth. Mix 1 package of unflavored gelatin with 3 tablespoons cold water and add it to the hot stock. Stir well. Pour the aspic over the fish. Cool the dish and refrigerate it until the aspic has set. Serve as a buffet dish or as a main course with buttered French bread.

BAKED FISH
serves 6

4 pounds dressed, whole fish (trout, mackerel, or salmon)	Salt and pepper to taste
½ cup melted butter	1 tsp caraway seeds
	2 Tbls lemon juice

Preheat oven to 350°. Split fish lengthwise and place it in a shallow baking dish with the melted butter. Sprinkle with salt, pepper, caraway seeds, and lemon juice. Bake for 25 minutes or until the fish flakes easily when tested with a fork.

Peasant women

FISH LOAF
serves 6

3	pounds boned and ground fish (carp, pike, salmon, or trout may be used)	3	beaten eggs
1½	cups bread crumbs soaked in	1	mashed clove garlic
1	cup milk		Salt and pepper to taste
		⅓	cup melted butter

Preheat oven to 350°. In a bowl, mix all the ingredients except butter together. Shape into 2 loaves and place them in a shallow baking pan. Brush the loaves with half of the melted butter and pour the remainder into the pan. Bake for 35–40 minutes.

CODFISH WITH POTATOES
serves 4

1½	pounds salted dry codfish	2	minced cloves garlic
3	quarts or more water		Salt and dark pepper to taste
4	medium potatoes, peeled		
5	Tbls vegetable oil or unsalted butter		

Place codfish in a large bowl. Add water to cover and refrigerate for 6 hours or overnight. Drain the fish, place it in a pot of fresh water, and simmer until tender—about 40 minutes. While the fish is cooking, quarter the potatoes, place in a separate pot, and cook until tender—about 20 minutes. Heat oil or butter and add garlic. Simmer for 2 minutes and remove from heat. Drain the fish and potatoes, place them into a heated serving bowl, pour hot oil over them, sprinkle with salt and pepper, and serve immediately.

Czech pottery

KACHNÁ S HRAŠKÉM
Duck With Peas
serves 6

1 4–5-pound duck
Salt and pepper to taste
3 Tbls butter
⅔ cup water
3 Tbls diced bacon

24 very small whole onions, or pearl
onions
1½ pounds fresh peas, or 2 10-ounce
packages frozen peas

Have the butcher cut the duck into serving pieces. Sprinkle duck
with salt and pepper. In a large skillet, sauté the pieces and cook
for 1 hour, or until almost tender, adding water as needed. Add
bacon, onions, and peas and cook for 20 minutes, or until vegetables are tender.

CHICKEN WITH MUSHROOMS
serves 6

2 2½–3-pound chickens, cut in serving pieces
5 Tbls butter
2 medium onions, thinly sliced
1½ cups sliced mushrooms

Salt and white pepper to taste
1 cup water
1⅓ cups sour cream
1½ Tbls flour

In a large skillet, brown chicken pieces in butter. Add the onion.
When the onion is limp, add mushrooms, salt, white pepper, and
water. Cover and simmer for 1 hour, or until tender. Remove the
chicken to a hot covered platter. Mix sour cream and flour, stir
into the juices in the skillet and bring to a boil. Serve sauce over
the chicken.

KUŘE ZADĚLÁVANÉ
Chicken Fricassee
serves 6

2 chickens (broilers or fryers), cut into serving pieces
   Salt and pepper to taste
6 Tbls butter
1 parsnip, sliced
1 medium onion, sliced
1 carrot, sliced
⅛ tsp nutmeg
½ lemon peel

2 cups water
4 Tbls flour
4 Tbls butter
1 cup sliced mushrooms
1 Tbls butter
3 Tbls heavy cream
1½ tsp minced parsley
1 beaten egg yolk
   Juice of ½ lemon

Sprinkle chicken pieces with salt and pepper. In a large skillet, brown chickens and vegetables in 6 tablespoons of butter. Add the nutmeg, lemon peel, and water. Cover the skillet and simmer for 1 hour, or until chicken is tender. Remove the chicken to a hot platter and keep it warm. Reserve the pan juices and vegetables. In a saucepan, melt 4 tablespoons of butter, add flour, and cook, stirring continuously, until flour is golden brown. Stir this mixture into the skillet where chickens were cooking. Simmer for 5–10 minutes. Strain the pan juices through a sieve and pour them over the chicken. Brown mushrooms in 1 tablespoon of butter, add cream and parsley and bring to a boil. Blend in egg yolk and lemon juice. Pour sauce over the chicken before serving.

PEČENÁ HUSÁ SÉ ZĚLIM
Roast Goose with Sauerkraut
serves 6

1   8–10 pound goose
1½   cups water
3½–4 pounds fresh sauerkraut
2   large onions, minced

2 red Delicious apples, grated
1 large baking potato, grated
   Salt and pepper to taste
1 Tbls caraway seeds

If goose is frozen, defrost it in the refrigerator for about 36 hours. Remove giblets. Pull and cut out all excess fat from inside the goose and from around the opening. Chop fat very fine, place in a skillet, and add the water. Cover and cook over medium heat for about 15 minutes. Uncover and cook until all water has cooked out and the fat has stopped sputtering. Strain the fat into a bowl and set aside. Discard the brown fat pieces. Drain sauerkraut, wash it thoroughly in cold water, then squeeze it as dry as possible. In a large skillet, heat ⅓ cup of the goose fat. Add minced onion and cook for about 2–3 minutes. Add sauerkraut, stir well, and cook uncovered for about 10 minutes, stirring frequently. Add apples, potatoes, salt and pepper to taste, and the caraway seeds. Mix well and simmer for 5 minutes. Set aside to cool.

Wash the goose inside and out. Drain well and pat dry with paper towels. Sprinkle inside the cavity with salt and pepper. Stuff the cavity with the sauerkraut mixture. Cover the cavity with a piece of foil and tie the legs together. Place the goose onto a well-greased rack in a large roasting pan, breast up. Brush the goose with melted goose grease. Use a meat thermometer. Insert it into the thickest part of the breast without touching the bone. Bake for about 2–2½ hours in a 350° oven until the thermometer reaches 185°, or until the fat from a punctured thigh runs pale yellow.

Place the goose onto a carving board or a platter. Cool for 15 minutes before carving. Remove the foil and cut away the string. Serve the goose surrounded by bread dumplings (see recipe on p. 132).

APPLE PANCAKE WITH CHICKEN LIVERS

serves 6

1 ½	cups milk	3	Tbls butter
6	eggs	1	pound chicken livers
1	cup flour	2	apples, peeled, cored, and cubed
½	cup beer	1	tsp cinnamon
1	tsp baking soda	1	cup sour cream (optional)

Preheat oven to 400°. Mix the milk and eggs in a blender at high speed. Add flour, beer, and baking soda. Mix again for at least 30 seconds, scraping the flour down from the sides of the blender. Blend again for 30 seconds. Heat a 10-inch nonstick frying pan and melt 3 tablespoons of butter in the pan. Place chicken livers in the pan, add apple cubes sprinkled with cinnamon, and pour the batter over the livers and apples. Bake in a preheated 400° oven for 15–20 minutes, or until golden brown and puffy. Sour cream may be served on the side.

SAUERKRAUT STEW

serves 8

10	strips of bacon	3	stalks of celery, grated
1½	pounds pork spareribs cut into 2-inch pieces	2	cloves minced garlic
			Salt and pepper to taste
1½	pounds veal cut into 1½-inch cubes	½	cup water
1½	pounds lean pork shoulder cut into 1½-inch cubes	2	chickens, cut into serving pieces
		4	pounds fresh sauerkraut
2	large onions, sliced into thin circles	½	tsp marjoram
3	carrots, grated	2	cups sour cream, or more as desired

Cut bacon into small pieces and place it in a large pot or dutch oven. Cook bacon until crisp. Pour off ⅓ of the fat and reserve. Add spareribs, veal, and pork meat. Cook on high heat, stirring often until the meat is browned on all sides. Reduce heat and add onions. Cover and cook, stirring occasionally, for about 10–15 minutes, or until the onions are golden brown. Add carrots, celery, garlic, and salt and pepper to taste. Cook, stirring occasionally, until the vegetables are tender. Add water and continue simmering. While the meat and vegetables are cooking, heat the remaining bacon drippings in a large skillet. Brown chicken pieces on all sides in the fat. Reduce heat and cook for 20 minutes longer, or until chicken pieces are tender. Drain off excess fat and reserve the fat and the chicken pieces.

Drain fresh sauerkraut well and rinse it with cold water in order to remove some of the tartness. Add the sauerkraut to the meat and vegetables and stir well. Add marjoram. Simmer, stirring occasionally, until the sauerkraut is browned and the meat is tender. Add the chicken pieces and, if the sauerkraut seems a bit dry, add 1–2 tablespoons of the reserved fat. Stir well. Simmer for 10 minutes longer. Refrigerate for 24 hours. Stir well and reheat before serving. If desired, serve with a bowl of sour cream on the side.

BEEF PATTIES IN CREAM
serves 5–6

4 slices white bread, with crust removed	¼ tsp thyme
1 cup milk	1 cup flour
1 large onion, minced	¼ cup butter
4 Tbls butter	1 cup sour cream
2 pounds ground beef	½ cup milk
2 eggs	½ pound sliced mushrooms
Salt and pepper to taste	Salt and pepper to taste

Soak bread in 1 cup of milk. Set aside. Sauté onion in 4 tablespoons of butter until it is just limp. In a bowl, combine ground beef, eggs, sautéed onion, bread and milk mixture, salt and pepper to taste, and thyme. Mix well. Make 3-inch oval ½-inch-thick patties and dredge them in flour. Brown the patties in butter slowly on both sides. Add sour cream mixed with milk and mushrooms. Add salt and pepper to taste and simmer for 30 minutes. Serve immediately, with noodles or dumplings.

HOVĚZÍ PEČENĚ S UZENKAMI
Roast Beef with Frankfurters
serves 6

3 frankfurters	½ cup butter or margarine
2½–3 pounds top round roast of beef	Salt and pepper to taste
1 large onion, sliced	2½ cups water
1 carrot, sliced	2 Tbls flour
1 parsnip, sliced	

Preheat oven to 350°. Cut frankfurters into lengthwise strips. Secure the strips to the roast with toothpicks. In a large skillet or oven-proof casserole, sauté vegetables in butter until they are slightly browned. Add meat and salt and pepper to the vegetables and brown the meat well. Add half the water, cover, and roast in a 350° oven for 2 hours, or until tender. Remove meat, dust the pan drippings with flour, and stir over the heat until brown. Add the rest of the water and simmer for 5 minutes. Strain the gravy through a sieve. Pour gravy over the sliced meat.

CABBAGE ROLLS
serves 6–7

½ cup rice
2 quarts water
1 large head of cabbage
1 pound ground beef
½ pound ground lean pork
3 eggs
½ cup minced sautéed onions
Salt and pepper to taste

½ cup oatmeal
½ cup milk
15–18 strips of bacon
1 cup white wine
1 cup prepared tomato sauce
2 cups sour cream
Salt and pepper to taste

Preheat oven to 350°. Wash rice in cold water. Add it to 1 quart of rapidly boiling salted water. Boil for 10 minutes and strain. Set aside. Core cabbage and drop into 1 quart of rapidly boiling water. Boil for 10 minutes. Drain and cool. Carefully remove the leaves and cut off the tough parts. In a bowl, combine beef, pork, eggs, onions, salt and pepper to taste, half-boiled rice, oatmeal, and milk. Mix well.

Spread each cabbage leaf with the meat mixture, so that it is about ½-inch thick. Fold the 2 sides to meet in the center, then roll up the cabbage. Wind a thin piece of bacon around each cabbage roll, place them into a baking dish, pour dry white wine over the rolls, and bake them in a 350° oven for 1½ hours, or until the bacon is well browned. Combine 1 cup of prepared tomato sauce with 2 cups of sour cream, beat with a whisk until smooth, and add salt and pepper to taste. Pour over the cabbage rolls and bake for 15–20 minutes.

SEKANÁ PEČENĚ
Meat Loaf
serves 8–10

2 pounds ground beef
1 pound ground pork
Salt and pepper to taste
3 eggs
4 Kaiser rolls (or any other hard rolls)
1 cup milk

¾ cup chopped bacon
1 large onion, diced
½ cup flour for handling meat loaf
¼ cup melted butter or margarine
1 cup meat broth (canned bouillon may be used)

In a bowl, mix meats, salt, pepper, and eggs together. Break up the rolls and soak in milk; then squeeze most of the liquid out. Chop the rolls and add them to the meat mixture along with half of the chopped bacon. Fry the remainder of the bacon and then brown

onion in the bacon drippings. Cool the bacon and onion and add
them to the meat mixture, mixing well. Flour your hands and
form the meat mixture into a roll. Pour the melted butter into a
baking pan. Place meat roll into the pan. Bake in a 350° oven for
1¾–2 hours, basting frequently with the meat broth.

SKOPOVÁ KÝTA NA SMETANĚ
Leg of Lamb with Sour Cream
serves 6–8

1	cup diced vegetables (celery, carrot, parsnip)	¼	tsp allspice
1	large onion, diced	1	bay leaf
⅓	cup butter or lard	¼	tsp thyme
3	pounds boned leg of lamb	⅛	tsp marjoram
2½	cups water	2	Tbls flour
	Salt to taste	1½	cups sour cream
6	peppercorns		Lemon juice or vinegar to taste

In a large skillet, sauté vegetables and onion in butter or lard. Add
meat and brown on all sides. Pour in half the water, add the
seasonings, cover, and simmer for 1 hour and 15 minutes. Add the
remaining water. Transfer lamb and vegetables to a baking dish
and bake uncovered in a 350q oven for 40–50 minutes. Remove
the meat. Mix flour with sour cream, add the mixture to the broth
in the pan, and simmer for 5 minutes. Strain gravy into a saucepan
and add lemon juice or vinegar. Bring to a boil and serve gravy
either poured over the meat or on the side.

SKOPOVÉ MASO S MRKVÍ
Lamb with Carrots
serves 6

2	pounds cubed shoulder of lamb	1¾	cups water, or more as needed
	Salt to taste	2	mashed garlic cloves
1	large onion, thinly sliced	2½	Tbls flour
½	cup butter	6–8	carrots, sliced

Salt meat to taste. Sauté onion in butter in a large skillet. Add
meat cubes and brown. Pour in ¾ cup of water, add garlic, cover,
and simmer for 2 hours, or until tender. Add water as needed.
Remove meat cubes. Add flour to the pan drippings, stirring until
brown. Add 1 cup water, bring to a boil, add carrots, and simmer
for 15–20 minutes, or until the carrots are tender.

KARLOVARSKÝ KOTOUČ
Veal Roast Karlsbad
serves 5–6

3 pounds veal shoulder cut into ¾-inch thick slices
Salt and pepper to taste
⅓ pound bacon strips
6 ounces thinly sliced ham

4 soft scrambled eggs—cooled
2 dill pickles, diced
½ cup butter
1 ¾ cup water
2 Tbls flour

Preheat oven to 350°. Have the butcher slice the veal shoulder. Pound veal slices lightly and sprinkle them with salt and pepper to taste. Cover each slice with layers of bacon, ham, eggs, and pickle. Roll up each slice and secure with string or toothpicks. In an oven-proof skillet, brown the veal rolls in butter. Add ¾ cup of water. Roast the rolls in a 350° oven for about 2 hours, basting often. Remove veal, add flour to the drippings, stir well until lightly browned. Add the remainder of the water and stir. Add veal and simmer for 5 minutes. Serve immediately.

BAKED POTATOES WITH MEAT
serves 6

6 large baking potatoes
Salt and pepper to taste
1 ½ cups diced cooked meat (veal, chicken, or beef)
1 medium onion, chopped and sautéed

*½ cup white sauce
⅓ cup melted butter
¼ cup grated Swiss cheese
1 Tbls minced parsley

Preheat oven to 450°. Wrap potatoes in foil and bake about 50 minutes, or until done. Turn the oven down to 350°. Cut about a ¼-inch-thick lengthwise slice off each potato and scoop out the inside. In a bowl, combine potato, salt, pepper, cooked meat, sautéed onion, and white sauce. Stuff potato shells with the mixture. Place them in a baking pan. Pour butter over potatoes and sprinkle with cheese and parsley. Bake at 350° for 30 minutes.

*White Sauce

2 Tbls flour
1 Tbls butter
½ cup milk

In a saucepan, melt butter and blend in flour. Gradually add milk, stirring continuously. Simmer, stirring frequently until the sauce thickens.

VEAL LIVER PÂTÉ
serves 8

1 medium onion, diced	3 beaten eggs
⅔ cup diced bacon	Salt and pepper to taste
¾ pound pork cut into 1-inch cubes	⅛ tsp each of thyme, tarragon, all-
1½ pounds veal liver cut into small	spice, crushed bay leaf
pieces	3 Tbls red wine
4 slices of bread soaked in	2–3 Tbls shortening
⅔ cup milk	

In a large skillet, fry the onion and bacon. Add pork, cover, and simmer until tender. Grind liver, cooked meat, and milk-soaked bread together in a meat grinder or a food processor. Pour into a bowl; add eggs, seasonings, and wine, and beat with a wooden spoon until smooth. Grease a loaf pan well with the shortening. Pour mixture into the loaf pan until it is three-quarters full. Wrap the loaf pan in foil and place into a large pot on a wire rack. Add water to come two-thirds of the way up the side of the loaf pan. Simmer 1½–2 hours. Cool, then refrigerate overnight. Run a knife around the pâté and unmold onto a platter. Serve sliced in ½-inch slices. This pâté will keep for 3 or 4 days in the refrigerator.

PORK CHOPS WITH APRICOTS
serves 6

6 center-cut pork chops, 1-inch thick	⅔ cup pale dry sherry
4 Tbls clarified butter or margarine	⅓ cup apricot brandy
(see recipe on page 37)	1 17-ounce can of whole peeled apri-
¼ tsp thyme	cots in heavy syrup
¼ tsp salt, or more to taste	1¼ Tbls cornstarch
¼ tsp white pepper	1 tsp Dijon mustard
⅛ tsp nutmeg	

Trim as much fat as possible from the pork chops. Heat butter or margarine in a large skillet with a cover. Brown the chops slightly on both sides and sprinkle them with seasonings. Add sherry and apricot brandy, cover, and simmer for 10–15 minutes, or until very tender, turning occasionally. Add a little more sherry if the liquid cooks down too much. Remove the chops to a platter, cover, and keep them warm. Drain apricots and reserve ⅔ cup of syrup. Mix the reserved syrup with cornstarch and mustard until well blended. Add to the skillet and blend with the liquid in the skillet, cooking until slightly thickened. Add apricots. Coat the apricots with sauce and cook 1–2 minutes. Return the chops to the skillet, turning to coat them with sauce. Simmer again for 1–2 minutes. Serve immediately.

NA KÁPAŘÉCH
Pork Chops with Capers
serves 6

12	½-inch thick pork chops, center cut	1	cup water
	Salt and pepper to taste	2	tsp caraway seeds
3	Tbls flour	3	Tbls capers
½	cup butter or lard		

Place pork chops on a cutting board, and using a small mallet pound each chop starting at the edge away from the bone. Then pound along the bone. This will partially loosen the meat from the bone. Be careful not to pound too hard or the meat will fall off. Sprinkle with salt, pepper, and flour. In a skillet, brown meat about 5–6 minutes on each side in butter. Set meat aside on a hot platter. Pour off half of the remaining fat and add water and caraway seeds. Stir well, bringing the liquid to a boil. Before serving, stir in capers. Serve sauce over the meat.

VEPŘOVÉ ŘÍZKY NEBO KOTLETY RYCHLÉ
Quick Pork Cutlets or Chops
serves 6

12	½-inch thick pork cutlets or chops	½	cup butter or lard
	Salt and pepper to taste	1	cup water
3	Tlbs flour	2	tsp caraway seeds

Loosen meat partially from bone by pounding (see preceding recipe for directions). Sprinkle with salt, pepper, and flour. In a skillet, brown meat about 3–4 minutes on each side in the butter. Set meat aside on a hot platter. Pour off half of the remaining fat and add water and caraway seeds. Stir well, bringing the liquid to a boil. Serve sauce over the meat.

VEPŘOVÁ PEČENĚ PEKANTNÍ
Roast Pork Piquant
serves 6

2 ½ pounds fresh boned picnic ham or pork butt	3 strips chopped bacon
Salt and pepper to taste	1 large onion, diced
4 strips bacon	2 cups water
4 thin slices cooked ham (about an ounce per slice)	2 carrots, thinly sliced
2 dill pickles, sliced into 2" × ½" strips (large)	2 small dill pickles, diced
	2 Tbls flour

Salt and pepper meat to taste. Cut bacon and cooked ham into wedges 2 inches long and ½ inch wide. Make slits in the meat large enough to hold the wedges of bacon, ham, and pickles. Push them into the slits. In an oven-proof large skillet, fry the chopped bacon. Add onion and brown. Add the meat and brown on all sides. Pour in ½ cup of the water, cover, and simmer 1 hour. Remove cover, add another ½ cup water, and bake in a 350° oven for 45–60 minutes. Place meat on a warm platter. Add carrots, pickles, and flour, mixed with 1 cup of water, to the baking pan and simmer for 5 minutes. Serve sauce over the sliced meat.

TELECÍ JÁTRA SMAŽENÁ
Breaded Calf's Liver
serves 6

2 pounds of ½-inch thick slices of calf's liver	3 beaten eggs
Salt and pepper to taste	1–2 cups bread crumbs
½ cup flour	1 cup shortening

Lightly pound liver with a mallet. Sprinkle it with salt and pepper. Dip liver slices in the flour, then into the eggs, and then into the bread crumbs. In a skillet, heat shortening and fry the liver slices until brown on all sides. Serve immediately.

Side Dishes . . . .

HOUSKOVE KNEDLIKY
Bread Dumplings
serves 12

10 pieces white bread, with crusts removed
5 Tbls butter
4 Tbls minced onion
¾ cup flour
¼ cup crisp crumbled bacon
3 Tbls minced parsley
Salt and pepper to taste
⅛ tsp nutmeg
⅓ cup milk

Cut the bread into ½-inch cubes to make about 3½ cups. In a large skillet, heat 4 tablespoons of butter and add bread cubes. Toss the cubes with 2 forks in butter until they are golden brown on all sides. Remove cubes from the skillet and place them in a bowl. Add the remaining butter to the skillet and sauté onions until slightly browned. Place onions in a large bowl. Add flour, bacon, parsley, salt, pepper, and nutmeg. Add milk to moisten the flour mixture. Knead lightly to form a soft dough. Add the bread cubes, gently folding them in. Shape the dough into 6–7-inch long and about 2-inch wide sausage-like rolls.

In a 9-inch saucepan, bring to a simmer just enough salted water to cover the rolls. Place rolls carefully into the simmering water. Simmer, covered, for about 25 minutes. Turn rolls carefully once, using two large spoons. Remove rolls with 2 slotted spoons and place them on paper towels to drain. While still hot, slice the rolls into ¾-inch slices. Slice with a thin string, Czech style. Serve with roast goose (see recipe on p. 122) and your favorite gravy.

MORKOVÉ
Marrow Dumplings
makes about 20–24 small dumplings

2 eggs
3 Tbls milk or cream
Salt and pepper to taste
½ pound marrow (from marrow bones), chopped
¼ tsp mace
⅛ tsp rosemary
2 cups bread crumbs, or more as needed

132

Beat eggs with milk, salt, and pepper. Add the remaining ingredients and mix into a stiff dough. Form into very small walnut-sized balls. Test the dough by boiling one dumpling. If the test dumpling crumbles, add more bread crumbs to the mixture and test another dumpling. Simmer dumplings for approximately 5–7 minutes. Use in soups or stews.

JÁTRŎVÉ
Liver Dumplings
makes about 20–24 small dumplings

3 Tbls butter	¼ tsp rosemary
Salt and pepper to taste	2¼ cups bread crumbs, or more as
2 eggs	needed
½ pound ground veal or chicken livers	

Cream butter, salt, and pepper with eggs. Add the remaining ingredients and mix into a stiff dough. Form one small, walnut-sized ball and test the dough by boiling this one dumpling. If the test dumpling crumbles, add more bread crumbs to the mixture and test another dumpling. Simmer dumplings for about 5–7 minutes. Use in soups and stews.

CABBAGE CASSEROLE
serves 8–10

This is a buffet dish or a luncheon dish; it is also wonderful as a vegetable with roasts.

1 large head cabbage	1 cup milk
3 cups water	¼ tsp pepper
1 tsp salt	Dash garlic powder
2 Tbls butter	1½ cups cooked farina (cream of wheat)
2 tsp flour	6 slices American cheese

Preheat oven to 400°. Core cabbage and cut it into slices. Bring water to a boil and add ½ teaspoon salt. Cook cabbage for 15 minutes; drain and cool. In a saucepan, melt butter, add flour, and stir until smooth. Slowly add milk and stir the mixture constantly until thickened. Stir in pepper, garlic powder, and remaining salt. Place one layer of cabbage into an 11″ × 18″ baking dish. Spread ¾ cup of farina over the cabbage and pour ¾ cup of the white sauce over it. Repeat with another layer of farina and then with a layer of cabbage. Pour remaining sauce over cabbage and spread the cheese over the top. Bake in a 400° oven for 35 minutes.

ZELENINOVY
Vegetable Pancake
serves 7–8

3 eggs whites	3 Tbls milk
3 egg yolks	1½ cups chopped cooked vegetables
4 Tbls melted butter	(asparagus, cauliflower, peas, and
⅔ cup all-purpose flour	broccoli)
Salt and pepper to taste	2 Tbls butter
⅛ tsp mace	3 Tbls flour

Preheat oven to 350°. Beat egg whites until stiff, then add 1 egg yolk at a time, blending well after each addition. Stirring constantly, slowly pour in the melted butter. Fold in flour and gently blend in the seasonings, milk, and vegetables. Butter an 8″ × 8″ baking pan well and dust it with flour. Fill pan with the batter and bake in preheated 350° oven for about 12–25 minutes until it is golden brown. Cool. Slice into strips and use in soups or as a side dish with meat or fowl.

TATROVY
Liver Pancakes for Soup
serves 7–8

3 Tbls butter or margarine	3 egg whites
⅛ tsp marjoram	1½ cups bread crumbs
Salt and pepper to taste	½ cup milk
3 egg yolks	3 Tbls butter
1⅓ cups finely ground veal or pork liver	3–4 Tbls bread crumbs

Preheat oven to 350°. Cream butter, marjoram, salt, and pepper with egg yolks. Add liver. Beat egg whites until very stiff. Mix 1½ cups of bread crumbs with milk. Fold egg whites and bread crumbs into liver mixture. Grease a 9–10-inch pie pan with butter and dust it with bread crumbs. Fill the pan with batter and bake in a pre-heated 350° oven for about 12–15 minutes until golden brown. Cool. Slice into thin strips and use in soups or serve in a separate dish as an accompaniment to soup.

HAM AND NOODLE CASSEROLE
serves 6–8

1	pound medium noodles	1	cup sour cream
¼	pound butter, melted	½	cup grated Parmesan cheese
1	pound boiled ham, diced	4	Tbls butter
5	eggs	4	Tbls flour
½	tsp salt	2	cups milk
¼	tsp pepper	3	egg yolks
	Pinch each of ground cloves and nutmeg	1	cup grated cheddar cheese
½	cup heavy cream		Salt and pepper to taste

Preheat oven to 350°. Cook noodles as directed on the package. Drain, add butter and ham, and toss together. Beat eggs and add salt, pepper, cloves, nutmeg, cream, and sour cream. Beat until smooth. Add to the noodles. Butter an oven-proof dish well and sprinkle it with Parmesan cheese. Place noodle mixture in the dish. Melt the 4 tablespoons of butter and add flour and stir. Add milk and stir until smooth and slightly thickened. Cool slightly and add egg yolks, cheddar cheese, and salt and pepper to taste. Mix well. Pour the cheese sauce over the noodles. Bake in a preheated 350° oven for 40–50 minutes.

. . . . *Desserts*

NOODLE PUDDING WITH CHERRIES AND NUTS
serves 6

3½	cups milk	½	cup ground walnuts
1	pound medium egg noodles	2	pounds pitted fresh cherries or 2 cans of sour pitted cherries, well drained
1	tsp salt		
1	pound butter	½	cup sugar, or more to taste
6	Tbls sugar	¼	cup cherry brandy
7	egg yolks		
1½	tsp vanilla		

Preheat oven to 350°. In a large pot, bring milk and salt to a boil. Add noodles and cook over low heat, stirring constantly. Cook until the milk has been almost absorbed. Add butter and cool.

Beat sugar with egg yolks. Add vanilla. Add cooled noodles and nuts to the egg mixture. Butter well a 9½ × 13½" pan with 2½" sides. Spread half of the noodles in the pan. If using canned cherries, drain them well. Pit the fresh cherries. Sprinkle cherries with sugar and cherry brandy. Spread cherries over the noodles and then spread remaining noodles over the cherries. Bake in a preheated 350° oven for 40–45 minutes until puffy and well browned.

RAISED FRUIT DUMPLINGS
12 dumplings

2 packages granulated yeast	2 tsp salt
1 Tbls sugar	
½ cup lukewarm water	*Filling
⅓ cup lukewarm milk	
½ tsp grated lemon peel	12 Italian plums or apricots, pitted
⅓ cup sugar	12 small cubes of sugar
½ tsp salt	
2–2½ cups unbleached all-purpose flour	Topping
3 egg yolks	12 Tbls unsalted melted butter
3–4 quarts water	⅔ cup granulated sugar, or more to taste
	1 tsp cinnamon

Mix yeast, sugar, and water in a small bowl. Set aside for 5 minutes. In a large bowl, combine milk, lemon peel, sugar, salt, nutmeg, yeast mixture, and 1 cup of flour. Mix lightly with a wooden spoon. Add the egg yolks one at a time, beating well after each addition. Add 1 or 1½ cups of flour, enough to make a medium-firm dough. Knead by hand or with a bread hook for about 1–2 minutes. If dough is sticky, add a bit more flour, ¼ cup at a time. Turn dough onto a floured board and knead it by pulling dough into a long ribbon and then pressing the two ends together. Repeat the pulling and folding motion 2–3 times. Then push dough away from you with the heel of your hand a few times. Continue kneading, adding a little flour if dough is sticky, until dough is blistery and elastic. This will take about 5–7 minutes. Form dough into a ball, place it in a well-buttered bowl, and turn it once to coat all sides. Cover bowl and let dough rise in a warm place for about 45 minutes or until doubled in bulk. Punch down. Roll dough out to a ¼-inch thickness on a well-floured board.

Cut dough into 12 4-inch squares. Place sugar cubes into plums or apricots, replacing the pits. Place a piece of fruit on each square. Fold corners of dough squares over the fruit and pinch them together. With floured hands, roll into a ball. Place the dumplings on a floured cookie sheet and let them rise for about 10 minutes. Bring water and salt to boil in a large pot. Carefully lower 6 dumplings into the boiling water. Cover pot and cook dumplings on medium heat for 5 minutes. Turn them over and boil 5 minutes longer. Remove them with a slotted spoon and drain on paper towels. Cover the dumplings to keep them warm. Cook the remaining dumplings. Place them on a heated platter. Pour the melted butter on the dumplings and sprinkle them with sugar and cinnamon. Serve hot.

Note: Instead of fresh fruit, 2 teaspoons of Damson plum jam or any other jam or preserves may be used. Eliminate the sugar cubes if you are using preserves. Cook as directed and use the topping.

NUT SQUARES
serves 10 (makes 24–30 squares)

1	cup unsalted butter	5	egg yolks
1½	cups sugar	3	whole eggs
¼	tsp salt	1½	cups coarsely ground walnuts
1½	cups sifted all-purpose flour		

Preheat oven to 300°. Cream unsalted butter. Mix together sugar, salt, and sifted all-purpose flour and add the mixture to butter, alternating it with yolks and whole eggs. Beat well after each addition. Fold in walnuts. Butter an 11″ × 17″ jelly roll pan well and line it with waxed paper. Butter the paper generously and sprinkle it with bread crumbs. Spread batter over the paper and smooth down the dough. Bake in a preheated 300° oven for 35 minutes, or until a cake tester comes out clean. If using topping, bake for 35 minutes only, cool slightly, and spread the topping on top. The topping will crack a bit after it has cooled.

Topping

4	egg whites	1	cup raisins
¾	cup sugar	½	cup cocoa
1	cup coarsely chopped walnuts		

Beat egg whites until stiff. Add sugar and beat until very stiff. Fold in chopped walnuts, raisins, and cocoa. Spread over the baked pastry and bake for 15 minutes longer in a 300° oven. Cool completely, remove from pan, peel off the paper, and slice into squares.

STUFFED BAKED APPLES, CZECH STYLE

serves 6

6 large baking apples	½ cup sugar
*1 cup ground roasted hazelnuts	½ cup honey
½ cup heavy cream	½ cup dark rum
½ cup chopped raisins soaked in	2–3 cups sweetened whipped cream
¼ cup dark rum	

Preheat oven to 400°. Cut the tops off apples and reserve tops. Core the apples, but do not peel them. In a bowl, combine and blend nuts, cream, raisins soaked in rum, and sugar. Stuff apples with the mixture and cover with the reserved apple tops. Place apples side by side in a deep baking dish. In a bowl, combine honey and rum. Pour the sauce over the apples. Bake for 30–35 minutes, basting apples often with sauce. Serve the apples hot with the whipped cream on the side or served them chilled, surrounded by the whipped cream.

* Roasted Hazelnuts

To roast hazelnuts, place them on a cookie sheet. Bake in a 350° oven for 10–15 minutes, or until the nuts are a pale golden brown and the skins rub off easily. Cool. Rub off skins and grind nuts in a blender. (Do not use a meat grinder.)

RICE SOUFFLÉ

serves 6

1 cup converted rice	½ cup sugar
1⅓ cups light cream	3 stiffly beaten egg whites
1 vanilla bean (or 3 tsp vanilla extract)	2 Tbls butter
1 Tbls grated lemon rind	1 Tbls bread crumbs
½ cup raisins	½ cup raspberry (or your favorite) syrup
3 egg yolks	

Preheat oven to 350°. In a saucepan, cook rice as directed on the package for 15 minutes. Drain. Add light cream and vanilla bean to the rice and cook until the liquid is almost absorbed, stirring often, for 5–6 minutes. Remove from heat, remove vanilla bean, and let rice cool. Add lemon rind and raisins. Beat egg yolks with sugar and fold into the rice mixture. Then fold in egg whites. Butter well and sprinkle with bread crumbs a 1½ quart baking dish with 3-inch sides. Bake in a preheated 350° oven for 40–50 minutes, or until an inserted knife comes out clean. Serve sprinkled with raspberry syrup or with any favorite syrup of your choice.

APPLE NOODLE SOUFFLÉ

serves 6

2	Tbls butter	⅔	cup sugar
1	Tbls sugar	4	Tbls melted butter
1	pound medium egg noodles	1	cup sour cream
2	cups light cream	1	cup light cream
½	vanilla bean (or 1½ tsp vanilla extract)	4	large apples, peeled, cored, and sliced
6	eggs	½	tsp cinnamon
		3	Tbls sugar

Preheat oven to 350°. Butter well and sprinkle with sugar a 2½ quart baking dish with 3-inch sides. Set aside. Cook noodles, as directed on the package, in salted water for 5–6 minutes. Drain nookles and put them back into the pot. Add light cream and vanilla bean and cook for 4–5 minutes stirring often, until most of the milk has been absorbed. Do not drain. In a bowl, beat eggs and sugar. Pour in melted butter, beating steadily until eggs are light and slightly thickened. In another bowl, beat sour cream with light cream. Combine the egg and sour cream mixtures. Place one-third of the cooked noodles into the baking dish. Pour one-third of the sour cream mixture over the noodles and place half of the apple slices over noodles. Sprinkle with half the cinnamon and sugar. Repeat the layers of noodles, sour cream mixture, apples, and cinnamon and sugar. Top with a final layer of noodles and sour cream mixture. Bake in a 350° preheated oven for 50–60 minutes, or until bubbly and well puffed.

POTATO APRICOT DUMPLINGS

serves 6–8

7	medium potatoes	12	small apricots
2	slightly beaten eggs	12	lumps sugar
	Salt and pepper to taste	4–6	quarts boiling water
3	cups unbleached all-purpose flour	⅔	cup melted butter
1	tsp baking powder		

In a pan, boil potatoes, drain, and refrigerate for 12–24 hours. Peel and grate potatoes into a large bowl. Add eggs, salt, pepper, flour, and baking powder. Knead dough until it is firm. Halve apricots and remove the pits. Place a lump of sugar where pit was. Wrap a piece of dough securely around each apricot. Make sure that dumplings are well sealed. Drop dumplings into boiling water and cook for 15–20 minutes. Remove them to a heated platter and sprinkle with melted butter.

RAISED DOUGH CAKE

serves 10–12

⅓	cup warm water	⅔	cup sugar
1½	packages granulated yeast	1	tsp salt
1	tsp sugar		Pinch each of ginger, nutmeg, and
5	egg yolks plus 1 egg		cinnamon
⅔	cup light cream	¼	pound sweet butter
3–4	cups sifted flour		

Preheat oven to 350°. Combine water, yeast, and sugar. Set aside for 5 minutes. Beat egg yolks and cream and add them to the yeast mixture. Sift the dry ingredients together and cut in butter. Add the yeast mixture and beat well. Chill overnight. Set dough in a warm place and let it rise until light. Punch down and let rise again. Roll dough into a rectangle ½-inch thick and spread it with the filling. Roll as for a jelly roll and place in a very well greased 9-inch Bundt pan. Let dough rise until light, and then bake cake in a 350° oven until done, about 1 hour. Invert on a rack, cool, and sprinkle with powdered sugar. Serve warm or cold.

Poppy Seed Filling

Combine ½ pound of ground poppy seeds (or use 1 jar of prepared poppy seed filling); ¾ cup sugar; 1 cup raisins; 1 teaspoon cinnamon; grated rind of 2 lemons; 1 apple, grated; and ¼ cup sour cream. Spread on dough.

Walnut Filling I

Combine ½ cup softened butter, ¾ cup brown sugar, 1 egg, ⅓ cup cream, 1 tsp cinnamon, and 2 ½ cups finely chopped walnuts. Proceed as with Poppy Seed Filling.

Walnut Filling II

Mix together ⅔ cup chopped walnuts, 4 Tbls granulated sugar, ½ tsp cinnamon, 1 Tbls cocoa. Spread on rolled cake as directed.

PEACH DUMPLING DESSERT

serves 8–10

Pastry

1 cup all-purpose unbleached flour	1 egg
¼ tsp salt	1 egg yolk beaten with
2 Tbls sugar	1 Tbls cream
6 Tbls butter or margarine	1 Tbls granulated sugar

In a bowl combine flour with salt and sugar. Cut in butter or margarine. Crumble butter and flour lightly with your fingers until it resembles a coarse meal. Add egg and knead lightly until pastry holds together. Shape ⅔ of the pastry into a ball. Wrap in wax paper and refrigerate for 1 hour. To the remaining ⅓ of the pastry add ½ teaspoon baking powder and 1 tablespoon milk and mix lightly. Leave in the bowl and do not refrigerate.

To Prepare Peaches

2   16-oz. jars or cans of whole spiced
    peaches (or 2 cans of cling peach
    halves)
¼   lb. unsalted butter or margarine
⅔   cup light brown sugar
⅔   cup roasting and finely ground
    hazelnuts

¼   tsp cinnamon
⅛   tsp nutmeg
½   cup of the canned juice
    Whipped cream (optional)

Preheat oven to 350°. Drain the whole peaches or the peach halves and set aside. Reserve ½ cup of the juice. In a saucepan melt butter with sugar, stirring continuously. Cook over low heat, stirring for 2–3 minutes until the mixture is very smooth and thickened. Add nuts, cinnimon, and nutmeg. Stir well and cook for 1 minute longer. Use a 2-quart ovenproof glass soufflé dish or a 9 × 5 × 2-inch oven-proof glass loaf pan. Spread half of the sugar mixture in the bottom of the dish. Place the peaches on top. Pour the remaining mixture over the peaches. Roll the reserved ⅓ of the pastry into walnut-sized pieces. Place the pastry pieces between the peaches. Pur the reserved peach juice over pastry and peaches.

On a lightly floured board roll out the refrigerated pastry into a square about ¼" thick. Place on top of the baking dish, letting the pastry overlap the dish on all sides by about ½ to 1 inch. Trim off the excess. Press the pastry firmly to the sides all around. Use the trimmed-off pieces for decoration. Make fancy cutouts or a braid and place on top of the pastry. Brush generously with egg yolk beaten with cream. Bake in preheated 350° oven for 30–35 minutes until delicately brown. Sprinkle with 1 tablespoon granulated sugar and place low under the broiler for 1–2 minutes.

Watch carefully while broiling, as the sugar burns easily. When the sugar has melted and browned, remove from oven and cool for about 5 minutes. Serve hot or cold with whipped cream on the side.

CHAPTER  4

The Land of the Magyars

HUNGARIANS consider the Danube to be their very own river, and its virtues and grandeur have been extolled in poetry and songs since time immemorial.

Along the Czech border near the Hungarian city of Gyor, the Danube, on its way to Budapest, swerves away from Slovakia and ripples between embankments dotted with ancient castles, sunny villages, and fertile fields.

Budapest is a city of timeless romanticism, soaring spires, and magnificent parks; it is divided by the majestically flowing Danube into the ancient city of Buda and the more modern city of Pest. Eight graceful bridges span the river and connect the two cities. On the Buda side, the Castle Hill towers over the Danube.   *143*

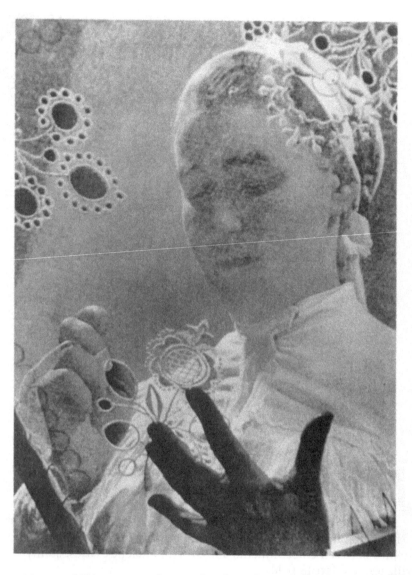

Woman of Kalosca region doing embroidery. This is sheer fabric and a special type of workmanship handed down through generations. Photo by Bill Sanders

The surrounding countryside, dominated by the former Royal Palace, stretches across the mile-long plateau and dwarfs the storybook houses, ancient churches, and picturesque squares of the Castle district. This is a small piece of terra firma steeped in antiquity and turbulent history through the centuries.

On the north side of the delicately Gothic Coronation Church stands the most recent addition to the landscape of the Castle district, the beautiful new Budapest Hilton. This marvel of modern engineering, with its baroque facade and ancient church tower separating the two wings of the hotel, blends perfectly with the medievel architecture of its surroundings.

The Budapest Hilton became the first structure of its kind in the world, mixing modern luxury with ancient treasure.

Béla Pintér, one of Hungary's foremost architects, was responsible for the tremendous task of blending ancient and modern styles in the design of the hotel, and incorporating it into the Buda skyline in a location where Hungary's rich past is written on every house, building, arch, gate, and statue.

The Budapest Hilton opened its doors January 1, 1977. Built into the perfectly modern lobby is the atrium of the ancient abbey, enclosed by a wall of glass. A Roman column of white marble towers in lonely magnificence in the corner of the lobby. This column was discovered under the monastery's 500-foot deep cellar. The corridors of the monastery link the two wings of the hotel.

Without destroying the fluid lines of the decor, the architect incorporated pieces of ancient arches, rosettes, and gates into the ceilings, walls, and archways. The two modern wings of the building are fused with the ancient church, as well as with the remnants of a college which later stood on the site. The interiors are so cleverly constructed that it is difficult to tell where ancient ends and modern begins. The decor is crisp and reflects a high level of sophistication.

History is so much a part of this hotel that it takes days to discover all the art treasures and monuments which have been effectively placed throughout the building.

On the sixth floor, in the loft of the tower of the original St. Nicholas Church, is the aptly-named Tower Restaurant. Here, huge iron chandeliers cast shadows on the medieval tapestry, handsome oak tables, and straight-backed knights' chairs. Even the food—some of which dates back to recipes from the fourteenth century—reflect the restaurant's medieval atmosphere. Stuffed pheasant with chestnut sauce, larded deer steak, noisette of venison, and escalope of goose liver a la King Mattyas are just a few of the delicacies. While dining, if you listen closely you can almost hear the pealing of the bells in the Tower, or the soft chants of the monks who, with heads bowed, once shuffled through the corridors of this venerable establishment.

The main dining room, the Kalocsa, is a complete antithesis to the somber beauty of the tower dining salon. It is incredibly bright and gay with a magnificent view of the Danube and Fisherman's Bastion, a Disney-like fantasy of parapets and turrets. The dazzling floral designs of artisans from the Kalocsa region abound on the walls, ceiling, and coordinating table linens and china.

The cuisine is purely and superbly Hungarian, including such specialties as Gulyás soup, Alföld catfish with paprika sauce, pork saddle stuffed with Debrecziner sausage and cabbage and beef pörkölt with tarhonya—all to be enjoyed against a background of vibrant gypsy music. The function rooms of the hotel are named for famous kings and dynasties of Hungary, and are decorated in period furnishings so that each gives a brief insight into Hungary's past.

Budapest today is one of the most westernized cities of the Eastern bloc nations. It has been magnificently restored and has regained most of its former opulence. The forested hills of Buda hide a multitude of villas and mansions, former dwellings of the wealthy and the nobility, which have now been subdivided into apartment buildings. The hills are also dotted with small, charming inns—*csardas*—serving some of the most delicious fare this side of heaven.

Sweeping toward the south, the river becomes shallow; it branches out into numerous arms, which encircle small inlets and vast, grassy islands. Once the navigation was impossible here, but as early as the Roman times, attempts have been made to tame the river, and today, deep, marked channels avoid the shallows.

The Danube has spawned a hearty breed of fishermen and river folk with their own particular lifestyles, legends, customs, and a way of preparing their catch. Even today, at night the banks of the Danube flicker with bonfires where the fishermen cook the *halaszle* fish soup, which has a tantalizing flavor and aroma all of its own. On the banks of the Danube stand thatch-covered *Halasz Csarda*, or fish inns, where fish is dished up in many marvelous ways.

Hungary is a small, enchanting country with towering mountains, fertile valleys, and grazing land that seems to stretch into infinity. Lush vines cover terraced hills, and immense orchards grow along wide rivers. The countryside is dotted with small inns and thatch-roofed cottages in which hearty, succulent fare is prepared and served.

The cuisine of Hungary is often underrated and misunderstood; it is not comprised solely of *gulyas, paprikas,* and sauerkraut. Rather, true Hungarian cookery consists of a blend of flavors and techniques inherited from Asian ancestors and acquired from many cultures. In the ninth century, under the banner of Chieftain Arpad, the seven tribes of Magyars traversed the vast Russian steppes, ascended the wild heights of the Carpathian Mountains, and swooped down into the fertile Pannonian plain. Herds of longhorn cattle were driven through the narrow gorges by Mongol horsemen, and they were followed by lumbering wagons and litters carrying noble ladies. The Magyars settled along the shores of the Danube on the site of the Roman camp of Aquincum. There, Chief Arpad bade his people to till the soil, raise cattle, and live in peace with their neighbors.

The hordes of Genghis Khan who pillaged Hungary in the thirteenth century also left their indelible marks on the country's gastronomy, but the most significant contribution was made by the Turks, who occupied the land for 150 years. They brought pepper pods, which at first were called Turkish peppers and were used only by the peasants to "pepper up" their simple fare, but, quite rapidly, the zestful red spice gained popularity and moved to the tables of the upper classes, eventually becoming the most outstanding feature of Hungarian cuisine.

In the fifteenth century, during the reign of King Mattyas and Queen Beatrice, many Mongol dishes benefited from the refinements given them by the queen's Italian kitchen staff, and several interesting cookbooks providing insight into the evolution of the Magyar cuisine were penned during that period. Dishes from Transylvania were held in great esteem by the aristocracy, and cooks from that mountainous land were at a premium. From Transylvania comes *fatanyeros,* a rather complicated presentation of a mixed grill in which a wooden platter is piled high with sautéed pork chops, small steaks, veal cutlets, lamb chops and sausages. It is decorated with mounds of rice, sliced beets, parsley, and shredded lettuce and is served flaming. *Tokaji fatanyeros* is a similar creation, but chicken and duck are substituted for the pork and steak.

As late as the eighteenth century, travelers to Hungary returned home with tales of legendary hospitality as well as of the eccentricities and implausible escapades of the unbridled Magyars. There were accounts of great feasts that lasted for many days, and the stories of drinking, dancing, and merrymaking were unparalleled in the civilized world. By the middle of the nineteenth century, praise of Hungarian culinary achievements began to be heard throughout Europe. Dumas *père*, who was a passionate amateur chef, was a great exponent of the culinary art of the Magyars, and the well-known German traveler and writer, J. G. Kohl, enthusiastically extolled the virtues of Budapest restaurants and inns. He was in ecstasy over the fare served at the Queen of England restaurant. Edward VII evidently found it to this liking also, for after a stay at the hostelry, he lured the chef away and took him back to England.

Many of the more substantial elements of Hungarian cookery owe their presence not so much to settlers and invaders as to the bounty of the land itself. Venison and game birds have long been devoured in great quantities by the Magyars, and their preparation was brought long ago to an exalted rank of culinary artistry.

No animal, however, is more beloved by Hungarian epicures than the fattened goose. All summer long, young girls and crones ply the greedy white birds with corn. After a few months, the birds can barely waddle, and their meat becomes tender and sweet. The geese are roasted or braised, and the cracklings made from the layers of fat and skin are eaten with bread or used to flavor other dishes. But it is the liver, the magnificent foie gras, that is the most precious morsel. Large and incredibly delicious, it can be sautéed, poached, smoked, wrapped in fat and baked, or made into pâté—and it is the epitome, the crowning glory, of Hungarian cuisine.

The prominence of pork in the Hungarian diet is the result of the short-legged, small, fat hogs that the Magyars brought with them from Asia. Everywhere in Hungary, from November through February, the predawn darkness of the farmyards is illuminated by straw bonfires beside which hogs are butchered. Children gather around the fires cooking pieces of fresh bacon speared on sticks and soaking up the drippings with wedges of crusty bread while the wonderful aroma of homemade sausages wafts through the chilly air. By evening, the chops and roasts have been cut and stored in the ice cellar; the bacon and hams have been hung in the smokehouse; and the back, head bones, feet, jaws, and ears are simmering in a kettle in preparation for *orja*, the pungent thick soup of Hungarian peasants. At suppertime, the *orja* kettle is set on the table along with a platter of pork cutlets and fresh sausages, a huge pan of stuffed cabbage, a bowl of *galuska* (dumplings) or *tarhonya* (egg pasta), and dishes of horseradish sauce.

Pastas and dumplings are vital components of Hungarian cookery, and among the pastas, *tarhonya* is probably the most characteristic. A firm egg dough is pressed through a sieve or grated and allowed to dry. The tiny pieces of dough are then roasted or sautéed in lard, sprinkled with paprika, and boiled in salted water. *Tarhonya* is served with numerous familiar Hungarian stews, and it is given to children in boiled milk, mixed with peas or mushrooms, and used for poultry stuffing as well.

Kocka, csusza, and *metélt* are all pastas, each of which is made in a different shape and served with various toppings. The most common pasta dish consists of small squares of dough that are boiled, drained, and topped with cottage cheese and hot lard with cracklings. Other toppings include walnuts, poppy seeds, sautéed cabbage or sauerkraut, and chopped meats.

Galuska, csipetke, and *nockeddli* are perhaps the favorite small dumplings, though also cherished is the *gomboć,* a dumpling of Slavic origin that is made from raised dough or potatoes and usually stuffed with apricots or plums.

Castle Hill, circa 17th Century

Many Hungarian dishes originated on the Puszta, the wide expanse of plain that extends east of the Danube toward the foothills of the Carpathian Mountains. Here, cowboys cook their *gulyas* in iron kettles suspended over log fires, and at night they sit huddled in great fur capes, assuaging their hunger with the slightly smoky *gulyas*, thick slices of bread, and wine poured from leather-encased decanters.

True *gulyas* is really a stew made from beef, onions, potatoes, and green peppers; it is accompanied by *csipetke* and is served, even in the best restaurants, from an iron or copper kettle. *Porkolt* is a similar, though somewhat thicker, stew made with lamb, beef, or pork, and it is served with *nockeddli*. *Paprikas*, prepared with pork, veal, chicken, or fish, belongs to the same family, but it usually has more sauce than *pörkölt*, and the sauce contains sour cream.

Stews and soups are the mainstays of Hungarian cuisine. The soups are thick and pungent, made from vegetables, fruits, meats, poultry, and game. There are purées and so-called sour soups, which incorporate sour cream and vinegar, and fruit soups made from cherries, raspberries, plums, apples, and apricots, which are served cold with generous dollops of sour cream. Hungarian lakes and rivers abound with fish, and the *fogas* of Lake Balaton is one of the best tasting. Customarily served whole, it is generally baked or poached and presented with great flair. Other freshwater fish go into *paprikas* in addition to being baked, grilled, sautéed, or simmered with vegetables.

Among the prominent seasonings found in Hungarian cookery are caraway seed, marjoram, dill, and thyme. Tarragon, which made the arduous journey with the Mongol tribes from Siberia, is widely used in Transylvania and the eastern provinces, and sour cream is used lavishly throughout the country. Sauces, soups, and vegetables are frequently thickened with a well-browned roux known as *rantas*.

Hungarian housewives usually have an extensive repertoire of stuffed vegetables, of which *töltött káposzta*, the inimitable stuffed cabbage, is undoubtedly the best known. It is made differently in almost every village. Stuffed kohlrabi, squash, onions, tomatoes, and peppers are also great favorites. Some are prepared with a version of béchamel sauce, whereas others assume an Italian or Turkish character and are made with a tomato sauce. Also typical of the many elaborate vegetable preparations, which are considered so important, is *fözelék*. This dish calls for braising vegetables in lard or simmering them and then mixing them with sweet or sour cream, a roux, and a bit of vinegar.

In the country, the fare is hardy, spicy, robust, and sometimes heavily laden with lard, onions, and paprika.

In Budapest, chefs produce more sophisticated specialties, excelling in the preparation of subtle sauces and exquisite pastries. *Dobos torta; Rigó Jancsi;* crêpes stuffed with nuts, strawberries, cheese, or apricots; chestnut purées with whipped cream; nut tortes; pastry balls filled with cream; square pies containing nuts or apples; an assortment of chocolate confections; and, of course, *rétes,* the incomparable strudels, are but a few among a fabulous array of Hungarian sweets.

In many restaurants, a special corner of the kitchen is set aside for girls or women whose sole occupation is to produce *rétes,* and almost every woman has her own jealously guarded recipes for these tempting delicacies. Girls learn early how to pull the dough into paper-thin transparent sheets and how to fill and bake it to crisp perfection. The *rétes* are filled with nuts, poppy seeds, apples, cherries, raspberries, cottage cheese, sautéed cabbage, or ground meat. One of the most delectable kinds is the *vargabélés,* or cobbler's cake, which consists of layers of strudel pastry filled with cottage cheese, sour cream, and noodles.

Dining in a Hungarian *csarda* (country inn) or restaurant is not only a gustatory experience; it is a total involvement of all the senses. The food may be regional or classical, but it is always served with great pomp, creating an appropriate aura for a fine gastronomic adventure.

Appetizers. . . . .

KÖRÖZÖTT
Liptauer Cheese Spread

½	pound farmers' cheese	2	tsp paprika
½	pound pot cheese	2	Tbls caraway seeds
¼	pound Feta cheese or Brindza, if available		Radishes
			Scallions
¼	pound softened butter		Green and red peppers
10	drops Worcestershire sauce		Green olives
½	tsp prepared mustard		Crackers or French bread
3	Tbls minced scallions—whites only		
1	tsp anchovy paste or 2 anchovies, mashed		

(Radishes, Scallions, Green and red peppers, Green olives, Crackers or French bread } garnish)

Press cheese through a fine sieve into a bowl. Sieve butter on top of the cheeses. Add Worcestershire sauce, mustard, scallions, anchovy paste, and paprika. Blend well into a smooth paste. Add caraway seeds and blend again. Refrigerate for 1 hour. Serve with garnishes and with crackers or sliced French bread.

CHOPPED CHICKEN LIVER PÂTÉ

2	medium onions chopped	3	hard-boiled eggs, chopped fine
4	Tbls melted butter	1	Tbls chopped scallions
1	tsp paprika	1	Tbls vegetable oil
2	pounds chicken liver (fresh, not frozen)	¼	cup pimientos
½	tsp salt, or more to taste	1	bunch scallions
¼	cup dry white wine	6	sprigs parsley
¼	tsp freshly ground black pepper	¼–½	cup capers

In a large skillet, sauté onions in half the butter until golden brown. Add the paprika, mix well, add livers and mix again until livers are coated completely. Cook livers for about 7 minutes on medium heat. Add salt and wine and cook for another 3–4 minutes. Cool the livers slightly, place in a blender, and blend to a smooth paste, adding some of the liquid from the skillet. Place in a bowl and add pepper, more salt if necessary, the rest of the

*The real goat's cheese is rarely available in the United States.

melted butter, chopped egg, and scallions. Mix well. Line a square loaf pan with plastic wrap. Spread some oil over the plastic wrap, which should extend well over the rim of the pan. Pack the pâté tightly into the pan. Fold overhanging wrap over the pâté. Refrigerate for at least 3 hours before serving. Place a plate over the pan, invert the pan, and slide out the pâté. Remove the wrap and decorate the pâté with pimientos, scallions, parsley, and capers. Serve with crackers or thinly sliced rye bread.

STUFFED EGGS

Use 6 eggs. Hard-boil eggs by bringing them to a rapid boil. Reduce heat and simmer for 5–7 minutes. Take off heat and let-stand for 15 minutes—you will have much creamier yolks this way. Peel eggs and cut them in half lengthwise or crosswise, as desired. Remove the yolks.

Filling

6 egg yolks	3 Tbls prepared mayonnaise
½ cup any liver pâté—or pâté de foie gras	1 Tbls minced capers
	1 Tbls minced dill
1 Tbls minced scallions	

Purée egg yolks and the pâté together. Add scallions, mayonnaise and capers. Fill egg whites by using a pastry bag with a tube. Place eggs on a platter. Prepare aspic, and glaze eggs with the aspic. Before glazing, decorate with pimientos, scallions, or more capers. Pour about 2–3 tablespoons of aspic over each egg half. Refrigerate until set. Repeat glazing and refrigerating until all the aspic has been used.

The Aspic

2 envelopes unflavored gelatin	¼ cup white wine
½ cup cold water	1 Tbls lemon juice
2 cups chicken broth	

Soften the gelatin in cold water. In a saucepan, combine broth and wine and heat to a boiling point. Add gelatin and stir until dissolved. Add lemon juice. Refrigerate until cold but not set.

STUFFED EGGS WITH CHICKEN LIVER PÂTÉ
serves 4

4 hard-cooked eggs
⅓ cup liver pâté (see recipe on page 152)
   or pâté de foie gras
1 tsp minced scallions

1 Tbls mayonnaise
   Salt and pepper to taste
1 Tbls minced parsley

Shell and slice eggs lengthwise. In a small bowl, mash egg yolks with a fork. Add pâté, scallions, mayonnaise, salt, and pepper and blend until very smooth. Fill the eggs. Decorate with parsley.

CRÊPES WITH HAM
serves 8–10

Crepe Batter

Makes 12 large or 18 small crepes

1 cup sifted all-purpose flour
⅛ tsp salt
3 large eggs plus 1 extra egg yolk
2 Tbls melted clarified butter (see recipe on page 37)

1½ cups milk
5 Tbls melted clarified butter (for baking crepes)

Sift flour and salt and place in a blender. Add eggs. Use the blender at low speed and add butter and milk, beating until the batter is the consistency of thick cream. Let batter stand for 1 hour before baking. Bake crêpes in a 5- or 6-inch well-buttered pan over medium-high heat. Pour a little of the batter into the pan and gently tip pan so that the batter runs evenly over the entire surface. Brown on one side, then turn and brown the other side. Stack crêpes on a warm platter. The crêpes may be refrigerated for as long as 3 days and reheated before using. They may also be frozen. Before freezing, place squares of wax paper between the crêpes. When defrosting, place them in a pan, cover pan with foil, and defrost in a 200° oven. Be sure they are completely defrosted before using.

Filling

1 pound cooked ham	¼ tsp white pepper (finely ground)
3 egg yolks, well beaten	½ tsp tarragon
1 cup sour cream	

Mince ham. Place into a bowl and add beaten egg yolks. In another bowl, beat sour cream and seasonings until the mixture is very smooth and add it to the ham mixture. Mix well. Spread about 1 tablespoon of ham on each crêpe. Fold crêpes envelope fashion, making small squares.

2 eggs, well beaten	½ cup or more clarified butter (see
2 cups bread crumbs	recipe on page 37)
2 cups flour	

Dip each crêpe into eggs, then into flour, then into egg again, and then into bread crumbs. Heat butter in a large skillet and fry crêpes until crisp and golden brown on both sides. Serve immediately. If you wish to keep the crêpes warm, place them on a heated platter in a preheated 250° oven.

Hungarian woodcarving. Photo by Bill Sanders

Soups . . . .

KALARABÉLEVES
Kohlrabi Soup
serves 6

4	Tbls butter	4	kohlrabies, peeled and diced
2	large onions, diced	3	Tbls butter
3	celery stalks, scraped and diced	2	Tbls flour
2½	quarts water	3	Tbls apple cider vinegar, or more to
2	large frying chicken, cut into serving pieces		taste
	Salt and pepper to taste	3	Tbls minced parsley and dill

In a large skillet, melt 4 tablespoons butter. Add onions and celery. Sauté until very tender, but not browned. Press through a fine sieve into a large pot. Add water, chicken, salt, and pepper. Cover pot and cook over medium heat for about 45 minutes, or until chicken is very tender. Remove chicken with a slotted spoon and place it in a bowl. Add kohlrabi to the soup in the pot and simmer while you remove the skin and bones from the chicken. Slice chicken into ½-inch pieces and add them to the soup. Cook over

Women of Kalosca region in traditional costumes. Photo by Bill Sanders

low heat until kohlrabi is tender. In a small skillet, melt butter, add flour, and cook, stirring constantly, until golden brown. Add 1 cup of hot soup to the flour mixture, stirring steadily. When the sauce thickens, add it to the soup pot. Add vinegar to taste. (Some prefer the soup on the tart side; others eliminate the vinegar completely.) Add more salt and pepper if desired. Serve hot, sprinkled with parsley and/or dill.

KAROLYI HALÁSZLÉ
Fish Soup, Karolyi Style
serves 8

1 large green pepper	1 ½ pounds carp, cut into 2½-inch slices
½ or more small very hot pepper	
2 carrots	1 ½ pounds bass, cut into 2½-inch slices
3 stalks of celery	
1 large mild onion	2 ½ quarts water
4 Tbls lard or bacon drippings	2 bay leaves
2 tsp sweet paprika	2–3 Tbls wine vinegar to taste
½ tsp salt	¼ tsp marjoram
2 pounds pike, cut into 2½-inch slices	1 cup or more sour cream for serving

Dice green and hot peppers, grate carrots, and coarsely chop celery and onion. In a heavy pot, sauté the vegetables in bacon drippings or lard until just limp. Add paprika and salt. Stir well. Sprinkle cut-up fish with additional salt and place on top of vegetables. Pour water over fish. Do not stir. Add bay leaves, vinegar, marjoram, and more salt to taste. Bring to a boil, reduce heat, and simmer for about 20 minutes, or until the fish flakes easily. Do not stir the soup; just shake the pot gently a few times. Taste for seasoning and add more salt, marjoram, and a little black pepper if desired.

Serving

With a slotted spoon, remove the fish and place into individual soup plates or a tureen. Strain liquid over fish. Take ½ cup of liquid and beat it well with the 1 cup of sour cream until smooth. Serve a sauce boat on the side. One or 2 tablespoons more of sour cream may be added to each serving of Halászlé, but this is optional.

MEGY LEVES
Cold Cherry Soup a la Budapest
serves 6–8

2 16-ounce cans sour pitted cherries	½ cup dry red wine
1 cup sugar or more to taste	2 Tbls lemon juice
1 cup water	1 Tbls grated lemon rind
1 stick of cinnamon	2 Tbls brandy
¼ tsp finely ground white pepper	1 cup sour cream
⅛ tsp salt	⅛ tsp cinnamon per cup of soup
2 Tbls cornstarch	

Do not drain cherries. Pour the contents of 2 cans of cherries into a saucepan and add sugar, water, cinnamon stick, pepper and salt. Simmer 5 minutes. Dissolve cornstarch in wine and add it to the soup. Simmer, stirring until slightly thickened. Remove cinnamon stick and discard. Add lemon juice, lemon rind, and brandy. Take some of the soup and mix it with sour cream until it is very smooth. Add sour cream mixture. Cool and then refrigerate. Serve in cups: Top with a teaspoon of sour cream and sprinkle with cinnamon.

HIDEG SZILVA LEVES
Cold Plum Soup
serves 6

1 30-ounce can of purple plums in heavy syrup	1 Tbls cornstarch
⅔ cup sugar	½ cup dry red wine
1 cup water	2 Tbls lemon juice
1 stick of cinnamon	1 tsp grated lemon
¼ tsp finely ground white pepper	1 cup sour cream
Pinch of salt	3 Tbls brandy
½ cup heavy cream	1 cup sour cream
	2 tsp cinnamon

Drain plums and reserve the syrup. Remove pits and shred plums into small pieces. Pour reserved syrup and plums into a saucepan and add sugar, water, cinnamon, white pepper, and salt. Simmer for 5–6 minutes, stirring occasionally. Add heavy cream. Mix cornstarch with wine and add to the plum mixture. Simmer, stirring constantly, until slightly thickened. Add lemon juice and grated lemon rind. In a small bowl, combine 1 cup sour cream, brandy, and about half the plum soup. Beat together, add to soup, and blend well. Chill before serving. Serve in cups: Top with a dab of sour cream and spinkle with cinnamon.

RAGOUT SOUP

serves 6

1	turkey gizzard	5	peppercoms
1	turkey liver	6	cups water
1	turkey heart	2	cups chopped fresh mushrooms
½	pound sweetbreads	2	Tbls butter
2	stalks celery, sliced into 3-inch pieces	3	Tbls flour
2	carrots, sliced	3	egg yolks
1	large onion, cut in half	1	cup sweet cream
1 ½	tsp salt		Paprika

In a large pot, combine turkey giblets, sweetbreads, celery, carrots, onion, salt, peppercorns, and water. Cook slowly until all ingredients are tender. Remove and discard the celery, carrots, and onion. Chop giblets and sweetbreads and return them to the soup. In a skillet, brown mushrooms in butter. Add flour and 1 cup of the soup. Continue cooking and stirring until the mixture is thickened and smooth. Add another cup of soup; then add the mushroom mixture to the soup in the pot. Heat to boiling. Mix egg yolks and cream and divide the mixture into 6 soup bowls; then pour on the hot soup and mix well. Sprinkle with paprika and serve.

Hungarian "cowboy"

HIDEG ÖSZIBARACK LEVES
Cold Peach Soup
serves 6–8

2	cups light brown sugar		5	cups Rhein wine or any other semi-sweet white wine
2	cups water			
*8	large very ripe peaches		¼	tsp cinnamon
3	quarts boiling water		⅛	tsp nutmeg
2	Tbls lemon juice		⅛	tsp salt
⅓	cup granulated sugar		2	cups whipped cream
	Grated rind of 1 lemon		¼	cup apricot or peach brandy
3	Tbls lemon juice			

In a saucepan cook brown sugar and water for 10 minutes; remove from heat and cool completely. Drop peaches into boiling water for 1 minute. Remove with a slotted spoon and peel them while they are still hot. Dice 3 of the peaches, place into a bowl, sprinkle with 2 tablespoons of lemon juice and ⅓ cup granulated sugar. Toss lightly and refrigerate. Slice remaining 5 peaches and purée in a blender until very smooth. Pour peach purée into a bowl, add lemon rind and 3 tablespoons juice, the sugar syrup, and wine. Mix well. Combine cinnamon, nutmeg, and salt with whipped cream, then fold the cream into the peach mixture until well-blended. Add brandy and whip briskly a few times with a whisk. Add the reserved diced peaches and chill for at least 2 hours before serving.

Note: If using canned peaches: Use 3 16-ounce cans of peeled cling peach halves packed in heavy syrup. Drain, but reserve the syrup. Dice 8 peach halves and refrigerate. Purée the rest. Take 2 cups of the syrup and cook for 5 minutes with ¾ cup light brown sugar and cool. Then follow the recipe for fresh peaches.

Grand Hotel Margitsziget, St. Margaret's Island, Budapest (pre-World War II)

UBORKA SALÁTA
Cucumber Salad
serves 10

6 large cucumbers	3 Tbls minced dill (optional)
2 tsp salt	Salt and coarsely ground black pepper
3 Tbls wine vinegar	Bibb or Boston lettuce
4 Tbls olive oil	Paprika
4 Tbls minced scallions	

Peel cucumbers and slice very, very thin. Place them into a bowl, add salt, and mix. Let stand in the refrigerator for 15 minutes. Drain and squeeze out the liquid. Add vinegar, oil, scallions, dill, salt, and pepper. Toss together and taste. Add more salt and vinegar if necessary. Separate lettuce leaves and line a serving dish with lettuce. Place the cucumbers on top and sprinkle them with paprika.

GREEN BEAN AND TOMATO SALAD
serves 6

2 pounds green beans	⅓ cup olive oil
Salted water to cover beans	2 Tbls wine vinegar
12 ripe tomatoes	1 Tbls Worcestershire sauce
Salt and pepper to taste	

Cook beans in salted boiling water for 7 minutes, leaving them whole. Chill for 2–3 hours. Cut tomatoes in eighths. Sprinkle with salt and pat them dry with paper towels. Pour oil, vinegar and Worcestershire sauce into a salad bowl. Mix well and add salt and pepper to taste. Add beans and tomatoes and mix again. Refrigerate for 1 hour.

BURGONYA SALÁTA
Hungarian Potato Salad
serves 6

6 large potatoes, cooked in jackets, peeled and sliced into thin circles
Salt and pepper to taste
¼ cup vegetable oil
½ cup apple cider vinegar
1 tsp paprika
2 Tbls dill, minced

1 large mild onion, sliced into thin circles
2 Italian peppers, sliced into thin circles
2 hard-cooked eggs, chopped
1 tsp paprika

Peel and slice potatoes while they are still hot. Place into a heated bowl, sprinkle with salt and pepper, and keep warm. In a jar, mix oil, vinegar, paprika, and dill. Shake well and pour over the warm potatoes. Place into a serving dish and place sliced onions and pepper rings on top. Chill. Sprinkle with chopped eggs and paprika.

ASPARAGUS SALAD
serves 6

36–42 stalks fresh asparagus
1 tsp salt, in water to cover asparagus
¾ cup vegetable oil

¼ cup wine vinegar
¼ tsp salt
¼ tsp pepper
1 tsp tarragon

Wash and scrape asparagus. Cook in a skillet with just enough salted water to cover, until tender. Drain, cool, then chill. In a jar, mix oil, vinegar, ¼ tsp salt, pepper and tarragon, and shake well. Pour over the asparagus and refrigerate for 1–2 hours before serving.

PARADICSOM ÉS ZÖLDBAB SALÁTA
Tomato and Green Bean Salad
serves 6–7

3 heads Bibb or 2 heads Boston lettuce
3 cups green beans, cooked and sliced
5 ripe tomatoes, thinly sliced

3 Tbls scallions, minced
3 Tbls parsley, minced
Salt and pepper to taste

Wash, drain, and break up lettuce. Place it into a salad bowl. Add green beans, tomatoes, scallions, and parsley. Sprinkle with salt and pepper to taste, toss lightly, and chill for 30 minutes.

Dressing

1 tsp prepared mustard	¼ cup wine vinegar
½ tsp salt	½ cup vegetable oil
½ tsp pepper	¼ cup sour cream
1 tsp paprika	2 eggs, minced and hard-cooked
1 tsp tarragon	Paprika

In a bowl combine mustard, salt, pepper, paprika, and tarragon. Add vinegar and oil and beat with a whisk until well-blended. Whisk in sour cream and beat until smooth. Chill. Whisk again just before using. Pour mixture over the salad. Sprinkle with minced eggs and paprika and serve immediately.

. . . . *Vegetables*

TEJFELES ZÖLDBAB
Green Beans with Sour Cream
serves 6

1 pound green beans, with ends and strings removed	1 tsp paprika
Salt to taste	½ cup milk
2 cups water	1 cup sour cream
3 Tbls vinegar	1 Tbls sugar
2 Tbls butter	1 Tbls vinegar, or more to taste
2 Tbls flour	Minced dill (optional)

Place green beans into a saucepan with salted water to cover, add vinegar, bring to a boil, and cook, uncovered, for about 25–30 minutes. Drain beans and set aside. Taste for salt and add more salt if desired. In a small saucepan, melt butter, add flour, and cook until bubbly. Add paprika and mix well. Add milk, stirring constantly. Cool the mixture. Beat in sour cream, sugar, and vinegar. Pour the sour cream mixture over the green beans and bring to boiling point, but do not let the mixture boil. If desired, sprinkle with minced dill.

RAKOTT BURGONYA
Layered Potatoes
serves 6

8 medium potatoes	1 Tbls flour
6 Hard-boiled eggs	2 cups sour cream
Salt and pepper to taste	1 cup bread crumbs
½ cup milk	4 Tbls melted butter
1 Tbls melted butter	½ tsp paprika

Boil the potatoes in their jackets until tender. Cool them slightly and peel. Slice the potatoes into ¼-inch thick slices. Peel hard-boiled eggs and slice thin. Sprinkle potatoes and eggs with salt and pepper. Mix together milk, melted butter, and flour. Beat in sour cream and continue beating until very smooth. Butter well an oven-proof baking dish suitable for serving. Place a layer of potatoes in the bottom of the dish, sprinkle with salt and pepper, layer eggs over the potatoes, and pour half of the sour cream mixture over eggs. Place another layer of potatoes and eggs on top of the sour cream mixture, and pour remaining sour cream mixture over the eggs. Finish with a layer of potatoes. Sprinkle with bread crumbs. Mix butter and paprika and sprinkle on top of bread crumbs. Bake in a 375° oven for 40–45 minutes, or until the crumbs are brown. Serve immediately.

SAUTÉED CABBAGE
serves 6

1 large onion, chopped	½ cup flour
⅓ cup chopped bacon	1 ½ cups water
2 heads Savoy cabbage, washed and drained	Salt and pepper to taste
	2 Tbls vinegar

In a large skillet, sauté onion with bacon. Cut Savoy cabbage into thin strips, add them to the skillet, and sauté for 15 minutes, until tender. Dust with flour, and add water, salt and pepper, and vinegar. Simmer 15 minutes.

Menu cover (top) and hotel itself—Budapest Hilton

LECSÓ TOJÁSSAL
Green Peppers and Tomatoes with Eggs
serves 6–8

3 medium onions, thinly sliced	9 firm tomatoes, sliced
½ cup butter	Salt and pepper to taste
9 green peppers, sliced	6 slightly beaten eggs

In a large skillet, sauté onions in butter. Add green peppers and cook for 10 minutes. Add tomatoes, seasonings, and continue cooking for 10 more minutes. Add eggs, stirring until the mixture sets. Serve with rolls or bread.

TÖKFŐZELÉK
Zucchini Hongroise
serves 6

2 pounds pared zucchini	1 tsp paprika
1 tsp salt	½ tsp salt
4 Tbls vinegar	½ cup heavy cream
5 Tbls butter	½ cup sour cream
2 Tbls flour	3 Tbls minced fresh dill

Cut off ends of the zucchini. Slice into ¼-inch lengthwise strips. Place in a bowl and sprinkle with salt and vinegar. Let stand for 15 minutes. Drain and squeeze the moisture out gently. Melt 3 tablespoons of butter in a saucepan, add zucchini, and simmer, covered, for about 6 minutes, until just tender. Stir occasionally. In another saucepan, melt remaining butter, add flour, and cook over low heat for 2–3 minutes. Do not brown. In a bowl, combine paprika, salt, and cream and beat with a whisk until smooth. Add sour cream and beat again until completely blended. Bring to a boil, simmer until slightly thickened, and remove from heat. Add dill and blend well. Serve immediately.

PONTY TÉJFELES TORMÁVAL
Carp in sour cream and horseradish sauce
serves 6

1 large onion, sliced	3 cups water
1 bell pepper, sliced	1 3–4-pound carp or 2 small carp, cleaned, but with head and tail on
2 carrots, scraped and sliced	2 Tbls flour
Thinly sliced green or red pepper rings } garnish	1 tsp paprika
Paprika	1 cup sour cream
2 stalks celery, cleaned and sliced	1 large horseradish, peeled and finely grated
10 peppercorns	
6 sprigs parsley and 4 scallions tied together	

Place all vegetables in a very large skillet or a fish poacher. Add peppercorns, parsley and scallions, and water. Cook for about 35–40 minutes. Place fish on top of the vegetables in the broth, cover skillet or poacher, and simmer gently for about 20–25 minutes—depending on the size of the fish—until the fish is tender but still firm enough to hold its shape. Remove fish gently onto a heated platter and keep it warm in a 150° oven. Strain the cooking liquid into a saucepan and boil until it has been reduced by about one-third. In a small bowl, beat flour, paprika, and sour cream together with a whisk until very smooth. Mix in horseradish. Bring the fish stock to a boil; reduce heat; and when it barely simmers, add the sour cream mixture, stirring constantly. Simmer for 2–3 minutes. If desired, add a little salt to taste. Pour sauce over the fish and serve. Garnish with thinly sliced green pepper rings and a sprinkle of paprika.

HAL NEMES MODRA
Fish Noble Style
serves 6

2 Tbls butter	Juice of 1 lemon
*6 fish steaks—cod, haddock, or white fish, about ¾" thick	½ pound small shrimp or shelled craw-fish tails, cooked
Salt to taste	3 Tbls butter
⅛ tsp coarsely ground pepper	2 Tbls flour
1 cup dry white wine	2 Tbls brandy

Use an oven-proof baking dish suitable for serving and butter it well. Place fish steaks into the baking dish. Sprinkle with salt and pepper. Pour wine and lemon juice over fish. Cover and bake in a 350° oven for 15 minutes. Spread shrimp over the fish. Cover and bake for an additional 10 minutes. While fish is baking make up the roux; in a small saucepan melt butter, add flour, and stir constantly while cooking until mixture is just turning golden. Pour off the cooking liquid and add to the roux, stirring constantly. Add brandy, then pour sauce back over the fish. Bake 5 minutes longer uncovered, then place for a few minutes under the broiler to brown the top. Serve immediately.

FISH ON A SPIT
serves 4

20 small fish—whiting, pike, perch, or red mullet	2 chopped tomatoes
	2 chopped green peppers
½ pound smoked bacon, cut into ½" slices	1 large mild onion, chopped (optional)
	Salt and pepper to taste
1–2 tsp paprika	2–3 Tbls wine vinegar
½ cup bacon drippings	

Thread 4–5 small fish on a skewer, alternating it with bacon slices. Sprinkle with a little paprika. Brush fish generously with bacon drippings. Cook over medium hot coals on a grill, turning often and brushing with more drippings. Cook until fish is golden brown and crisp. Have a water-quencher handy to douse flare ups. To broil in the oven, place skewers into a baking pan on a grill.

* This dish in Hungary is made with "Fogas," the delicious perch-pike fish found in Lake Balaton.

Pour water into the baking pan and place pan about 6 inches away from heat. Broil, brushing occasionally with drippings. Serve with chopped tomatoes, peppers, and onions, which have been sprinkled with salt, pepper, and vinegar.

Hungarian peasant women

PONTY FÜSZÉRMARTÁSSAL
Deviled Carp
serves 6

¼ cup butter
1 large onion, diced
2½ Tbls paprika
2 small green peppers, diced
1 16-ounce can tomatoes, peeled, drained, and chopped

⅓ cup dry white wine
1 6-pound carp, sliced into 1-inch steaks
Salt and pepper to taste
2 Tbls flour
⅔ cup sour cream

Preheat oven to 350°. In a medium skillet, melt butter and sauté onion until limp. Remove from heat and add paprika. Return to heat and add peppers and tomatoes. Cover and simmer for 5 minutes. Add wine and bring to a boil, reduce heat. Place vegetables in a shallow, well-buttered baking dish. Place fish on top of the vegetables. Sprinkle with salt and pepper and cover with the rest of the vegetables. Bake fish for about 20 minutes, or until fish flakes easily when tested with a fork. Meanwhile, beat together flour and sour cream, add the mixture to the skillet, and stir with the broth in the skillet. Simmer for 5 minutes, stirring continuously, until thickened. Place fish on a hot platter and pour sauce over the fish.

Hungarian herdsman from Hortobagy.
Photo by Bill Sanders

Kalosca woman doing free-hand painting for embroidery patterns. Photo by Bill Sanders

FISH PAPRIKÁS

serves 6

3	Tbls shortening	6	slices
3	large onions, chopped	2	tsp salt
2	Tbls water	1	cup water
1½	Tbls paprika	½	cup sour cream
2	pounds whitefish or bass, cut into		

Heat shortening in a deep skillet. Sauté onions for 5 minutes, add 2 tablespoons of water, and steam for another 5 minutes. Add paprika and stir. Immediately add the fish and stir so that the fish is coated with onions and paprika. Add salt and cook over low heat, adding the cupful of water 1 tablespoon at a time. Be careful that the fish does not stick to the skillet. When all the water has been added, cook over low heat until fish flakes easily when pricked with a fork (about 20–25 minutes). Remove fish from pan and place it on a preheated serving dish. Add sour cream to the sauce in the skillet and heat, but do not boil. Pour sauce over the fish and serve.

TÖLTÖTT CSUKA
Baked Stuffed Pike
serves 6

3 Tbls diced bacon	Salt and pepper to taste
⅓ cup diced onion	⅔ cup diced onion
⅔ cup chopped fresh mushrooms	2 mashed garlic cloves
1 cup bread crumbs soaked in	½ cup melted butter
⅓ cup milk	¾ cup sour cream
6 mashed anchovies	2 Tbls lemon juice
1 ½ Tbls diced parsley	2 Tsp paprika
5–6 -pound pike, cleaned and scaled, with head and tail on	Salt and pepper to taste

Preheat oven to 450°. In a skillet, sauté bacon until fat begins to sizzle, add onions, and sauté for 3 minutes. Add mushrooms and cook for about 4 minutes. Spoon mixture into a large bowl. Add soaked bread crumbs, anchovies, and parsley, mixing until smooth. Wash and dry the fish inside and out. Fill with the mixture and season. Secure with small skewers and string. Line a baking pan with foil, place fish on foil, and place the diced onions and garlic around fish. Pour melted butter over fish. Bake, basting often with the juices, for 45–50 minutes, or until fish feels firm when pressed lightly with a finger. Use the foil to remove fish from pan to a hot platter. Pour pan juices into a small saucepan and place on low heat. Beat sour cream, lemon juice, paprika, salt, and pepper together in a bowl. Stir into the saucepan and continue to stir until the sauce is heated, but do not let it boil. Pour sauce over the fish.

View of Budapest, circa 17–18th Century

FIATAL SULT LIBA
Roasted Young Goose
serves 6

1	8–10 pound young goose	3	sprigs dill and 3 sprigs parsley tied together with a string
	Salt and pepper to taste		
1	tsp marjoram	3	small hard dinner rolls (Kaiser rolls)
1	small onion, cut in half	4	ounces salt pork

If goose is frozen, defrost it in the refrigerator for about 36 hours. Wash in cold water and pat dry with paper towels. Sprinkle with salt and pepper on outside and inside. Sprinkle with marjoram on the inside. Place onion and dill and parsley in the cavity. Place hard rolls inside the cavity. The rolls are not a stuffing, but they will absorb the fat as the goose bakes. Place goose in a baking pan on a grill, breast side up. Tie legs together and tuck under wings. Pierce the skin in several places with a fork in order to let the fat ooze out. Bake in a 375° oven for 1 hour. Rub goose all over with salt pork, and pierce the skin again in several places. Reduce heat to 325° and bake for an additional 2 ½ hours, or until the leg joint moves freely. Or insert a thermometer into the thickest part of the breast without touching the bone: When thermometer reaches 185°, the goose is done. While the goose is baking, rub it several times with the salt pork. Remove goose from the oven, discard rolls and vegetables from the cavity, let it cool for 10 minutes, and then carve. Serve goose with vegetables (for example, the green beans recipe on page 68), dumplings (a good choice is the recipe on page 91), and a salad.

MUSTÁROS CSIRKE
Chicken with Mustard
serves 6

1	large broiler or frying chicken, cut into serving pieces	3–4	Tbls Dijon mustard
2	cups water, or more if needed	3	Tbls butter, softened
	Salt and pepper to taste	2	Tbls flour
1	carrot, scraped	1	cup heavy whipping cream
1	small onion, sliced		Salt and pepper to taste

Place cut-up chicken into a large skillet, add water, salt and pepper to taste, carrot, and onion. Cover, bring to a boil, and cook until chicken is tender. Let chicken cool in the liquid. Remove chicken from liquid and skin and bone cooked chicken. Pour about ½ cup of the cooking liquid into a baking dish and place chicken into the dish. Spread mustard over chicken pieces. Blend butter and flour together into a walnut-sized piece, kneading it well. Heat cream, but do not boil it. Add the flour and butter mixture to cream and mix until completely blended and smooth. Add salt and pepper to taste and pour sauce over the chicken. Bake in a 350° oven for 15–20 minutes.

RIZSES KACSA
Duck with Rice
serves 4

2	ducklings, quartered		tsp dried marjoram	
2	Tbls lard, shortening, or goose fat	3	cups water, or more as needed	
1	large onion, diced	3	Tbls minced parsley	
2	stalks celery, diced		Sprigs of parsley	
1	parsnip, scraped and diced		Small rings of onion	garnish
1 ¼	cup long-grained rice		Thin rings of green	
	Salt and pepper to taste		or red pepper	
1	tsp fresh minced marjoram or ½			

Wash ducklings and quarter them yourself, or have the butcher do it. In a large skillet, heat lard or shortening, add duck pieces, and sauté, covered, for about 35–40 minutes, turning the pieces often, until the duck feels very tender. Remove duck pieces from skillet and cool them. Bone duck pieces and cut the meat into 1 ½-inch pieces. Set aside. Cook onion, celery, and parsnip in the same skillet where the ducks were cooked. When vegetables are just tender but not browned, add rice and cook, stirring constantly, until rice turns golden. Add salt and pepper to taste, marjoram, and water. Cover and simmer until rice is tender. Return duck pieces to the skillet and stir until duck is coated with rice. If rice seems dry, add more water. Cover skillet and cook over low heat for about 25 minutes, stirring occasionally. Be careful or the rice may burn. Sprinkle with parsley and serve on a heated platter and garnish with sprigs of parsley, onion rings, and pepper rings.

CHICKEN PAPRIKÁS
serves 4

1	cut-up frying chicken	1	clove
	Salt to taste	½	cup chicken broth, or more if needed
4	Tbls butter	1	cup sour cream
1	large onion, diced	1	Tbls flour
1	Tbls paprika	1	tsp paprika

Clean chicken pieces and pat them dry with paper towels. Sprinkle them with salt. In a large skillet, heat butter. Add onions and cook until just transparent. Reduce heat and add paprika and clove. Stir and cook over low heat for 2–3 minutes. Increase heat, add chicken, and stir well to coat with onions. Cook over medium heat, stirring occasionally, for 10–15 minutes. Add chicken broth and cook for 30–35 minutes, stirring occasionally, until chicken is very tender. In a small bowl, combine sour cream, flour, paprika, and ½ cup of the sauce that formed around the chicken. Beat with a whisk until smooth. Add to the chicken and stir well. If sauce seems too thick add a little broth or water. Cook for 3–4 minutes. Serve with pinched noodles (see page 188).

TENDER "SHE" TURKEY
serves 6–8

1 small turkey, 8–10 pounds	¼ tsp allspice
Salt and pepper to taste	½ tsp dry mustard
⅓ cup pale dry sherry	¼ tsp crushed fennel seed
2 Tbls lemon juice	¼ tsp nutmeg

Preheat oven to 450°. Wash turkey and pat it dry with paper towels. Sprinkle with salt and pepper. Mix sherry, lemon juice, and seasonings. Brush turkey inside with the mixture. Stuff turkey and cover the opening with a piece of foil. Place on a rack, breast up, in a baking pan and brush generously with sherry mixture. Stick a meat thermometer into the breast without touching the bone. Bake in a preheated oven at 450° for 35 minutes. Baste every 15 minutes. Reduce heat to 350° and bake for at least 3 hours, or until the thermometer shows 185°. Baste very often, but do not baste for the last 35 minutes. Remove turkey to a heated platter and let stand for 15 minutes before carving. A good choice for serving would be prunes stuffed with almonds, page 186.

Chestnut Stuffing

2 large onions, minced	1 tsp salt
3–4 Tbls butter	½ tsp poultry seasoning
2 stalks celery, minced	¼ tsp pepper
10 strips bacon, diced	¼ tsp thyme
3 cups bread croutons or prepared bread stuffing	¼ tsp basil
*2 cans of whole chestnuts (this will not work with puree; do not use water chestnuts)	1 cup chicken broth (approximately)

Sauté onions in butter, add celery, and cook until both are just limp. Cook bacon in a separate skillet until it is golden brown and crisp. Remove bacon and crumble it. Drain off one-half of the fat. Add croutons, drained chestnuts, onion mixture, seasonings, and crumbled bacon. Toss together and add the chicken broth. Add just enough to moisten the stuffing. Stuff the cavity of the body with stuffing.

Note: You may cook your own chestnuts. You will need about 1 ½–2 pounds unshelled chestnuts. Cut a gash in the flat part of the chestnuts, cook in about 2 quarts water for 40 minutes, shell, and chop.

OMELET WITH CHICKEN LIVERS AND MUSHROOMS
serves 2–3

3 Tbls butter or margarine	½ tsp salt
1 large onion, finely chopped	¼ tsp black pepper
1 Tbls paprika	¼ cup Madeira
1 pound chicken livers	2 Tbls minced parsley
6 large mushrooms, sliced	

Recipe for basic omelet is on page 9. Melt butter in a large skillet, add the onions, and sauté until slightly browned. Add paprika, stir well, increase heat, and immediately add chicken livers and mushrooms. Cook, stirring occasionally, until the livers lose their pink color. Add salt, pepper, and Madeira. Stir well, reduce heat, cover, and simmer until livers are done, but still tender. Taste for seasoning, cover, and set aside.

In an omelet pan, make up the basic omelet. Spread ½ of the chicken livers over the omelet. Fold omelet over, slide it onto a platter, and spread the remaining livers over the omelet. Sprinkle omelet with parsley and serve immediately.

Fish Inn, Pearl of the Danube, on banks of the river south of Budapest

HUNGARIAN BOGRÁCS GULYAS
Goulash
serves 6

1 large onion, finely chopped	2 ½ pounds top round of beef, cut into
5 Tbls vegetable shortening	1-inch cubes
1 tsp caraway seeds	Salt to taste
1 crushed clove garlic	2-3 cups water
2 Tbls paprika	4 large potatoes, peeled and diced

Sauté onion in vegetable shortening in a large pot until golden brown. Add caraway seeds and garlic and sauté for 1–2 minutes. Pull the pot off heat, add paprika, and stir until onions are coated with paprika. Reheat the mixture carefully, but do not burn the paprika. Add meat and mix well until pieces are completely coated with the onions and paprika mixture. Add salt and ½ cup of water and stir well. Cover tightly and simmer, adding water as needed and stirring occasionally. Cook for 1 ½ hours. Add enough water to cover the beef. Add potatoes. Cover and cook for about 15 minutes, or until the potatoes are tender. While potatoes are cooking, make up the small dumplings.

Dumplings

⅔ cup unbleached all-purpose flour
1 slightly beaten egg
¼ tsp salt

In a bowl, combine flour, egg, and salt. Knead into a firm hard dough. Roll out into a long strip. Pinch off small pieces and drop them into the goulash soup. Simmer for 5–6 minutes, until the dumplings rise to the surface. Serve immediately.

MEAT LOAF WITH SOUR CREAM
serves 8–10

2	pounds ground beef	1	large onion, diced
1	pound ground pork	3	Tbls flour for shaping meat loaf
	Salt and pepper to taste	⅓	cup diced bacon
3	eggs	1	cup beef broth
4	hard dinner rolls	1½	Tbls flour
1	cup hot milk	1¼	cups sour cream
¾	cup chopped bacon		

Preheat oven to 350°. In a bowl, mix the meats, salt, and pepper. Add eggs. Soak rolls in milk, squeeze most of the moisture out, chop, and add them to the meat mixture along with half the bacon. In a skillet, fry the rest of the bacon and brown onion. Allow these to cool and add them to the meat mixture, mixing well. Flour your hands and form the mixture into a roll. In the bottom of a roasting pan, place bacon and onion. Set the meat loaf on top of this mixture. Roast for 1 ½–2 hours, basting frequently with beef broth. Remove meat loaf from roasting pan to a hot serving platter. Mix flour with sour cream and stir the mixture into the pan. Simmer for 5 minutes, strain, and serve with the meat loaf.

Castle at Esztergom along the Danube

STEAK ESZTERHÁZY
serves 6

6	sirloin steaks 1-inch thick	2	carrots, grated
½	cup flour	½	pound sliced mushrooms
1	tsp salt	¼	cup minced parsley
½	tsp pepper	½	cup white wine
2	Tbls paprika	1	cup sour cream
¼	cup butter	3	Tbls capers
2	large onions, chopped		

Remove all fat from the steaks. Pat them dry with paper towels. Dip steaks into flour mixed with salt, papper, and paprika. In a large skillet, melt butter and brown steaks quickly on both sides. Add onions, carrots, mushrooms, and parsley. Cover and simmer for 10 minutes, stirring a few times. Add wine and simmer for 15–20 minutes, or until steaks are very tender. Remove the steaks to a heated platter. Add sour cream and capers to the skillet. Heat and pour over the steaks. Serve immediately.

TÖLTÖTT KÁPOSZTA
Hungarian Stuffed Cabbage
serves 10

2	large cabbages	**Filling**	
5	slices bacon, cut into pieces		
¼	pound salt pork sliced into 2-inch slices	1	pound ground pork
2	large onions, finely chopped	1	pound ground chuck
2	Tbls paprika	2	eggs
1	clove crushed garlic	½	cup uncooked rice
	Salt and pepper	½	cup ice water
½	cup water	1	clove crushed garlic
2	pounds raw sauerkraut, drained	3	Tbls sautéed onions
2	Tbls caraway seeds	½	cup liquid from the sauerkraut
		3	Tbls butter
		2	Tbls flour
			Salt and pepper to taste
		1½	cups sour cream

Remove and discard wilted outer leaves from cabbage. Carefully core the cabbage. Place it in a deep bowl and pour boiling water over cabbage. Let it soak while preparing the filling. Use a very large, heavy pot with a tight cover. Put bacon and salt pork into the pot. Add onions and sauté until onions just start to brown. Remove 3 tablesponns of the mixture and add to the meat filling. Add paprika to the remaining onions and stir well. Add garlic, salt and pepper, and water. Cover and simmer for 15 minutes. Drain sauerkraut, reserving the juice. Rinse the kraut and add to onions, along with caraway seeds. Cover pot and let the mixture simmer.

Filling

Place ground pork and ground chuck into a bowl and add the rest of the ingredients, except for sour cream, butter, and flour. Mix well with your hands until very well blended and smooth.
Remove cabbage from hot water and gently spread it apart. One by one, carefully remove the leaves. Be careful not to tear them. Cut off the thick, heavy part of each leaf. You should have about 12–15 leaves. Place approximatley 2 tablespoons of the meat filling on each leaf. Tuck in the end and roll up carefully. Push stuffed cabbage down into the sauerkraut, put the rest of rolls on top, and add a little more water if necessary. Taste. If you wish a sharper taste, add some sauerkraut juice. Cook for 2 hours. Add salt and pepper if needed. In a saucepan, melt butter, add flour, and cook, stirring constantly, until slightly browned. Add 1 cup of the cooking liquid from the cabbage and stir until very smooth. Add the mixture to the cabbage and mix with the sauce. Simmer for 10 minutes. Pour sour cream into a bowl, add 1 cup of gravy, and stir until smooth. Pour sour cream into the pot over cabbage, stir gently, and simmer for 5–7 minutes. If desired, serve more sour cream on the side. Serve with buttered rye or pumpernickel. This is an excellent buffet dish or dinner dish.

Hungarian pottery

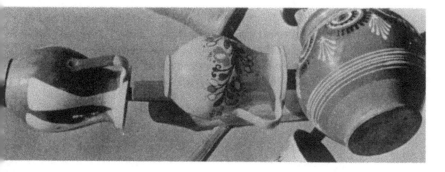

SERTÉS SZELETEK LECSÓVAL
Pork Chops with Lecso
serves 6

1 cup flour
1 tsp paprika
6 loin pork chops
Salt to taste
3 Tbls vegetable shortening or oil
¼ cup water
4 Tbls vegetable shortening or oil

1 large onion
2 green peppers
2 large chopped tomatoes
Salt and pepper to taste
1 pound ½-inch pieces Hungarian sausage (Polish sausage may be substituted)

Mix flour with paprika. Sprinkle pork chops with salt and dredge them in flour mixture. Sauté chops in 3 tablespoons of vegetable shortening until they are delicately browned on both sides. Add water and cook the chops, turning occasionally, until tender. Slice onion into very thin circles and slice peppers into 1 ½-inch slices. Heat the vegetable shortening and sauté onions and peppers until tender (about 5 minutes). Add tomatoes, salt, pepper, and Hungarian sausage. Cover and simmer for 10 minutes. Pour the mixture over chops, cover skillet, and simmer for 10 minutes longer.

KOHLRABI BAKED WITH HAM
serves 6

½ cup butter
6 kohlrabi, diced
Salt and pepper to taste
2 Tbls butter
¾ pound ham, chopped
2 Tbls minced parsley

4 egg yolks
1¼ cups cream
3 Tbls flour
Salt and pepper to taste
⅛ tsp basil

Preheat oven to 350°. In a skillet, melt butter and sauté kohlrabi with salt and pepper for 10 minutes. Grease a casserole with butter. Layer kohlrabi, ham, and parsley, ending with a layer of kohlrabi. In a small bowl, beat egg yolks, cream, flour, and seasonings. Pour over kohlrabi. Bake for 35 minutes.

TÖLTÖTT MARHA TEKERCS
Beef Roulades
serves 6–8

10	slices bacon, diced
1	cup diced onions
⅓	tsp diced garlic
¾	pound lean ground beef
¾	pound ground veal
	Salt and pepper to taste
2 ½	Tbls paprika
	Dash marjoram
4	slightly beaten eggs
3–4	pounds top round of beef, cut into 10 slices, each ¼" thick

2	cups diced onions
¾	tsp diced garlic
1 ⅓	Tbls sweet Hungarian paprika
1 ⅓	cups beef stock (canned may be used)
1 ⅓	cups tomato purée
2 ½	bay leaves
	Salt and pepper to taste

In a large skillet, fry bacon until slightly crisp. Remove with a slotted spoon to a bowl. Reserve the fat, using about 2 tablespoons in the skillet. Sauté onions and garlic until lightly colored; add them to fried bacon. Thoroughly combine the bacon-onion-garlic mixture with beef, veal, seasonings, and eggs. Set aside. Heat a couple of tablespoons of the reserved bacon fat in the skillet. Brown beef slices lightly on both sides and remove them to a platter. Heat a tablespoon of bacon fat in the skillet. Sauté onions and garlic until lightly colored. Remove skillet from burner and add paprika, coating onions and garlic. Return to burner and add the stock. Stirring constantly, bring to a boil. Add tomato purée and seasonings. Cover and simmer. Place a couple of tablespoons of the mixture on each beef slice, roll up, and secure with a cord. Add the remaining mixture to the sauce, bring to a boil, and add beef rolls. Cover and simmer on low heat until beef is tender, about 45 minutes. Remove beef rolls to a hot serving platter. Remove bay leaves from sauce and pour sauce over the meat.

EYE ROUND ROAST, MISKOLC STYLE
serves 10

5	pounds eye round roast	4	Tbls butter or margarine
3-4	slices bacon, cut into small pieces	2	large onions, diced
2-3	cloves slivered garlic	2	Tbls paprika
	unseasoned meat tenderizer (optional)	½-1	cup water, or more as needed
		3	onions, diced
1½	tsp salt	3	green peppers, diced
½	tsp black pepper	3	tomatoes, diced
½	tsp basil		Salt and pepper
2-3	Tbls olive oil		

With a sharp knife, make 20–25 small incisions in the meat. Place a piece of bacon and a sliver of garlic into each incision. Rub roast with tenderizer on all sides and then rub with salt, black pepper, basil, and olive oil. Wrap in foil and refrigerate for 3–4 hours or overnight. In a dutch oven or a heavy pot, melt butter, add onions, and cook until just limp. Add paprika and blend well. Increase heat and place roast into the pot. Reduce heat and cook for 15 minutes, turning frequently. Add water, ¼ cup at a time, and cook about 15–20 minutes per pound (for rare).* (The original recipe calls for well-done meat.) Cook for 2–3 hours, adding water as needed, and turn the roast frequently.

Twenty minutes before the roast is done, add onions and green peppers, cover, and cook for 12 minutes. Add tomatoes and cook for 8 minutes longer, or until the vegetables are tender. Sprinkle with salt and pepper. Remove roast and slice into thin slices. Serve on a heated platter surrounded with the vegetables. Serve with buttered noodles, rice, or pinched noodles.

*To test for doneness, insert a meat thermometer half-way into the meat and leave in for 5 minutes. Be sure the pot is uncovered while the thermometer is in. Thermometer should read medium or well-done. You also may make a small incision in the meat to check for doneness.

SUCKLING PIG, HUNGARIAN STYLE

serves 10

1 10–12 pound suckling pig, cleaned and dressed (or use smallest available size)

2 tsp salt

3 cloves garlic, mashed

⅔ cup lard

1 medium onion, stuck with 4 cloves

4 peppercorns

2 apples cut in half

3 Tbls wine vinegar (more or less to taste)

Rub inside and outside of the pig with salt and mashed cloves or garlic. Rub outside with lard. Place into a large roasting pan onto a rack. Place onion stuck with cloves, peppercorns, and apples into the cavity. Bake in a 325° oven for 2½–3 hours, or until tender, basting occasionally with pan juices. If you have a rotisserie, place the piglet on the spit and bake in oven or over coals until tender, brushing occasionally with more lard and with vinegar. Remove from spit or oven and let cool for 10 minutes before serving.

Montenegro –Yugoslavian lace embroidery. Photo by Bill Sanders

Side Dishes . . . .

TRANSYLVANIAN BREAD
makes 3 loaves

2½	cups water	3	packages granulated yeast
1	Tbls salt	½	cup warm water
3	Tbls sugar	1	cup water, lukewarm
½	cup butter	¼	cup softened butter
10	cups flour, sifted		

In a saucepan, combine water, salt, sugar, and butter. Bring to a boil, set aside, and cool. Sift flour into a large bowl. Dissolve yeast in warm water. When dissolved, stir the yeast mixture and 2½ cups water into the flour. Now add the cooled water and sugar mixture. Mix well with a wooden spoon until the dough no longer sticks to the spoon—about 10 minutes. Turn onto a floured board and knead for 5 minutes. Rub dough with softened butter. Place dough in a large bowl. Cover with a towel and let dough rise until doubled, about 1¼ hours. When the dough has doubled, punch it down and divide it into three parts. Butter 3 9-inch cake pans and place dough in pans. Cover and let rise again until doubled, about 1 hour. Preheat oven to 450°. When ready to bake, cut into the top of each loaf lightly with a sharp knife to make the sign of the cross. Bake at 450° for 10 minutes, then lower the heat to 350° and continue baking until bread is browned and done, about another 35–45 minutes.

PRUNES STUFFED WITH ALMONDS
serves 6–8

2	pounds pitted prunes	½	tsp cinnamon
*½–¾	pound blanched almonds	½	tsp nutmeg
4	cups red wine (ruby port may be used)	½	tsp ginger

Stuff each prune with a whole blanched almond. Place prunes into a saucepan, add wine and seasonings, and simmer for 10–15 minutes over low heat until the prunes are tender. Serve with roast turkey (see recipe on page 176).

*To blanch almonds

Place whole almonds into a bowl and pour boiling water to cover over them. Let stand for 5–10 minutes. Cool until lukewarm and rub the skins off the almonds.

EGG BARLEY
Tarhonya
serves 6

3	cups unbleached all-purpose flour	6	Tbls butter
3	eggs, slightly beaten	1–2	tsp paprika
1–2	egg yolks	3	quarts water
1	tsp salt	1	tbls salt

Sift flour into a bowl and add eggs, 1 egg yolk, and salt. Do not crumble but knead these ingredients together into a very firm dough. If dough does not stick together, flour may be too dry. If so, add half an egg yolk or, if needed, a whole egg yolk. Press together and knead until a firm dough is formed. Cover and let rest for 10 minutes. Grate dough on the widest side of the grater. Spread grated tarhonya on foil and let dry for 24 hours, stirring occasionally. Melt the butter, add 1–2 teaspoons of paprika, and sauté the tarhonya until brown and crunchy. If you are preparing them ahead of serving time, let them cool and store in an airtight container. Bring 3 quarts of water to a boil, add salt, drop in the tarhonya, reduce the heat, and cook until tender, about 10 minutes. Drain and toss with butter.

King Mattyas Well, courtyard of Budapest Hilton

NOODLES WITH POPPY SEEDS
serves 6

1	pound medium egg noodles	½	cup sugar
1	cup milk	¼	cup honey
*1 ½	cups blanched, dried, and ground poppy seeds		

Cook noodles as directed on the package until tender. Drain well. In a saucepan, heat milk to boiling point. Remove from heat, add poppy seeds, sugar, and honey, and stir well. Simmer for about 5 minutes. Stir into the hot noodles and serve immediately.

*To blanch poppy seeds

Place seeds into a bowl. Pour boiling water over them and let stand 12 hours. Drain well and squeeze out as much liquid as possible. Grind through the finest blade of a meat grinder, or use a poppy seed grinder if you have one available. In most Hungarian stores, they will grind the poppy seeds, but be sure the seeds are fresh.

PINCHED NOODLES
serves 10

2 ½	cups unbleached all-purpose flour	*A little water	
½	tsp salt	4	quarts water for boiling
2	Tbls vinegar	1	Tbls salt
3	eggs		

Sift flour and salt onto a board and push them together, forming a cone. Make a well in the center and pour the vinegar and the eggs into the center. Knead together until the dough is very stiff, shiny, and elastic. In a large kettle, bring 4 quarts water to boil. Pinch off tiny pieces of dough, about the size of a hazelnut, and drop them into the boiling salted water. Cook for about 10–15 minutes, or until tender. Serve with butter.
*If the dough feels too crumbly and dry, add water, a teaspoon at a time, just to bind the dough together. Be careful not to make the dough too sticky.

TEPÉRTÖS POGÁCSA
Crackling Biscuits
makes about 30 biscuits

1 package granulated yeast	⅓ cup sour cream
1 tsp sugar	3 egg yolks
¼ cup lukewarm water	¼ cup rum
3 cups unbleached, all-purpose flour	12 ounces diced salt pork
½ tsp salt	1 cup water
2 tsp baking powder	2 Tbsp water
½ cup milk	3 Tbsp flour
6 Tbsp butter	1 beaten egg

Dissolve yeast and sugar in ¼ cup of lukewarm water. Set aside. Place flour into a bowl. Add salt and baking powder. In a saucepan, heat milk and add butter, stirring until melted. Add sour cream and beat with a whisk until smooth. Add the milk mixture to flour along with yeast. Mix until well blended. Add egg yolks and rum. Knead for 2–3 minutes, until the dough is smooth and elastic. Place dough in a greased bowl, cover, and let it rise in a warm place for about 45 minutes or until doubled in bulk. While dough is rising, make up the cracklings.
Place salt pork into a skillet with 1 cup water. Cook uncovered over medium-high heat, stirring occasionally, until pieces turn golden in color. Remove them with a slotted spoon and place them into another skillet. Sprinkle with 2 tablespoons of water. Continue cooking, stirring frequently, until golden brown on all sides. Drain cracklings on paper towels and cool them. Mince cracklings and mix with 3 tablespoons of flour. Roll the dough out on a lightly floured board into a rectangle about ½-inch thick. Spread cracklings over dough. Fold one third of the rectangle over the cracklings, then fold the other third over it. Turn the dough with the open end towards you. Roll out again into about a 6″ × 12″ rectangle and fold into thirds. Wrap in wax paper and refrigerate for 30 minutes. Roll out into a rectangle and fold into thirds. Repeat the rolling and folding. Rewrap the dough into plastic and wax paper and refrigerate for 1 hour before baking. Roll dough out to ¾-inch thickness. Cut into rounds with a 2-inch cookie cutter. Score the top of the biscuits in a criss-cross fashion. Place on a lightly greased baking sheet. Cover and let rise for about 30–40 minutes. Brush with beaten egg and bake in a preheated 350° oven for 25–30 minutes, or until golden brown.

Desserts . . . .

CRÊPES WITH APRICOT FILLING
serves 6

Crêpe Batter

1 ¼ cups flour
⅛ tsp salt
4 large eggs
2 Tbls melted clarified butter (see recipe on page 37)

1 ½ cups milk
½ cup melted clarified butter (for baking the crêpes)

Sift flour and salt together and place in a bowl or blender. Add eggs. Blend at low speed, adding butter and milk and beating until the batter is the consistency of thin cream. Let batter stand for 1 hour before baking. Makes 20 5-inch crepes.

Bake the crêpes in a 5-inch well-buttered crêpe pan over medium-high heat. Pour 2–3 tablespoons of batter into the pan and tip it so that batter runs evenly over the entire surface. Brown on one side; then turn and brown the other side. Stack the crêpes on a warm platter. The crêpes may be refrigerated for as long as 3 days, warmed up, and used. They may also be frozen: to freeze, place pieces of wax paper between the crêpes and wrap in foil. Be sure they are completely defrosted before using. Defrost in the refrigerator overnight or wrap in foil and defrost in a 200° oven for about 20 minutes.

Filling

1 cup apricot preserves or jam
3 Tbls rum
½ cup ground walnuts

Mix preserves, rum, and walnuts together. Spread about 2 tablespoons of the apricot mixture onto a crêpe. Roll up cigar fashion. Place in a well-buttered dish and heat in a 350° oven for 10 minutes. Sprinkle with powdered sugar and serve immediately.

190

CSOKOLADÉS PALACSINTA
Chocolate Crêpes
serves 8

5 Tbls butter	1 Tbls rum
¾ flour, sifted	6 eggs, separated
½ tsp salt	4 ounces semisweet chocolate, grated
¼ cup sugar	4 Tbls seedless raspberry jam
2 ½ cups milk	Clarified butter for baking (see rec-
1 tsp vanilla	ipe on page 37)

In an enamelled saucepan, melt butter, add flour and salt, and stir well. Add sugar and stir. Cook, stirring constantly, until bubbles appear. Add milk, beating with a whisk to prevent clumping. Continue beating over low heat until thickened. Remove from heat and cool slightly. Add vanilla and rum. Blend in egg yolks. Beat egg whites until stiff but not dry. Fold into the batter. Bake 6-inch pancakes. Use a crêpe pan. Butter the pan. Pour about 2 tablespoons of batter into the pan and tilt the pan right and left in a circular motion to spread the batter. Brown the crêpes on both sides. Handle very carefully: These pancakes are very tender.
Place a pancake in a well-buttered baking pan. Spread the pancake with a little jam. Grate chocolate and sprinkle a little over the pancake. Place another pancake on top. Continue with 2–3 more pancakes (5 in a stack), spreading each with jam and sprinkling each with chocolate. You will have about 4 stacks in all.

Topping

3 egg whites	½ tsp vanilla
⅛ tsp cream of tartar	½ cup crushed hazelnuts or walnuts
4 Tbls sugar	

Beat egg whites with cream of tartar until stiff. Add sugar and vanilla and beat until very stiff. Fold in nuts, spread meringue over the stacks of pancakes, and bake in a preheated 350° oven 25 minutes. Serve cut into wedges.

DIÓS PITÉ
Hungarian Nut Cake
serves 8–10

½   pound sweet butter or margarine
2   cups sifted flour
⅓   cup ice water

The butter must be very cold, but not frozen. Place butter on a cutting board and add flour. Using a very large knife or a cleaver, cut the flour and butter together. Do not handle or knead—just use the knife. When flour and butter are well blended, add a little water, about 3 tablespoons at a time. Continue chopping until the dough starts sticking together. This takes about 15 minutes. Now, press the dough down slightly and fold over and chop again. Press down again, and fold and chop. Repeat this process 3 times. Wrap dough in wax paper and refrigerate for at least 3 hours, or overnight.

Filling

3   cups ground walnuts
¾   cup milk
¾   cup granulated sugar
1   tsp vanilla extract
⅔   cup apricot preserves
1   cup white raisins soaked in ½ cup rum or brandy

1   egg
1   Tbl cream or evaporated milk
    Powdered vanilla sugar for decorating, if desired (see recipe on page 37)

Put ground walnuts into a saucepan and add milk and sugar. Simmer for 15 minutes, or until very thick. Stir frequently. Be careful; the mixture burns easily. Add vanilla, apricot preserves, and raisins. Blend well and cook a little longer, until the filling is very thick. Stir frequently to prevent scorching. Cool completely before using.

Divide the dough into 3 sections. Take one section at a time and roll out on a lightly floured board to a 10″ × 14″ rectangle about ¼-inch thick. Preheat oven to 350°. Butter well and sprinkle with flour a baking dish or jelly roll pan. Line the dish with dough. Spread one-half of the filling over dough. Be sure it is very smooth. If your filling is too thick, add a few drops of rum or brandy and stir well. Cover the filling with the second leaf of dough and then spread remaining filling over dough and smooth down again.

Cover with the third leaf and trim the edges. The edges do not have to be sealed, just trimmed.

Beat egg with cream and brush the mixture generously over the dough. Bake in a preheated 350° oven for 35–40 minutes, or until the top is golden brown. If you wish, after the cake is baked, sprinkle it with powdered vanilla sugar.

Inn at Matraszentlaszlo. Photo by Bill Sanders

KEPVISELÖFÁNK
Cream Puffs
serves 8–10

This is quite a different technique for making cream puffs.

Pastry

⅓ cup butter	½ tsp salt
⅔ cup milk	1 tsp grated lemon rind
1 tsp vanilla extract	6 egg yolks
⅔ cup flour	

Preheat oven to 500°. Place butter and milk in the top of a double boiler. Let the butter melt completely. Add vanilla, flour, salt, and lemon rind. Beat with a wooden spoon until the batter leaves the sides of the pan and forms a ball. Remove from heat and add egg yolks, one at a time, beating well after each addition. Chill for 1 hour. Grease a jelly roll pan well. Place heaping tablespoonfuls of the batter about 3–4 inches apart on the pan. Bake in a preheated 500° oven for 10 minutes. Reduce heat to 425° and bake 10 minutes longer. Reduce heat to 350° and bake 10 minutes longer. Cool. Cut puffs in half lengthwise. Scoop out any soft batter. Fill the puffs and cover them with the tops.

Filling

½ pint whipping cream
½ cup or more powdered vanilla sugar
   (see recipe on page 37)

Whip cream until slightly stiffened. Add sugar and whip until stiff. Do not overwhip or you will have butter.

Glaze

1 cup seedless raspberry jam
½ cup sugar
1 Tbls water

In a small saucepan, combine jam, sugar, and water and simmer over low heat, stirring occasionally, for 5–7 minutes. Spread the syrup over the puffs. Cool and serve immediately.

DOBOS TORTE

serves 8–10

Cake batter

1   cup sifted flour
6   egg yolks
½   cup granulated vanilla sugar (see page 37)

1   tsp grated lemon rind
6   egg whites
⅛   tsp cream of tartar

Preheat oven to 350°. Butter lightly six 9-inch cake pans and line bottoms with circles of wax paper. Butter the wax paper and set pans aside. Divide flour into 4 parts and set aside. Beat egg yolks with ¼ cup vanilla sugar until thick and lemon-colored. Add grated lemon rind. Beat egg whites until soft peaks appear, add cream of tartar and ¼ cup vanilla sugar. Beat for about 5 minutes until very, very stiff. Add the egg yolk mixture to egg whites. Sift ¼ cup of flour at a time over the egg mixture, blending lightly after each addition, until all the flour is used up. Spread equal amounts of batter about ¼-inch thick into each prepared cake pan. Bake in a 350° oven for about 10–15 minutes or until lightly browned. Cool for 5 minutes. Remove from pans and peel off the wax paper. Cool for another 10 minutes on a flat surface. Select the best-looking layer and set aside. Spread the remaining five layers with the filling.

Filling

¼   pound unsalted butter
1   cup confectioners' vanilla sugar
5   oz semi-sweet chocolate, melted in double boiler and cooled
2   egg yolks

½   cup heavy cream
1   Tbls cornstarch
¼   cup sugar
1   tsp vanilla extract

Cream butter and vanilla sugar until very light and fluffy. Beat in the melted chocolate. Using the same double boiler in which you melted the chocolate over slightly simmering water, beat together egg yolks, cream, cornstarch, sugar and vanilla. Beat for at least 3–4 minutes. Remove from heat and beat until mixture is thick and creamy. Cool. Add chocolate and beat some more. Chill, but do not let it harden.
Spread each round with the chocolate cream and place one on top of the other. Spread the sides of the cake with the cream and place

the glazed round on top. Decorate with whole and chopped roasted hazelnuts or walnuts. Refrigerate for at least 12 hours before serving.

Caramel glaze

1 **cup sugar**
⅓ **cup water**
⅓ **cup light corn syrup**

In a saucepan combine 1 cup sugar, water and corn syrup. Cook until sugar is completely melted. Reduce heat and cook until it turns golden brown, about 275° on a candy thermometer. Place the saucepan over hot water to prevent syrup from becoming hard. Spread the layer you have set aside with the glaze. Before the glaze is completely set, dip a knife into very hot water and cut through the glaze, making wedges. Each wedge becomes a serving piece. This facilitates cutting the cake later.

KIFÖTT TURÓSRÉTES
Boiled Cheese Strudel
serves 6

2 **cups sifted all-purpose flour**	1 **egg yolk**
⅓ **cup lukewarm water**	½ **tsp salt**
1 **large egg**	

In a bowl, combine flour, water, egg, egg yolk, and salt. Blend well. Then knead on a lightly floured board until dough is smooth and elastic. Cover with an inverted bowl and let rest for 15 minutes. While dough is resting, make the filling.

Filling

5 **Tbls butter**	4 **Tbls sour cream**
5 **Tbls sugar**	4 **Tbls fine bread crumbs**
2 **eggs**	4 **quarts water**
2 **egg yolks**	1 **Tbls salt**
Grated rind of 1 lemon	**Sour cream and sugar for topping**
1½ **cups sieved pot cheese**	

In a bowl, beat butter with sugar until very smooth. Add eggs and egg yolks one at a time, beating well after each addition. Add lemon rind, pot cheese, sour cream, and bread crumbs. Blend well. Roll out dough on a lightly floured board until paper-thin. Spread filling evenly over the dough, leaving about 1½–2-inch border. Roll tightly, jelly roll fashion. Press the ends firmly together. Spread out a napkin and brush the napkin generously with butter; then roll the dough into the napkin.

Tie ends securely with a string. Then bend the napkin into a horseshoe shape and tie ends of napkin together. In a large pot, bring water and 1 tablespoon of salt to a boil. Place napkin with dough into the pot. Bring to a boil again, reduce heat, and simmer for 40 minutes. Remove strudel from the water and put on a drain board. Take off the napkin, place strudel on a platter, and slice it into 2–3-inch slices. Top with sour cream and sugar and serve immediately.

Refrigerate the unused portion. To reheat, steam over hot water for 15–20 minutes.

CHEESE FRUIT DUMPLINGS

serves 6

3	Tbls butter	3	quarts boiling water
1	egg	½	cup melted butter
⅔	cup farmers' cheese	⅓–½	cup sugar
	Salt to taste	2	tsp cinnamon
⅔	cup milk		
2	cups all-purpose unbleached flour		
1½	pounds fresh firm fruit (pitted cherries, sliced apples, sliced apricots)		

In a bowl, cream butter, egg, and cheese together thoroughly. Add salt and milk. Slowly add flour, forming a fairly stiff dough. Tear off pieces of dough a little less than ¼-inch thick to wrap around the fruit. Seal the dough well. Drop the dumplings into boiling water, turning them once during 7 minutes of cooking. Remove to a heated serving platter. If desired, sprinkle with melted butter, sugar, and cinnamon.

APPLE OR CHERRY STRUDEL

makes 1 strudel—6–8 slices

*1 package defrosted filo (strudel dough)

½ lb melted clarified butter (see recipe on page 37)

⅓ cup bread crumbs

⅓ cup sugar

** Apple filling or

***Cherry filling

Preheat oven to 350°. Spread a slightly damp cloth on the counter. Remove dough from package. Place 2 strudel leaves on the damp cloth. Brush with butter and sprinkle with half the crumbs and half the sugar. Place 2 more leaves on top, brush with butter, and sprinkle with remaining crumbs and sugar. Spread either fruit filling over the dough, leaving a 2-inch border. Fold dough leaves along the side borders over the filling and seal well; then roll up the strudel like a jelly roll. Place on a buttered baking sheet or jelly roll pan, seam side down. Brush strudel with butter. Bake for 25–30 minutes, until golden brown. Serve hot or cold.

To freeze the strudel: Butter a double thickness of foil, place the unbaked strudel on foil, butter the strudel, and wrap it up. Freeze. Do not defrost; unwrap and bake still frozen in a 350° preheated oven on a cookie sheet for 35–40 minutes, or until golden brown. *Rewrap remaining strudel dough, place into the freezer until next time.

**Apple Filling

3 tart apples, peeled and cored

½ cup sugar

½ tsp cinnamon

⅛ tsp nutmeg

⅓ cup raisins

½ cup chopped almonds

½ tsp almond extract

½ cup chopped walnuts (optional)

Slice apples very thin. Toss lightly with sugar. Add the rest of the ingredients and stir. Fill the strudel as directed.

***Cherry Filling

1 can well-drained sour pitted cherries
   or
1 pound pitted sweet fresh cherries

½ cup sugar

⅓ cup chopped walnuts

½ tsp cinnamon

½ Tbls vanilla sugar (see recipe on page 37) or ½ tsp vanilla extract

¼ cup cherry preserves

Combine all ingredients. Fill the strudel as directed.

GOLDEN DUMPLINGS
serves 8–10

2	packages of yeast	1	cup scalded milk
2	tsp sugar	5	cups flour
½	cup warm water	4	large eggs
½	cup butter	½	tsp vanilla
⅔	cup sugar	1	tsp orange rind
1	tsp salt		

Dissolve yeast and 2 teaspoons of sugar in warm water. Combine butter, ⅔ cup of sugar, and salt. Pour the scalded milk over butter and sugar and stir to melt the butter. Cool. Add yeast and 2 cups of flour. Beat in eggs and beat dough thoroughly. Add the rest of the flour, vanilla, and orange rind to make a soft dough. Turn the dough out onto a floured breadboard and knead well. Place it in a buttered bowl, cover, and let rise until doubled in bulk. Punch down and turn dough out onto a floured board. Roll dough out to a thickness of ½-inch. Cut into circles with a 2 or 2 ½-inch cookie cutter. Dip each of the circles of dough first into melted butter and then into the filling. Put the pieces in layers in a buttered 10-inch tube pan. Sprinkle each layer with more melted butter and with raisins, if desired. Sprinkle the top layer with more melted butter and nuts. Cover and let dough rise again until almost doubled. Bake in a 375° oven for approximately 45 minutes, or until it is browned and a cake tester comes out clean.

Filling

1	cup melted butter	4	Tbls cocoa
1	tsp cinnamon	1	cup sugar
1	cup finely crushed walnuts	1	cup raisins

Set melted butter aside. In a bowl, mix cinnamon, nuts, cocoa, and sugar. Reserve the raisins.

CRÊPES A LA BUDAPEST
Basic Crêpes
serves 6–8

¾ cup plus 3 Tbls sifted all-purpose
  flour
⅛ tsp salt
3 large eggs
2 Tbls melted clarified butter (see
  recipe on page 37)

1½ cups milk
1 Tbl sugar
4 Tbls melted butter mixed with
2 Tbls vegetable oil (for greasing the
  pan)

Sift flour and salt together and place in a bowl or blender. Add eggs, using blender at low speed. Add butter, milk, and sugar and beat until batter is the consistency of thick cream. For beat results, let batter stand for one hour before baking. Makes 16 5-inch crêpes. Bake crêpes in a 5-inch well-buttered pan over medium-high heat. Pour a little batter into the pan and tip the pan so the batter runs evenly over the entire surface. Brown on one side; then turn and brown on the other side. Stack crêpes on a warm platter. The crêpes may be refrigerated for as long as three days, warmed up, and used. They may also be frozen. Be sure they are completely defrosted before using. Defrost overnight in the refrigerator.

Topping

2 cups sugar
2 cups ground hazelnuts or walnuts
2 tsps lemon rind

6 Tbls rum
1 tsp rum flavoring
6 Tbls raisins (optional)

Mix ingredients together. Place one crêpe into a buttered dish or baking pan and spread it with the sugar mixture. Stack 6 crêpes, spreading sugar mixture between each crepe. Place crêpes into a 350° preheated oven. Bake 15 to 20 minutes. Makes two stacks of 6 crepes.

Sauce

10 ounces semisweet chocolate
½ cup rum
1 ⅓ cup sour cream

Melt chocolate in a double boiler. Add rum and sour cream and blend well. Serve the crêpes topped with this chocolate sauce.

THE VÁR NUT TORTE
serves 8–10

½ pound butter or margarine	1 Tbl grated orange rind
2 cups dark brown sugar	1 tsp orange flavoring
6 whole eggs (use large eggs)	½ cup sour cream
2 cups sifted flour	1 cup very finely ground walnuts
1 tsp vanilla extract	2 cups coarsely ground walnuts
½ tsp almond extract	3 tsp double acting baking powder

Preheat oven to 350°. Have all ingredients at room temperature—that is, leave eggs, butter, and sour cream out of the refrigerator for at least 1 hour or longer.

In a large glass or pottery bowl, cream butter with an electric beater until very fluffy. Add 1 cup of sugar and cream for 1 minute, or until sugar is completely absorbed. Add the second cup of sugar and cream for at least 3–4 minutes, until very smooth and fluffy. Add eggs one at a time, beating well after each addition, until they are completely absorbed. Add flour, vanilla, almond extract, orange rind, and orange flavoring. Blend well. Add sour cream and finely chopped walnuts. Blend. Fold in coarsely ground nuts and baking powder. Beat with firm strokes with a wooden spoon for one minute.

Preheat oven to 350°. Grease well a 9–10-inch loaf pan and sprinkle with bread crumbs. Fill half full with the batter and bake for 40 minutes. Reduce heat to 325° and bake an additional 15 minutes. Test with a cake tester. If it comes out clean, the cake is done. Remove cake from the oven and cool for 25 minutes. Loosen around the edges with a sharp knife and invert the cake onto a platter. Cool completely, but do not refrigerate. Cut in two lengthwise.

Filling

4 Tbls rum
⅔ cup raspberry jam
   A flat piece of semisweet chocolate
   about 4 inches long for decoration

Sprinkle both sections of cake with the rum. Spread half the raspberry jam on the bottom section, cover with the other section, and spread the remaining raspberry jam on top. Decorate with chocolate curls. You can make curls by using a vegetable peeler on a flat piece of semisweet chocolate at least 4 inches long.

CHAPTER 5

YUGOSLAVIA:
Crossroads
of the Balkans

P AST Budapest, the Danube flows almost due south through the great plains toward Yugoslavia. Near the capital city of Belgrade, it is joined with Yugoslavia's longest river, the Sava. This union creates an unforgettable wide expanse of water that swirls past Belgrade through the province of Serbia and the fertile rich lands of Vojvodina plain. Then the Danube starts to climb again, cutting a spectacular gorge known as "Djerdap," or the Iron Gate, through the surrounding mountains and forming the boundary between Yugoslavia and Rumania. Steep cliffs rise almost vertically on both sides of the river. There are treacherous rapids and swirling vortex. For centuries, men avoided the raging torrents; then, teams of horses and a railroad pulled barges and boats upstream against the surge of the current. Today, a hydroelectric dam tamed the rapids and made the river navigable through the Iron Gate.

Belgrade does not have the charm of Vienna or the beauty of Budapest, but it is a pleasant city—busy and bustling with wide avenues and much greenery, all dominated by the impressive old Turkish fortress of Kalemagdan.

Yugoslavia itself is an enigmatic country of contrasts. For centuries, armies have clashed on its soil, and peoples of diverse nationalities have settled on its river banks among the towering mountains and the shores of the Mediterranean Sea. Romans, Greeks, Slavs, Huns, Austrians, Hungarians, Italians, and Turks: All have left an indelible mark on the development and character of the country and its people.

Today, Yugoslavia is divided into six republics: Serbia, Croatia, Slovenia, Montenegro, Macedonia, and Bosnia-Herzogovina.

There are three major religions in Yugoslavia: Serbian Orthodox, Catholics, and Moslems. To complicate things, the various ethnic groups not only speak different languages and dialects but have different alphabets—the Cyrillic-Slav and the Roman. In Belgrade, newspapers and books are published in Cyrillic, whereas in Zagreb, papers and books are in Roman letters.

The Serbs, Croats, and Slovenians, who all live in the northern part of the country, comprise a loosely defined group with one strong bond—that of being descendants of ancient Slav tribes. Here, the Austro-Hungarian influence is evident in architecture and culture. Montenegro, Macedonia, and Bosnia are predominantly Moslem, and all have "the Mark of the Turk." Men in red fezzes or even turbans sit in open air *cafans*, sipping the pungent Turkish coffee, and some women still cover their faces, in spite of the fact that veils have been banned for decades. Dark brooding mountains tower in central Yugoslavia. They are picturesque and untamed, and there are high pastures, forbidding in winter, that are covered with wild blooming cyclamen in spring. The Dalmatian coast, which stretches along the Mediterranean, has the color and splendor of the Italian Renaissance. Spalato, or Split, and the walled-in city of Dubrovnik, formerly called Raguza, may be two of the most beautiful cities on the Mediterranean coast. Dubrovnik is still a completely walled-in city and can be entered by one of several fortified gates.

It is difficult to classify Yugoslavian cooking as one cuisine, for it is as complex as the country itself. The food reflects the Central European, Middle Eastern, and Mediterranean heritage of the people. Dalmatian ham tastes very much like the Italian proscuitto. *Cassata*, the many layered ice cream, is as available in Belgrade as it is in Naples. Turkish coffee is served all over the country. The greatest favorites are the *rajnici*—veal and pork kebabs—and *cevapcici*—grilled ground beef sausages. *Planinski sir* is a hard mountain cheese that is strung on skewers and grilled over a fire, Albanian style. *Baclava* and *strudel* as well as *Dobostorte* and *pita* bread are seen side by side in bakery windows. *Kadaif*—long thin noodles soaked in heavy syrup—are another Turkish dessert, as in *dul-pita*—a nutty strudel-like pastry.

Cheese is eaten by Yugoslavians before and after a meal, and

Yugoslavian pottery

the hard Parmigiano cheese is grated and used in cooking exactly like Parmesan is used by the Italians. Cheese is customarily served with *pogaca*—small rolls which are very much like their Hungarian counterparts, *Tepertös Pogácsa*. However, in some parts of the country *pogaca* are made into long thin strips, baked in clay ovens, and served hot with cheese or *kajmak*. Most housewives make their own *kajmak*. They boil part milk and part cream together, cook it, and then remove the cream from the top and place it into a wooden tub called a *cabrica*. The milk is boiled for two, three, or four days, and every day, the skimmed-off cream is poured into the tub. The fresh *kajmak* is mild-tasting and light cream-colored. When salt is added and it is fermented, it turns a caramel color and acquires a strong flavor.

Lamb and young goats are turned on the spit over hot fires, and in many villages, the bread is still baked the ancient way on a hot clay plate covered with a dome onto which burning coals are placed. *Pasulj*—a bean and pork dish—*Gjuvech*—potted chicken and vegetables—and *Sljiva Slatko*—very sweet plum preserves—are some of the most popular dishes all over the country.

Yugoslavia is a nostalgic land. Traditions and customs are deeply rooted in its people, and in the high mountains or hidden valleys, people cling to their ancestral beliefs, not quite accepting the new, the modern, the different.

Appetizers . . . .

HEARTY BLINI
Rich Pancakes
serves 7–8

2 packages yeast	3 eggs, well beaten
½ cup warm water	1 tsp salt
½ cup whole wheat or buckwheat flour (optional)	1 Tbls sugar
2½ cups all-purpose flour	¼ cup melted butter
3 cups milk, lukewarm	2 egg whites
	Melted butter for frying

In a small bowl, mix yeast, ½ cup water, and ½ cup all-purpose flour. Let batter rise for 10 minutes. In a large bowl, combine whole wheat flour, all-purpose flour, milk, and yeast. Beat with a wooden spoon for 1 minute. Add eggs, salt, sugar, and butter. Beat for at least 5 minutes. Cover and let batter rise in a warm place for 2 ½–3 hours. Beat egg whites until stiff and fold into batter. Cover and let rest for 45 minutes.

Butter a 5 or 6-inch crêpe pan or an omelet pan well, or use a 12-inch heavy skillet. Heat the skillet or pan and pour in about 3 tablespoons of batter for each pancake. You can bake 3 pancakes at a time in the 12-inch pan. Fry 2–3 minutes on one side, brush with butter, turn over, and brown on the other side. Stack on a platter and keep warm in a 200° oven. Serve the blini hot, with melted butter and a bowl of sour cream.

Yugoslavian potter. Photo by Bill Sanders

LENTEN PIE
serves 10

Pastry

3 cups all-purpose flour, sifted	4 hard-boiled egg yolks
1 tsp salt	2 raw egg yolks
½ pound unsalted butter, slightly softened	2 whole eggs

Sift flour into a bowl and add salt. Make a well in the center and add unsalted butter, slightly softened. Press hard-boiled egg yolks through a sieve and add them to the flour mixture. Add raw egg yolks and whole eggs. Work butter and eggs into the flour, starting in the center, until all flour is absorbed and the pastry is smooth. Shape the pastry into a ball, wrap into wax paper, and refrigerate for 2–3 hours.

Filling

2 ounces dry mushrooms soaked in	2 pounds filet of sole, cut into 2 ½-inch
2 cups of hot water	pieces
4 cups cooked rice	Salt and pepper
½ cup sautéed chopped onions	Melted butter
¼ cup chicken broth	Egg wash
¼ cup heavy cream	1 egg
4 Tbls minced dill	1 Tbl heavy cream
Salt and pepper to taste	

Preheat oven to 350°. Soak mushrooms in hot water for 30 minutes. In a bowl, combine rice, onions, chicken broth, and heavy cream. Drain the mushrooms and chop them coarsely. Add to rice, along with dill and salt and pepper to taste. Cut up filet of sole into 2 ½-inch pieces and sprinkle the pieces with salt and pepper. Divide pastry in half. Roll out one half of the pastry on a floured board so that it is ¼-inch thick and about 11″ × 16″ in size. Trim off all sides evenly. Reserve the trimmed off pastry. Butter a jelly roll pan well and sprinkle it generously with flour. Place the rolled out pastry into the pan. Spread the rice mixture on the pastry, leaving about 1 inch of pastry around the filling. Place pieces of fish on top of rice mixture. Brush them generously with melted butter. Roll out the second half of the pastry so that it is ¼-inch thick and about 12″ × 18″ in size. Cover the filling with the pastry and press edges of pastry together firmly. Then roll the pastry border up firmly all around the pie. Roll the trimmed-off pastry into a long strip about 3 inches wide, and about 18" long. Cut into 1" strips lengthwise and braid them. Place braid on top of pie.

Beat egg with heavy cream and brush pie with egg wash. Make two 1-inch slashes in the pie. Bake in a preheated 350° oven for 40 minutes, or until golden brown. Some melted butter may accumulate in the jelly roll pan; just pour it off. This pastry comes out rather crisp, so let it cool a little before slicing.

BOSNIAN STUFFED CABBAGE ROLLS
makes approximately 16–20 rolls

The cabbage rolls may be served as appetizers. Serve 2 rolls per person. They make a delicious buffet dish or tasty hors d'oeuvres.

1	large head of cabbage	¼	tsp oregano
4	cups hot water	¼	tsp tarragon
1	tsp salt	½	cup chicken broth
1	pound very lean ground chuck	⅔	cup of your favorite tomato and meat sauce (spaghetti sauce)
½	cup cooked rice	½	cup catsup
4	Tbls bread crumbs	3	Tbls butter or margarine
4	Tbls light cream	½	cup finely ground Parmesan cheese
1	egg		
¼	tsp black pepper		

Preheat oven to 400°. Core the cabbage. Place it into a pot and pour hot water over it. Add salt and bring to a boil. Simmer cabbage for 15 minutes. Drain and let cool. In a bowl, combine ground chuck, rice, crumbs, milk, egg, and seasonings. Blend well, preferably with your hands. Gently separate cabbage leaves. Cut the larger leaves in two. Cut off the thick center stem. The finished rolls should not be over 2 ½ inches long. Place about 1 tablespoon of meat mixture on the edge of a cabbage leaf, tuck in the sides, and roll up tightly. Butter a baking dish well and place the rolls close together into dish. Pour chicken broth over rolls; then pour on tomato sauce and catsup. Distribute the sauce evenly over the rolls. Dot with butter. Bake in a preheated 400° oven for 45 minutes. Sprinkle with Parmesan cheese and bake for 5 minutes longer. Serve hot.

SRPSKI AJVAR
Serbian Vegetable Caviar
serves 4–6

5   large whole green peppers
2   medium whole eggplants
    Salt and pepper to taste
5   cloves minced garlic (or less to taste)

4   Tbls lemon juice
1   cup vegetable oil
3   Tbls minced parsley

Preheat oven to 500°. Place green peppers and eggplants into a baking pan and bake them in a 500° oven. Remove peppers after 25 minutes and set them aside. Continue baking eggplants until tender—about 10–15 minutes longer—and remove from oven. To loosen the skins of the eggplants, wrap them in a damp towel for 10 minutes. Peel peppers by pulling off skin; remove ribs and seeds. Dice peppers and place them in a glass or china bowl. Peel and dice eggplants, squeezing them dry with a towel. Place them in the bowl with the peppers. Add salt, pepper, garlic, lemon juice, and oil and mix well. Refrigerate for 1–2 hours. Garnish with parsley before serving.

MONTENEGRO OMELET
serves 6

8   eggs
3   Tbls light cream
½   tsp salt

⅛   tsp white pepper
¼   tsp thyme
3   Tbls butter

Omelet

Beat eggs with cream and seasonings. Melt butter in a 9-inch skillet. Cook omelet until the underside is golden brown. Place a large plate over the skillet and turn the omelet upside down onto the plate. Scrape any bits of egg from skillet. If necessary, add 1 tablespoon of butter to the skillet. Slide omelet back into skillet uncooked side down. Cook until eggs are set. Cut into 6 wedges and serve with the sauce.

Montenegro Sauce

3 Tbls olive oil	1 16-ounce can whole tomatoes, drained and chopped
1 Tbls butter	1 tsp salt
2 cloves mashed garlic	⅛ tsp red hot pepper flakes
1 medium onion, finely chopped	½ cup red wine
1 green pepper, finely chopped	2 Tbls brandy
2 ribs celery, finely chopped	

In a large skillet, heat oil and butter, add garlic, onion, green pepper, and celery, and cook until vegetables are limp but not brown. Add tomatoes and seasonings. Cook, stirring occasionally, for 5 minutes. Add wine; stir, and cook, covered, over low heat for 10 minutes. Uncover; add brandy; and cook, stirring occasionally, for 15 minutes.

FILO CHEESE OR MEAT PIES
serves 6–8

1 package of Filo dough (strudel dough)
½ pound melted clarified butter or margarine (see recipe on page 37)

Meat Filling

1 pound raw lamb, ground twice	¾ cup lemon juice
1 large onion, minced	Salt and pepper to taste
½ cup pine nuts	1 Tbls allspice

Preheat oven to 350°. Blend ingredients together and refrigerate for ½ hour. Open package of filo dough. Spread a damp cloth or towel on the counter. Take 2 leaves of the dough and place them on the cloth. Cut leaves into 3–4 inch strips. Place 2 strips together, brush them with melted butter, and place 2 more strips on top. Brush with butter. Place meat or cheese filling on the end of the leaves. Begin at the right end of the long strip. Fold the corner of the strip downward to create a triangle. Then fold the triangle upward, and to the right, then downward again. You are folding back and forth, exactly the same way a flag is folded to create a triangle. Place on a well-buttered cookie sheet. Brush the triangles generously with butter and bake in a 350° preheated oven for 20–25 minutes, or until golden brown.

The triangles may be frozen unbaked. Place triangles on a greased double sheet of foil, brush tops with butter, seal, and freeze. Bake directly out of the freezer, without defrosting, for 30–35 minutes.

Cheese Filling

1	pound pot cheese	2	well-beaten eggs
¼	pound Feta cheese	⅛	tsp white pepper
3	Tbls melted butter		

Press the cheeses through a fine sieve. Add butter, eggs, and pepper and blend well. Make pastry triangles, as for the meat filling.

Soups . . . .

CANTALOUPE SOUP

serves 6

	Juice of 2 lemons		Juice of 1 orange
½	cup honey	½	cup white wine
¼	tsp fresh grated nutmeg	24	watermelon balls
1	large ripe cantaloupe, cut into small pieces	½	cup whipped cream

In a blender, mix lemon juice, honey, and nutmeg with cantaloupe pieces. Blend in orange juice and wine. Chill thoroughly. Mix well before serving. Put 2 or 3 melon balls in each chilled soup plate, pour soup over them, and garnish each plate with 1 teaspoon of whipped cream.

SOUP ZAGREB STYLE

serves 6

5 pig trotters (pigs' feet)	1½ pounds potatoes, peeled and quartered
5 cups water	
2 carrots, chopped	3 Tbls bacon drippings
1 large onion, chopped	3 Tbls flour
1 stalk celery, chopped	Juice of 1 lemon
1 parsnip, chopped	Salt and pepper to taste

Have the butcher quarter the pigs' feet. Wash the feet well. Place them into a soup pot. Add carrots, onion, celery, and parsnip. Cook for 1 ½ hours or until meat is tender. Add potatoes and cook for about 20 minutes until potatoes are tender. In a small saucepan combine bacon drippings and flour and cook, stirring constantly until mixture is golden in color. Add some of the hot soup to the flour mixture. Stir flour mixture and add to the soup, and mix well. Add lemon juice and salt and pepper to taste.

Smederevo, a fortress on the Danube

LAMB SOUP WITH ZUCCHINI
serves 6

1	pound lamb with marrow bone	½	pound zucchini, peeled and chopped
6	cups water	2	mashed garlic cloves
1	tsp salt	½	very hot pepper, minced
	Freshly ground black pepper	¼	tsp cinnamon
6	Tbls raw rice	2–3	Tbls chopped fresh mint

Place lamb in a medium-sized saucepan. Add water, salt, and pepper. Cover and simmer for 1 ½ hours. Discard the bone and cut the lamb into 1-inch cubes. Return lamb to the saucepan with the cooking liquid. Add rice and zucchini, along with garlic and hot pepper. Cover and simmer for 20 minutes. Sprinkle the soup with cinnamon and mint just before serving.

Salads . . . .

SPRING SALAD
serves 4–5

For the Salad:

4–5	heads of bibb lettuce	½	cup chopped green olives
2	16-ounce cans of artichokes, well drained	½	cup chopped black olives
2	green peppers, sliced into thin strips	24	Italian or cherry tomatoes, halved
10	minced scallions	½	tsp oregano
1	cup minced parsley	½	tsp basil
2	bunches watercress, with leaves removed	½	tsp black pepper
			Salt to taste
		½	cup grated Parmesan cheese

For the Dressing:

1	cup olive oil	½	tsp salt
2	cloves mashed garlic	1	tsp Italian seasoning
⅓	cup wine vinegar	2	Tbls minced capers
1	tsp dry mustard	2	Tbls minced dill pickles

Separate lettuce leaves and wash them well. Shake off excess water. Wrap them loosely into paper towels and refrigerate them for at least 1 hour. While lettuce is crisping, prepare the dressing. In a cup, combine oil and garlic and let stand for at least 2 hours. In a jar with a tight lid or a bottle, combine vinegar, mustard, salt, and Italian Seasoning and shake until well blended. Add oil, garlic, capers, and pickles and shake well again. Use one-half of the dressing for the salad. Keep the remainder refrigerated. Shake well before using.

Place lettuce into a large bowl. Drain artichokes well and cut each into 4 slices. Add the rest of the ingredients, except for the Parmesan cheese. Sprinkle with ½ cup of dressing, toss lightly, taste for seasoning, and, if necessary, add more dressing and salt and pepper. Sprinkle with Parmesan cheese and toss. Serve immediately.

RED BEET SALAD
serves 6

8–10	red beets	2	Tbls scallions, minced
	Salted water to cover	⅛	tsp nutmeg
¼	cup wine vinegar or more to taste	⅛	tsp ginger
½	cup vegetable oil	2	tsp horseradish
2	tsp sugar or more to taste		Salt and pepper to taste

Cook beets in salted water until tender. Peel beets and slice julienne (into thin strips). In a bowl beat together all ingredients and pour over the beets. Marinate beets overnight in the dressing in the refrigerator.

Yugoslavian pottery

MUSHROOMS WITH SPINACH
serves 6

1	small onion, diced	¼	cup water
2	Tbls butter	1	9-ounce package frozen chopped
3	pounds mushrooms, sliced		spinach, defrosted
1 ½	tsp caraway seeds		Salt and pepper to taste
1 ½	Tbls diced parsley	¾	cup sour cream
1	cup croutons		

In a large pot, cover cabbage heads with salted water and cook until barely tender—about 15 minutes. Remove them from water and allow them to cool. Carefully core cabbages and cut them into 2–2½-inch wide wedges. Dip cabbage wedges into flour that has been mixed with salt and pepper, then into beaten eggs, and then into bread crumbs. Heat oil in a deep large pot and fry cabbage wedges until they are crisp and brown on all sides—about 5 minutes. Serve hot with Kaimak (See recipe on page 230).

DINSTANI CELER
Stewed Celery
serves 6

8	stalks of celery hearts
2	Tbls butter
1 ½	Tbls powdered sugar
2–3	cups chicken broth

Preheat oven to 350°. Clean celery stalks and cut them in half. Butter a 1-quart oven-proof dish and sprinkle it with sugar. Arrange celery in dish and add just enough broth to cover celery. Cover baking dish and bake for 30 minutes, or until the celery is tender.

MIXED VEGETABLES
serves 6

2 Tbls butter	2 crushed cloves garlic
14–16 baby carrots, peeled (use fresh or frozen carrots)	1 Tbls lemon
	½ tsp basil
3 stalks celery, sliced	¼ tsp black pepper
1 package frozen peas or 1 ½ cups shelled fresh peas	2 chicken bouillon cubes
	2 Tbls water
1 large onion, finely chopped	
3 medium zucchini, sliced into circles	

In a saucepan, melt butter and cook carrots and celery over low heat for 4–5 minutes. Add all other vegetables, lemon, and spices. Cook for 2 minutes, stirring once or twice. Sprinkle with crushed chicken broth cubes. Add water and stir gently, but do not crush the vegetables. Cook for 5 more minutes. The vegetables should still be crisp and retain their bright color. Serve with fish or meat.

EGGPLANT CROQUETTES
serves 6–7

2 large eggplants, peeled	Salt and cayenne pepper to taste
4–6 cups water	⅛ tsp nutmeg
Salt to taste	2 beaten eggs
1 cup minced parsley	½ cup grated Gruyere cheese
2 minced cloves garlic	1 cup bread crumbs
2 Tbls minced scallions	2–4 cups oil for frying

Halve the eggplants lengthwise. Place them into a pot of cold salted water. Bring to a boil, reduce heat, and cook for 5–7 minutes. Drain eggplants and squeeze the water out of them. Purée them in a vegetable mill or a blender. Mix the purée thoroughly with minced parsley, garlic, scallions, salt, cayenne pepper, and nutmeg. Add and mix beaten eggs, Gruyere cheese, and bread crumbs well. Heat oil in a deep pan or deep-fat fryer. Drop a teaspoon of eggplant mixture into hot oil and fry on both sides until well browned.

POHANI KELJ
Deep-fried Cabbage
serves 6

2	heads of cabbage	½	tsp pepper
	Salt to taste	3	beaten eggs
1–2	cups flour	1–2	cups fine bread crumbs
½	tsp salt	2	cups vegetable oil

In a large pot, cover cabbage heads with salted water and cook until barely tender—about 15 minutes. Remove them from water and allow them to cool. Carefully core cabbages and cut them into 2–2½-inch wide wedges. Dip cabbage wedges into flour that has been mixed with salt and pepper, then into beaten eggs, and then into bread crumbs. Heat oil in a deep large pot and fry cabbage wedges until they are crisp and brown on all sides—about 5 minutes. Serve hot with Kaimak (see recipe on page 230).

Fish . . . .

BRODET NA DALMATINSKI NAĆIN
Fish, Dalmatian Style
serves 6

5	pounds scrod or carp, cut into 12 steaks	2½	cups tomatoes, peeled, seeded, and chopped
½	tsp salt	1	cup dry white wine
¼	tsp pepper	1½	Tbls vinegar
1	cup flour, or more as needed	1½	tsp chopped chili or jalapeno peppers
6	Tbls butter	2	Tbls minced scallions
3	Tbls vegetable oil		
1½	lbs onions, very thinly sliced		

Mix salt, pepper, and flour. Dip fish steaks into the flour and shake off the excess. Melt half the butter and oil in a large skillet. Lightly brown the fish, about 2½–3 minutes on each side. Remove them to a platter. In the skillet, heat remaining butter and oil, add onions, and sauté them until just transparent. Add the rest of the ingredients and bring the mixture to a boil. Add fish, cover, and simmer 15 minutes. Place fish on a heated platter; pour sauce over the fish and sprinkle with scallions.

RIBANI DŹUVEĆ
Fish and Vegetables
serves 8

1 large eggplant, thinly sliced	3 large boiling potatoes, peeled and thinly sliced
2 Tbls salt	½ cup long grain rice
½ cup oil	1 cup water
3 large diced onions.	3 pounds red snapper or scrod fillets
1 tsp paprika	3 large tomatoes, thinly sliced
3 green bell peppers, sliced into strips	Salt and pepper to taste
3 zucchini, sliced into strips	

Wash eggplant, and without paring, slice it very thinly. Spread on a board and sprinkle with salt. Let it stand for 15 minutes, then blot with paper towels.

In a large skillet sauté onions in oil until they are just starting to turn pale gold. Sprinkle with paprika. Stir well. Add peppers, zucchini, eggplant, potatoes, and rice. Add ½ cup water and cook for 30–35 minutes, stirring gently once in a while.

Place vegetables and rice into a deep baking dish. Place fish fillets on top of the vegetables and sprinkle with salt and pepper. Pour the remaining ½ cup water over fish and vegetables. Place sliced tomatoes over fish, and sprinkle with some more salt and pepper. Cover baking dish and bake in a 350° oven for 35 minutes. Uncover and bake for an additional 10 minutes. Serve hot, or, if you wish, cool, then chill and serve cold.

Peasant women in Yugoslavian costumes

FISH VOIVODINA
serves 6

3 pounds pike or perch, cleaned and
with backbone removed
Salt and pepper to taste
⅓ cup vegetable oil

1 Tbls butter
½ pound sliced mushrooms
1 cup sour cream

Cut fish into 3-inch pieces. Sprinkle with salt and pepper. Heat oil in a large skillet and cook fish until brown on all sides. Butter a baking dish and cook fish until brown on all sides. Butter a baking dish well. Spread a layer of fish in the bottom of the baking dish, cover with a layer of mushrooms, then spread another layer of fish and finish with mushrooms. Spread sour cream over mushrooms and bake in a 350° oven for 25 minutes.

SHRIMP IN BRANDY DALMATIA

2 pounds large shrimp, shelled and
deveined
1 cup flour
⅛ tsp pepper
1 tsp paprika
¼ tsp oregano
4 Tbls oil

3 cloves garlic, chopped
2 Tbls parsley, minced
3 Tbls brandy
2 Tbls flour
½ cup chicken broth (canned or
powdered)
½ cup dry white vermouth

Pat shrimp dry with paper towels. Mix flour, pepper, paprika, and oregano and coat shrimp in the mixture.
Heat oil in a large skillet. Add garlic and parsley and cook for about 5 seconds. Add shrimp and sauté until golden brown on all sides. Add brandy and shake the skillet. Blend flour mixture with the broth until smooth and add to skillet along with vermouth. Stir lightly and cook for about 6–7 minutes. Serve immediately with rice.

CHEVAVSHA ARNAUT
Yugoslavian Chicken
serves 4–5

1	medium eggplant, pared	1	3–4-pound cut-up chicken
2	cups boiling water		Salt and pepper to taste
3	Tbls butter	½	tsp oregano
2	green peppers, diced	½	tsp basil
2	tomatoes, diced	3	Tbls butter
2	onions, diced		Salt and pepper to taste

Slice eggplant into ½-inch circles; then quarter each circle. Place the pieces into a bowl and pour boiling water over the eggplant. Let stand for 15 minutes. Drain eggplant pieces and pat them dry with paper towels. In a large pot or Dutch oven, melt 3 tablespoons of butter and add half of the eggplant, along with peppers, tomatoes, and onions. Sprinkle with salt, black pepper, and with half the oregano and basil. Place chicken on top of vegetables and sprinkle the pieces with salt and pepper. Put remaining vegetables on top of chicken and dot with 3 tablespoons of butter. Sprinkle with salt, pepper, and remaining oregano and basil. Simmer, covered, for 1½ hours, stirring occasionally from the bottom up so that vegetables do not stick to the pot. Serve with rice.

Fortress of Kali-Magdan, Belgrade

221

CHICKEN WITH VEGETABLES
serves 4

3–3 ½ pound roasting chicken, quartered
  Salt and pepper and paprika to taste
5 slices bacon
2 medium onions, diced
2 green peppers, diced
3 carrots, grated

3 stalks celery, diced
2 cups diced potatoes
  Salt and pepper to taste
½ tsp tarragon
½ pound mushrooms, sliced
¼ cup white wine
½ cup minced parsley

Rub chicken with salt, pepper, and paprika. Cook bacon in a large pot until crisp. Remove the pieces and reserve the fat. Brown chicken on all sides in bacon fat. Remove chicken to a platter. Brown onions and peppers in the pot where the chicken was cooking. Add carrots, celery, and potatoes. Sprinkle with salt and pepper and stir well. Place chicken over the vegetables. Sprinkle with tarragon. Cover and cook for 20 minutes. Add mushrooms. Cover and cook for 30–40 minutes, or until the chicken is very tender. Add white wine to chicken. Stir well. Simmer for 5 minutes. Crumble crisp bacon and sprinkle, along with parsley, over chicken. Serve the chicken on a platter, surrounded with vegetables. Accompany the dish with noodles or rice.

PILEĆI RISOTO
Chicken with Rice
serves 6

3 Tbls vegetable oil
2 medium onions, thinly sliced
2 chickens, cut into serving pieces
  Salt and pepper to taste
1 tsp paprika

1 cup chicken broth
5 large tomatoes, peeled and sliced
1 cup rice
18 clams in shells

In a large pot, heat oil and sauté onions until limp. Add chicken, salt, pepper, and paprika, and simmer for 20 minutes. Add half the chicken broth and the tomatoes. In a saucepan, boil rice in salted water for 10 minutes only. Drain rice and add it to the chicken with the remainder of the broth. Place clams on top of chicken and rice and boil for 10 minutes, or until rice is tender. Simmer until clams open. Serve immediately.

PEĆENA ĆURKA NADEVENA PEĆURKAMA
Roast Turkey with Mushroom Stuffing
serves 6

12 slices bacon	¼ tsp mace
1 pound mushrooms, finely chopped	5 slices bread, with crusts removed
1 bay leaf	⅔ cup warm water
Salt and pepper to taste	1 small turkey, about 6–7 pounds
¼ tsp sage	½ cup white wine

Preheat oven to 320°. Chop half the bacon and sauté it in a skillet. Add mushrooms, bay leaf, salt, pepper, sage, and mace. Cook for 10–15 minutes. Set aside to cool. In a bowl, soak bread in warm water, squeeze out excess liquid, and add cooled mushrooms. Stuff turkey with the mixture. Secure the opening with small skewers. Place remaining bacon strips over the turkey. Place turkey on a rack in a baking pan and bake for 3½–4 hours in a 325° oven, or until turkey legs move freely. Baste, using turkey juices and white wine. Serve on a warm platter.

Pottery kiln

Meat . . . .

POT ROAST DUBROVNIK STYLE
serves 6–8

4–5	pounds brisket, top round, or chuck	1	cup tomato sauce
½	cup flour	1	cup chopped parsley
	Salt and pepper to taste	½	cup dry red wine
¼	cup olive oil, or any other oil	3	Tbls chopped capers
1	large onion, thinly sliced	¼	cup chopped green olives
2–3	cloves mashed garlic	6–8	thin slices of Provolone or Fontina cheese
5	scraped carrots, thinly sliced into circles	½	pound pasta shells
4	tomatoes, chopped	3	Tbls butter

For this recipe, you may use almost any cut of meat, but brisket is the best. Dredge the meat thoroughly in flour and sprinkle it with salt and pepper. Heat oil in a large pot or Dutch oven, add meat, and brown it on both sides. Add onion and garlic, reduce heat, and cook for 35 minutes, turning meat often. Add carrots and seasoning and cook ½ hour longer. Add tomatoes, tomato sauce, and parsley. Cook for 1½ hours, or until meat is very tender. Add wine, capers and green olives and cook for 15 minutes. Place thinly sliced cheese on top of meat, cover, and simmer until cheese is melted. Remove the meat to a heated platter and keep warm.

Cook pasta shells as directed on the package, drain well, add 3 tablespoons of butter, place the shells into the sauce, and bring to a boil. Remove from heat. Surround thinly sliced meat with shells and sauce. Serve Parmesan cheese on the side.

CEVAPĆIĆI
Ground Beef and Lamb Sausages
serves 6

1 pound ground beef	½ cup cold water
1 pound ground lamb	Salt and pepper to taste
2 cloves minced garlic	Finely chopped onions
1 Tbls minced parsley	

Place all ingredients into a bowl and mix lightly with 2 forks. Shape into 2½–3-inch long and about 1½-inch wide sausages. Grill over hot coals on a grill or broil in an oven, turning once until they are well browned. The little sausages may also be threaded on skewers and then grilled. Serve them with chopped onions.

RAZNJIĆI
Veal and Pork Shish Kebab
serves 4–6

1 pound veal cut into 1½-inch cubes	2 Tbls wine vinegar
	Salt and pepper to taste
1 pound pork cut into 1½-inch cubes	1 large onion, thinly sliced
	16–20 bay leaves
2 Tbls olive oil	1 onion, minced

Place all ingredients into a bowl and mix lightly with 2 forks. Shape into 2½–3-inch long and about 1½-inch wide sausages. Grill over hot coals on a grill or broil in an oven, turning once until they are well browned. The little sausages may also be threaded on skewers and then grilled. Serve them with chopped onions.

LOVAĆKI DJUVEĆ
Hunter's Stew
serves 6–8

10	slices bacon	4½	pounds cubed beef chuck
2	cups diced onions		Salt and pepper to taste
2	cloves minced garlic	1⅓	cups converted rice
1⅓	cups scraped, finely chopped carrots	⅔–1	cup more water
2½	cups water	2	large green peppers, thinly sliced
⅓	cup red wine vinegar	1½	cups beef broth

In a large skillet, fry bacon until slightly crisp. Remove bacon from skillet and reserve. Pour off most of the fat from the skillet. Add onions and sauté till just transparent. Add garlic and carrots and cook for 5 minutes. Return reserved bacon and add water, vinegar, beef cubes, salt, and pepper. Cover and simmer on low heat for 1 hour. Add more water if needed. Stir rice in slowly, add peppers and beef broth, and bring to a boil. Reduce heat, cover, and simmer for about 25 minutes, until rice is tender but not watery.

ROLLED BEEFSTEAKS
serves 6

6	slices ½-inch thick round steak	2	Tbls flour
	Salt and pepper to taste	4	Tbls butter
⅓	pound sliced bacon	1	large onion, thinly sliced
3	diced pickles	2½	cups water
1	cup diced cooked smoked ham		

Even out the edges on round steak and pound until thin. Slices of steak should be about 4 × 5", ¼-inch thick. Season the slices with salt and pepper. Cover steaks with sliced bacon. Mix pickles with diced ham and spread over bacon. Roll each steak up and fasten with skewers or toothpicks. Dust steak rolls with flour, place in a frying pan, and brown in butter. Remove meat and fry onion. Return steak rolls to pan, add half the water, cover, and simmer for 1 hour, or until tender. Add water as the broth evaporates. Remove skewers or toothpicks before serving.

BRAISED BEEF
serves 6

3 pounds beef brisket	Salt and pepper to taste
½ cup butter or bacon fat	2½ cups water
2 large or 3 medium onions, diced	2 Tbls flour

Tenderize meat by pounding. In a large skillet, brown the onion in fat and add meat, salt, and pepper. Pour 1 cup of the water over meat and simmer for 2½ hours, or until tender. Remove meat. Dust pan drippings with flour and stir over heat until brown. Add the rest of the water and simmer for 5 minutes. Slice meat and serve it in the gravy with dumplings, potatoes, rice, or noodles.

RIĆET
Beans with Smoked Pork
serves 4

½ pound navy beans	2 Tbls vegetable oil
½ pound smoked spareribs	½ tsp paprika
¼ pound barley	Salt and pepper to taste
1 small onion, diced	¼ cup chopped parsley

Soak beans in water overnight. Drain beans. Place beans in a pot, cover with water, and cook for 2 hours, or until tender. Cut spareribs into serving pieces, place in a pot with water to cover, and boil for 35 minutes. In a saucepan, cook barley, as directed on the package, until tender. Drain the beans, reserving the cooking liquid. Mix beans with barley, adding about 1 cup of cooking liquid. Add to the spareribs. Sauté onion in oil and add to the bean mixture. Add paprika, salt, and pepper. Cover the pot and simmer for 15 minutes. Garnish with parsley.

YUGOSLAVIAN MEAT PIE
serves 8

2	cups unbleached all-purpose flour	⅛	tsp ground nutmeg
2	lightly beaten eggs	2	whole cloves
¼	cup warm olive oil	⅛	tsp dry mustard
1	Tbls margarine	1	bay leaf
⅛–1	tsp warm water	1	tsp chopped parsley
1	medium onion, chopped	¼	cup white wine
1	Tbls olive oil	2	pounds ¼-inch cubed beef, veal, or
1	chopped clove garlic		pork
¼	tsp salt	1	Tbls margarine
⅛	tsp black ground pepper	1	beaten egg yolk
⅛	tsp cinnamon		

In a bowl, mix flour, eggs, ¼ cup warm olive oil, margarine, and water together. Work the dough so that it is soft and not dry. Add more water if necessary. Wrap the dough with a slightly damp cloth and allow it to rest at room temperature for 1 hour.

While dough is resting, prepare the filling.

Sauté onion in 1 tablespoon of olive oil until lightly golden. Add garlic and let it brown. Add salt, pepper, cinnamon, nutmeg, cloves, dry mustard, bay leaf, parsley, and white wine. Cook for about 5 minutes. Put in the meat cubes and cook at medium heat until meat is tender—about 40 minutes. Stir often. Set aside and allow to cool. Butter two 10-inch pie tins well with 1 tablespoon of margarine. Roll out the dough and make 4 pastry shells. Line the pie tins with a bottom crust. Fill pastry shells with the meat mixture and cover with a top crust. Brush each top crust well with beaten egg yolk and bake in a preheated 350° oven for about 40 minutes, or until the crust is golden brown.

VEAL ESCALOPS DUBROVNIK STYLE
serves 5

2	onions, diced	2	egg yolks
1	dozen mushroom caps	2	cups whipped cream, unsweetened
¼	pound butter	½	cup Parmesan cheese
2	bay leaves	16	scallops of veal (silver dollar size)
	Pinch of rosemary	1	cup dry sherry
2	cups rice	1	cup brown sauce (canned may be
3	cups chicken broth		used)
	Salt and pepper to taste		

Preheat oven to 400°. In a skillet or an oven-proof dish, sauté onions and mushrooms in 4 tablespoons of butter. Season with bay leaves and rosemary. Simmer for 15 minutes. Add rice and stir for one minute. Add chicken broth and season with salt and pepper. Cover. When the mixture reaches the boiling point, cover skillet and place it in the oven for approximately 25–30 minutes at 400°, or until rice is tender. When rice is cooked, cool it and then put in a blender to purée. Add egg yolks, unsweetened whipped cream, and Parmesan cheese. Place this blend into a pastry bag and set aside.

Sauté scallops of veal in a skillet in the remaining butter. Brown on both sides. When browned, place scallops on a serving dish. Add sherry to the skillet and cook until the liquid is reduced by half. Add brown sauce and simmer.

Squeeze rice mixture in the pastry bag over the veal in a criss-cross fasion. Sprinkle some Parmesan cheese over the top. Place dish under the broiler until the top is golden brown. Encircle veal with the sauce. Serve hot.

VEAL ROLLS

serves 4–6

1	pound veal tenderloin (scallops)	5	Tbls butter
12	very thin slices of cooked ham	2	large onions, thinly sliced
4–5	cloves mashed garlic	½	pound mushrooms, thinly sliced
	cups grated Romano cheese 1 ½	1	cup red port wine

Pound veal scallops to ⅛-inch thickness. Place a slice of the cooked ham on top of each veal scallop. Spread garlic on top of ham. Next, sprinkle some grated cheese on ham. Roll each scallop up and secure each roll with toothpicks. Sauté onions and mushrooms in 2 tablespoons of butter. Brown rolls in a skillet in 3 tablespoons of butter. Add sautéed onions, mushrooms, and wine and simmer for 15 minutes on a low heat. Serve immediately.

YOUNG LAMB BOILED IN MILK
serves 6

3 pounds leg of lamb
   Salt and pepper to taste
1 tsp rosemary
2 cups milk

2   cups whipping cream
2   Tbls chopped parsley
*1½ cups Kaimak

Rub lamb with salt, pepper, and rosemary. Place lamb in a large pot, add milk and cream, and slowly bring to a boil. Simmer until lamb is tender, about 1½–2 hours. Place lamb on a warm platter and discard the cooking liquid. Sprinkle lamb with parsley and serve it with Kaimak.

*Kaimak

½ cup Feta cheese
1 cup sour cream
1 cup softened cream cheese

Press Feta cheese through a sieve. In a bowl, beat cheeses and sour cream together until smooth. Serve with the lamb.

DJUVEĆ
Lamb Chop and Vegetable Casserole
serves 6

6 1-inch thick loin lamb chops
   Salt and pepper to taste
¼ tsp thyme
4 Tbls shortening
4 cups thinly sliced onions
3 cloves minced garlic
½ cup chicken broth

6   large potatoes, peeled and sliced ¼-inch thick
4   large rings of sliced green pepper
10 medium tomatoes, peeled and sliced ¼-inch thick
    Salt, pepper, and thyme to taste
1   crumbled bay leaf

Preheat oven to 350°. Rub lamb chops with salt, pepper, and thyme. In a large skillet, heat shortening; brown chops lightly on each side. Remove chops from skillet and place them on a heated platter. Sauté onions and garlic in the same skillet until lightly colored. Remove them with a slotted spoon and set them aside. Add chicken broth to skillet, bring to a boil, stir, and remove from heat. Spread half of onion mixture in the bottom of a deep baking dish. Add potatoes, green peppers, and half the tomatoes and seasonings. Add the rest of the onion-garlic mixture and tomatoes.

Pour broth from the skillet into the baking pan. Place lamb chops on top. Cover them with foil and bake them in a 350° oven for 25 minutes. Remove foil and bake for 15 minutes longer.

EGGPLANT CASSEROLE, YUGO STYLE
serves 8

2 ½	pounds ground beef	2	16-ounce cans whole, peeled to-
¼	cup olive oil		matoes, drained
2	large eggplants	½	tsp salt, or more to taste
1	Tbls salt	¼	tsp black pepper
1	cup or more olive oil	¼	tsp oregano
2	large onions, thinly sliced	¼	tsp rosemary
3	green peppers, thinly sliced	¼	tsp basil
2	cloves garlic, crushed		Salt and pepper to taste
2	Tbls olive oil		

Preheat oven to 350°. Sauté ground beef in ¼ cup of oil, stirring continuously to prevent lumping. Set aside. Slice the eggplant into ½-inch thick circles, place onto a board or wax paper, and sprinkle with 1 tablespoon of salt. Let stand for 20–30 minutes. Pat well with a paper towel. Brown slices on both sides in 1 cup or more of oil. Sauté onions and peppers in 2 tablespoons of oil. Add minced garlic. Chop drained tomatoes. Use a fireproof or earthenware baking dish. Place a layer of eggplant in the bottom of the pot, follow with a layer of meat, then a layer of onions and peppers, and then the tomatoes. Continue with the layers until all the ingredients are used up. Fill dish to about 2 inches from the top: Do not overfill. Sprinkle each layer with a little salt and pepper, oregano, rosemary, and basil. Bake in a 350° oven for 60 minutes.

For the Custard

3	eggs	1	Tbls minced scallions
½	cup light cream	¼	tsp salt
¼	cup sour cream		Pinch black pepper
2	tsp minced parsley		

Beat together eggs, cream, sour cream, parsley, scallions, salt, and pepper. With 2 forks, separate the center of the casserole, making a 2–3-inch space. Pour custard into the space and bake for 20 minutes more, or until the custard is set and the top is well browned.

Side Dishes . . . .

POPOLIJA
Noodles with Vegetables
serves 8–10

1	pound medium egg noodles	1½	cups heavy cream
7	Tbls butter	4	Tbls butter
2	Tbls olive oil	¼	tsp nutmeg
½	pound mushrooms, sliced	¼	tsp white pepper
5	zucchini, thinly sliced		Salt to taste
	Salt and pepper to taste	5	egg yolks
½	cup dry white wine	2	cups grated Parmesan cheese

Preheat oven to 350°. Cook egg noodles as directed on the package. Drain them and add 4 tablespoons of butter. In a skillet, sauté sliced mushrooms and zucchini in 3 tablespoons of butter and the oil. Add salt and pepper to taste. Drain well and return to the skillet. Add wine and simmer for 5 minutes. Add mushrooms and zucchini to the noodles and toss together. In the top of a double boiler, mix cream, 4 tablespoons of butter, nutmeg, white pepper, and salt together. When butter is melted, add egg yolks, beating continuously until slightly thickened, like a custard. Add 1½ cups of grated Parmesan cheese and stir until the cheese is melted. Pour sauce over the noodles, toss lightly, place into a baking dish, sprinkle with ½ cup of grated Parmesan cheese, and bake for 10 minutes in a 350° oven.

FLEKIĆE Ś KUPUSOM
Noodles with Shredded Cabbage
serves 4–6

¼ cup vegetable oil
1 medium head cabbage, shredded
  Salt and pepper to taste
1 pound wide noodles

In a skillet, heat oil and sauté cabbage, which has been sprinkled with salt and pepper, until slightly brown. Cook noodles in salted water as directed on the package, but reduce cooking time by 5 minutes. Thoroughly rinse and drain noodles. Add noodles to the cabbage and cook until noodles are very tender.

SPICED FARINA DUMPLINGS
makes about 2 dozen dumplings

⅔	cup milk	2	beaten eggs
½	cup farina	⅛	tsp allspice
	Salt to taste	4	cups or more of your favorite bouil-
2 ½	Tbls butter		lon (chicken or beef)

In a saucepan, slowly bring milk, farina, and salt to a boil and stir the mixture until it is thick. Allow it to cool and add butter, eggs, and allspice. Drop the batter from a wet teaspoon into boiling soup. Simmer for 5 minutes. Serve in soup or with stew.

POTATO AND SPINACH DUMPLINGS
makes about 3 dozen dumplings

7	medium potatoes, peeled		Finely ground black pepper to taste
1 ½	cups cream of wheat, uncooked	⅛	tsp nutmeg
	Salt to taste	2 ¼	cups unbleached all-purpose flour
1	slightly beaten egg	¼	tsp baking powder
1	egg yolk	2	cups diced toasted bread crumbs
1	10-ounce package frozen chopped spinach, defrosted	4	quarts boiling salted water
2	cloves mashed garlic	⅔	cup melted butter

In a pan, boil the potatoes until tender, drain them, and place them into a large bowl. Immediately add cream of wheat and salt and mash until smooth. Stir in egg and egg yolk. Squeeze spinach between two paper towels to remove some of the moisture. Stir in spinach, garlic, pepper, nutmeg, flour, and baking powder and mix well. Add bread cubes and knead. The dough will be sticky. Form into 3-inch balls. Drop dumplings into boiling salted water. When the water begins to boil again, cover and simmer for 15 minutes. Remove to a heated platter and sprinkle with melted butter. You can serve this recipe with meat, poultry, or just with a salad.

POTATO CASSEROLE
serves 6

8 medium potatoes, peeled
3 hard-cooked eggs, sliced
1½ pounds sliced sausage—Kilbasi

Salt and pepper to taste
1 cup light cream

Preheat oven to 375°. Cut the potatoes in ¼-inch thick slices. Grease an oven-proof casserole dish. Cover the casserole bottom with 2 layers of potato slices. Add a layer of egg slices and a layer of sausage slices and sprinkle with salt and pepper. Continue with layers, ending with potato slices. Bake in a 375° oven for 20 minutes. Add cream, reduce heat to 325°, and bake for 25–30 minutes, or until the potatoes are tender and golden brown.

Desserts . . . .

YUGOSLAVIAN HONEY CAKE
serves 8–10

1½ cups natural honey
1 tsp cinnamon
½ tsp nutmeg
¼ tsp cloves
¼ pound unsalted butter
2 tsp baking soda
1 cup dark brown sugar
6 egg yolks
4½ cups all-purpose flour

¾ tsp salt
2 tsp double-acting baking powder
1 cup raisins
½ cup currants
½ cup chopped dates
¼ cup candied orange peel
1 cup coarsely ground walnuts
6 egg whites
3 Tbls sugar

Preheat oven to 350°. Butter well two 7-inch loaf pans and sprinkle them generously with flour. Shake out excess flour and set the pans aside. In a saucepan, combine honey, cinnamon, nutmeg, and ground cloves. Bring to a boil, reduce heat, and simmer for 2 minutes. Set aside to cool. In a bowl, beat butter, baking soda, and sugar together until smooth and fluffy. Add egg yolks to butter mixture one at a time, beating well after each addition. Add flour, salt, baking powder, and honey to the butter mixture. Beat together with a wooden spoon until smooth. Add raisins, currants, dates, orange peel, and walnuts and mix well. Beat egg whites until stiff, add sugar, and beat until very stiff. Fold the egg whites gently into the mixture. Put batter into the loaf pans. Bake in a 350° preheated oven for 1–1½ hours or until a cake tester comes out clean. Cool the cakes in the pans. Run a knife around the cake, unmold onto a plate, cover, and let stand for 48 hours before using. Decorate with candied fruit.

ARNAUT CANDY
serves about 24

2 cups honey	1 cup finely crushed vanilla wafers
1¼ cups sugar	¼–½ cup orange juice
4 cups coarsely crushed roasted hazelnuts or walnuts	

In a saucepan, combine honey and sugar. Stir well and bring to a boil. Reduce heat and simmer, stirring constantly, until the mixture reaches 265° on a candy thermometer (hard ball stage). Be careful: The honey rises fast and may run over. Pour the syrup into a bowl and add hazelnuts or walnuts and crushed vanilla wafers. Mix well.

Use a plastic cutting board, or a cookie sheet. Moisten the surface thoroughly with orange juice. Spread honey mixture on the board, about ½-inch thick. Moisten your hands with more juice and smooth out the mixture with your palms. Let stand for 1–2 hours. Then cut into 1" × 2" pieces. Wrap each piece in wax paper or place each piece in a small paper cup. Refrigerate. Keep uneaten candy refrigerated.

Variation

Roast 1 cup of sesame seeds, sprinkle on top of the warm confection, and press down slightly until the seeds adhere.

CHEESE CRÊPES SLOVAKIAN
serves about 6–8

2 eggs	½ cup clarified melted butter (see recipe
1 Tbls melted butter	on page 37)
⅔ cup milk	½ cup powdered sugar
⅔ cup flour	½ cup sour cream
¼ tsp salt	

In a blender, blend eggs, butter, milk, flour, and salt until smooth. The batter should be as thick as heavy cream. Refrigerate for 30 minutes. Brush a 6-inch crêpe pan or a heavy skillet with butter. Pour about 2½ tablespoons of batter into the pan, rotating the pan to spread the batter. Cook crêpe on one side only, until crêpe is lightly browned on the bottom. Place crêpe brown side up on a platter. Repeat until all the batter has been used up. Place 2 tablespoons of cheese filling on the browned side of the crêpe. Fold crêpes so that edges are tucked in and sides overlap. Heat the remaining butter in a large skillet. Sauté crêpes, seam side down, until golden brown. Turn and brown the underside. Keep the cooked crêpes warm while cooking the rest. Sprinkle with powdered sugar. Serve hot, topped with sour cream.

Filling

1 cup ricotta cheese	2 slightly beaten egg yolks
1 3-ounce package softened cream	1 Tbls sugar
cheese	½ tsp vanilla extract
1 tsp grated lemon rind	

In a small bowl, beat all ingredients together until smooth and creamy. Cover and refrigerate.

CUSTARD CAKE
serves 6

4 cups milk	1 tsp vanilla
⅔ cup farina (cream of wheat)	½ tsp rum extract
½ tsp salt	⅔ cup raisins soaked in
¼ cup butter	½ cup rum
6 eggs	1 cup diced citron (optional)
1 cup sugar	1 cup coarsely crushed walnuts

Preheat oven to 375°. Bring milk to a boil and add the farina, stirring constantly. Reduce heat and simmer, stirring until thickened. Add salt and butter and stir until butter is melted and absorbed. Beat the eggs with sugar, vanilla, and rum extract until very thick. Stir slowly into the farina. While the farina is cooking, soak raisins in rum. Add raisins, citron, and walnuts to the farina. Spread the farina in an 8″ × 12″ well-buttered baking dish and bake in a preheated 375° oven for 45–50 minutes, or until an inserted knife comes out clean.

Syrup:

In a sauce pan, combine ½ cup of sugar with 1 cup water, 3 tablespoons of lemon juice, lemon peel, and a cinnamon stick. Bring to a boil and simmer for 10 minutes. Cool slightly and add 3 tablespoons of rum. Pour syrup over the farina. Cool and then refrigerate. Cut into squares and lift the squares out with a spatula.

Variation: Farina custard in pastry

Make up the farina mixture as before, but eliminate the raisins, citron, and nuts. Melt ½ pound of butter or margarine. Use ½ pound of filo dough.
Butter a 9″ × 14″ baking dish well. Place 6 filo leaves into the baking dish. Butter each leaf generously. Pour farina mixture over pastry. Cover with 6 more buttered filo sheets. Cut through the top of the pastry with a sharp knife, making 2-inch squares. Bake in a preheated 350° oven for 30 minutes, reduce heat to 300°, and bake for 30 minutes longer. Make up syrup as above and cool it. Pour the cool syrup over the hot pastry. Cut into squares, making sure that you cut through to the bottom. Makes about 36 pieces.
Note: Filo pastry is available in Greek and Arabic groceries and also in some Italian groceries and gourmet stores.

LEMON-NUT CRESCENT
makes 2 nut rolls

1	cup milk	2	eggs
1 ½	packages dry yeast	1	cup sugar
⅓	cup sugar	¼	tsp cinnamon
3	cups unbleached all-purpose flour	2	tsp grated lemon rind
1	tsp salt	3	cups grated walnuts
⅓	cup butter	1	Tbls melted butter
2	egg yolks	½	cup powdered vanilla sugar (see recipe on page 37)
	Grated rind of 1 lemon		
⅓	cup butter		

Warm ¼ cup of the milk and add yeast, 1 teaspoon sugar, and ⅓ cup flour. Stir to form a soft paste and let set for 10 minutes. In a bowl, cream butter and the remaining sugar. Beat in egg yolks and add lemon rind. Gradually stir in the remaining milk. Mix in the yeast mixture, salt, and flour. The dough shouldn't be too soft. Add 2–3 tablespoons more flour if necessary. Cover bowl with a towel and let dough rise until doubled in bulk. In another bowl, cream butter, beat in eggs, sugar, cinnamon, lemon rind, and half the grated walnuts. Divide dough into 2 equal parts. On a floured board, roll dough out into a rectangle about ½-inch thick. Spread filling on dough and sprinkle it with grated walnuts. Roll up the dough tightly. Secure ends and seam well. Place the roll on a buttered baking sheet, seam down, in the shape of a crescent. Repeat with the second half of the dough. Preheat oven to 325°. Let rolls rise in a warm place for 15 minutes. Bake for 30–35 minutes. Brush with butter and sprinkle with powdered sugar.

Note: Dough may be cut into smaller parts, filled, and rolled to make smaller crescents.

CREAM CAKE WITH CHERRIES
serves 6–8

The Glaze

1	cup black cherry preserves
½	cup sugar
1	Tbls water

In a saucepan, combine all ingredients, bring to a boil, and simmer for 5–7 minutes. Pour the glaze into a 1½-quart charlotte mold or an 8-inch cake pan. Turn and tilt the pan until bottom and sides are coated with the glaze. Refrigerate until glaze is set.

The Cream

3 cups milk	6–8 ½-inch slices of pound cake
6 eggs	½ cup cherry preserves
⅔ cup granulated sugar	1 cup whipped cream

Preheat oven to 350°. Scald milk. Beat eggs with sugar until lemon-colored. Add the scalded milk and stir. Place 3–4 slices of pound cake in the bottom of the glazed mold or pan. Pour ½ of the egg mixture over the cake. Let stand for 2–3 minutes. Place another layer of cake over the first one and pour the remaining egg mixture over the cake. The cake will float up, forming the top layer. Set mold into a pan of hot water. Bake in a preheated 350° oven for 50 minutes, or until an inserted knife comes out clean. Cool for 1 hour. Then refrigerate for at least 3–4 hours, or overnight. Unmold onto a platter. There will be liquid in the pan, which will run down the sides of the cake. The pound cake may not be visible at all; it will be incorporated into the custard, giving it a rich heavy texture.

Decorate the cake with additional cherry preserves and whipped cream.

ALMOND TART
serves 6–8

Tart Shell

1 can almond paste
2 unbeaten egg whites
1 tsp almond extract

In a bowl, mix almond paste, egg whites, and almond extract until very smooth. Press the almond paste into an 8–9-inch pie pan, spreading it evenly and as thinly as possible. Set aside.

Filling

1 ¼	envelopes unflavored gelatin
⅓	cup cold water
1 ½	cups milk
1	can almond paste
4	egg yolks
⅔	cups sugar

½	tsp almond extract
½	cup brandy
3	cups sweetened whipped cream
½	cup slivered blanched and toasted almonds

Soften gelatin in cold water. Scald milk in the top of a double boiler. Cut almond paste into small pieces, add to milk, and blend well. Beat egg yolks with sugar until thick and light. Add them to the milk, blending very fast. Place the mixture over simmering water, stirring constantly until slightly thickened. Add gelatin and remove from heat. Cool slightly. Add almond extract and brandy. Refrigerate until the mixture is just beginning to set. Fold in 1 cup of whipped cream. Refrigerate until completely set. Spread the remaining whipped cream on top. Sprinkle with slivered almonds.

CHAPTER 6

RUMANIA:
The Land
of the Delta

P AST Belgrade and near the Dubova cleft, the Danube is bordered by Yugoslavia and Rumania. The waters flow majestically be an ancient Roman sundial and surveyors pole visibly etched on a rock on the banks of the river, and on the Yugoslavian side Roman inscriptions still glorify construction of a Roman road along the Danube. This was the great marching route of the Romans toward the beautiful city of Dacia. The Roman legions which conquered the Dacians gave the country their name, their language, and much of their cultural legacy. Rumania is a Latin country among its Slavic and Hungarian neighbors, and Rumanian is a romance language richly interspersed with Slavic, German, and Greek words.

However, as strong as the Roman influence was on Rumanian destiny, it was the Greeks who brought their religion, priests, and culture to the land. Cyrillic alphabet was used until the early 1800s, after which it was changed to the Latin lettering.

The Danube skirts the southern border of Rumania with the crescent-like sweep of the Carpathian Mountains, providing a natural barrier to the north. The mountains are filled with legends, myths, and mystery, and volumes could be written about this semicircular, soaring piece of terra firma. There are wild gorges, shockingly white chalk caves, and sensational ski trails. There are fairytale forests filled with wild game, mushrooms, berries, and crumbling ancient ruins of castles and fortifications.

In the 10th century Transylvania was occupied by the Hungarians, who came from central Asia. With coming of the Hungarians, Rumanians, who at that time were called Vlachs, were driven south from their mountainous land and settled in the territory later called Wallachia. Others migrated to lovely garden-like lands of Moldavia, and not until 1859 were Wallachia and Moldavia united to become the country we now know as Rumania.

Hungarians, who were determined to stabilize Transylvania, brought German settlers from the Rhineland to the region. The Germans built walled-in cities and villages reminiscent of their homeland. Today there are still German-speaking areas in the mountains and valleys of Rumania, where people retained their Teutonic heritage and traditions. Greeks, Hungarians, Germans, Slavs, and Turks all contributed a great deal to the development of Rumania, but the land changed hands so many times that many of the country folk did not know from month to month who their current rulers were.

Today Rumania is an enchanting place with rolling hills, lush green meadows, vast orchards, and towering mountains. The countryside is dotted with tiny villages—each with its own distinct character and friendly inhabitants. The peasants cling to their traditions, their own way of life, their songs, native costumes, and handicrafts, which are the pride of the country. Monasteries and churches are also part of the landscape. Some of the churches are so ancient that it seems a miracle that the brilliantly hued frescoes, although protected from rain and snow by overhangs, have remained so bright and new for centuries. Rumania is also a land of spas. There are 160 resorts and ten thousand guests flock there each year to seek health and vigor.

Today Rumania may be considered a leader in the health spa and resort industry, and is a delightful oasis for recuperation in our age of pills and drugs. The resorts are scattered throughout the country from the sunny Black Sea to the snow-capped Carpathian peaks.

It is land of garden cities, and Bucarest, its capital, is filled with lush greenery. Bucarest is also a city of ancient monasteries and churches with characteristic onion-like domes and walls painted in brilliant colors. It is a sophisticated city—a large yet romantic metropolis filled with museums, fine restaurants, and cafés.

Once called "little Paris," Bucarest was indeed a pied-a-terre of Francophiles. French was the second language spoken by most cosmopolitan inhabitants. Before World War II, Rumanians (who in looks and mannerisms resemble Italians), would promenade along the wide boulevards before lunch and dinner admiring the beautiful girls and elegant women. The streets were lined with outdoor cafes in summer and at night strains of gypsy music and spirited orchestras reverberated through the city. At the famed "Ikra Bar" (Caviar Bar) at least forty varieties of the precious fish eggs were sold by the white-coated owner. All one had to do was select a favorite type of caviar. The caviar was served chilled with stark simplicity in cans with a spoon alongside and with a dish of chopped onions, sliced lemon, thin crackers, and champagne. Some of the devotees could consume up to a pound of fresh magnificent caviar at a sitting—luxury personified. Today Bucarest is less bustling, more streamlined, and the people seem to be preoccupied, but at night there is still gypsy music, songs, and fine food and wine to be had at a favorite tavern or restaurant.

Fish and seafood are plentiful brought in from the Danube delta and the Black Sea, and Rumanian cooks have created many original dishes with subtle seasoning and marvelous taste. The Rumanian cuisine in general has come under strong Slavic, Hungarian, and Turkish influence. Still today, *Tuica,* the midday meal, is substantial. It is customary to have a hearty soup made of vegetables, meat, or fish, a soup similar to the Russian borscht, or the favorite *ciorba de perisore*—meatball soup.

Spit-roasted chickens, veal, lamb, and fish are in great demand, served with fresh vegetables, potatoes or *mamaliga* (boiled cornmeal which is often served instead of bread or potatoes). Stuffed grape leaves and cabbage are also usually on the menu. Yogurt and ewe cheese *(brindsa)* are eaten almost with every meal, or as snacks with *mamaliga*. Most of Rumania's rivers originate in the high Carpathian Mountains and flow into the Danube, which swells and widens as it races toward the Black Sea. In the southeast, in an area called Dobruja, the Danube swings north, where it branches out into the three arms creating the delta. The delta scenery has a misty haunting quality—it is covered with waterplants and hides many animal species and flocks of birds which inhabit the swampy refuge.

Today the serenity of the delta is invaded by large wooden dugouts which carry curious natives and tourists through the lily ponds of the delta. The dugouts slide among high reeds and there are eerie bird calls and splashing of water, and croaking frogs to add to the strangeness of this faraway place. The northernmost branch of the Danube flows into the Black Sea in the Ukraine, adding yet another country and another dimension to this fascinating river.

Appetizers. . . . .

BAKED CHEESE
serves 6

1½ cups flour	½ tsp baking powder
1 egg plus 1 egg yolk	1 pound Fontina or Edam cheese
⅓ cup dry white wine, or more as needed	2 cups or more of vegetable oil for frying

In a bowl, mix flour, egg, egg yolk, wine, and baking powder together, making a thick batter. The batter should be the consistency of a very thick cream. Add more wine if it is too thick. Cut the cheese into 1½-inch squares about ½-inch thick. Dip each piece of cheese into the batter, coating it completely. In a large skillet, heat oil until a haze appears, then drop the cheese pieces into the oil and fry them on both sides until golden brown. Place on a paper towel and serve immediately.

RED CAVIAR MOLD

serves 6

- 1 package unflavored gelatin
- 3 Tbls dry sherry
- 3 Tbls fresh lemon juice
- 6 hard-cooked eggs
- 1½ cups mayonnaise
- ½ tsp dry mustard
- 3 -ounce jar lumpfish red caviar (or salmon)
  Snipped parsley
  Lemon slices

Generously grease a 2-cup mold. Soften gelatin in sherry and lemon juice in small heatproof container for about 5 minutes, then place over low heat until dissolved, stirring several times. Chop eggs in a food processor or blender. Transfer them to mixing bowl. Stir in gelatin, mayonnaise, and mustard, and mix thoroughly. Gently fold in caviar until well-blended. Turn into mold, cover, and refrigerate until firm. Unmold and garnish with snipped parsley. Surround with crackers or thin slices of black bread.

Rumanian pottery workshop

BESSARABIAN PANCAKES
makes about 36 pancakes

Batter

4	eggs	3	Tbls melted butter
1 ½	cups sifted flour	1	cup light cream
½	tsp salt	1	cup club soda

Put eggs into a blender and add flour, salt, butter, and cream. Blend for a few seconds. Scrape the flour from the sides of the blender and then add club soda. Blend again for a few seconds. Let stand for 1 hour. Butter well two 5 inch crêpe pans, and heat. Pour about 2–3 tablespoons of batter into each pan. Bake on one side until slightly browned, turn, and bake on the other side. The pancakes should be very pale in color. Stack them on a warm platter.

Filling

1	pound pot cheese	¼	tsp white pepper
½	cup shredded Gruyere cheese	2	10-ounce pkgs frozen chopped spinach, defrosted and well drained
½	cup grated Parmesan cheese		Slightly beaten egg white
3	Tbls butter		Clarified butter (see recipe on page 37)
½	tsp salt, or more if needed		
¼	tsp Italian seasoning		
1	clove garlic, crushed (optional)		

In a bowl, combine pot cheese, Gruyere cheese, Parmesan cheese, butter, salt, Italian seasoning, garlic, white pepper, and spinach. Place 2 tablespoons of filling in the center of each pancake, brush the inside rim of the pancake with slightly beaten egg white, fold it over, and press down on the edge, sealing the pancake. Fry in clarified butter until golden brown on both sides. Serve immediately.

RUMANIAN CAVIAR
serves 6

3 eggplants	Salt and pepper to taste
5 Tbls vegetable oil	2 tsp paprika
3 Tbls lemon juice	2 medium onions, finely diced

Preheat oven to 400°. Do not peel or slice eggplants. Place whole eggplants into a baking pan and bake in a 400° oven until very tender, about 1 hour. Let eggplants cool for a few minutes. Peel the eggplants. Purée eggplant pulp in a blender. Add oil, lemon juice, salt, pepper, and paprika and blend until the mixture is smooth. Place the purée into a bowl and add onion. Mix well. Use as a spread on raw vegetables, bread, or crackers.

Rumanian woodcarver

Soups . . . .

RUMANIAN BEAN SOUP
serves 6

1 pound great northern beans	2 Tbls shortening or lard
Water to cover	2 Tbls flour
¾ pound smoked pork plus a ham bone	1 tsp paprika
1 large onion, thinly sliced	2–3 Tbls vinegar, or more to taste
	Salt and pepper to taste

Place beans into a bowl and pour enough water over them to cover. Let them stand for at least 12 hours. Pour off the water. Put beans into a pot and pour on fresh water to cover. Add smoked pork and ham bone, cover pot, and simmer for 2–3 hours, or until beans are tender. In a skillet, sauté onion in lard or shortening until pale golden brown. Add flour and paprika and stir well. Cook until slightly thickened. Add onion mixture to the soup and cook, stirring occasionally, until slightly thickened. Remove the smoked pork and cut it into small pieces. Return it to the pot. Add vinegar and salt and pepper to taste. Bring to a boil and serve hot over noodles.

COLD TOMATO AND DILL SOUP
serves 6

4 large ripe tomatoes, peeled and chopped	2 Tbls tomato paste
4 cups boiling water	½ cup cooked rice
2 cloves of garlic, minced	1 cup chicken borth
1 mild onion, chopped	1 cup heavy cream
Salt and pepper to taste	2 Tbls scallions and dill, minced } garnish
2 Tbls dill, minced	

Drop the tomatoes into boiling water for about 30 seconds. Remove with a slotted spoon, peel off the skin, and chop. Put tomatoes, garlic, onion, salt and pepper, and dill into a saucepan. Stir well, cover, and simmer for about 10 minutes. Add tomato paste and rice. Cook 10 minutes longer. Cool for a few minutes and purée in a blender. Add chicken broth and cream and blend for a few seconds longer. Chill for 2–3 hours. Stir before serving.

Serve garnished with dill and scallions.

APPLE SOUP

serves 6

3	carrots, scraped and diced	6	large apples, cored, peeled, and sliced
2	stalks celery, cleaned and diced		
1	kohlrabi, peeled and diced	3	Tbls flour
1	green pepper, diced	⅓	cup light cream
1	tomato, diced	2	Tbls light brown sugar, or more to taste
3	Tbls oil		
8	cups chicken broth	2–3	Tbls lemon juice to taste
	Salt and pepper to taste	½	tsp grated lemon rind

Place all vegetables into a large pot. Add oil and stir well. Sauté for 5–6 minutes, stirring often. If needed, add ½ cup of chicken broth. When vegetables are just barely tender, add the remaining broth and salt and pepper to taste. Simmer soup for 1 hour, then add apples and cook over medium heat for about 15 minutes. In a small bowl, beat together flour, cream, and brown sugar until very smooth. Add to soup, stir well, and bring to a boil. Add lemon juice and rind, reduce heat, and simmer for a few minutes, until the soup is slightly thickened. You may wish to add more lemon and sugar to taste.

Rumanian dancers, Danube region, in national costumes

Salads . . . .

ZUCCHINI SALAD
serves 4

4–5 young tender zucchini	4 Tbls vegetable oil
3 young carrots, scraped	2–3 Tbls lemon juice or vinegar, or
2 Tbls minced dill	more to taste
2 Tbls minced parsley	Salt and pepper to taste
2 Tbls minced scallions	

Do not pare zucchini. Grate them, using the largest side of a grater, into a bowl. Grate carrots. Add dill, parsley, and scallions and toss lightly. Add oil and lemon juice or vinegar to taste. Add salt and pepper to taste and toss lightly together.

TOMATO SALAD
serves 6

4 large tomatoes	2 Tbls vinegar
4 green bell peppers	4 Tbls minced parsley
2 large mild onions	Salt and pepper to taste
3 Tbls oil	

Wash and dice tomatoes, Place them in a bowl. Slice green peppers into very thin strips and slice the onion into thinnest possible rings. Add them to the tomatoes and toss lightly. Add oil, vinegar, parsley, and salt and pepper to taste. Toss again. Chill for 1 hour before serving.

BLACK OLIVE, SARDINE, AND TOMATO SALAD

serves 6

8–9	large ripe tomatoes		Salt and pepper to taste
2	large mild onions	24	small sardines, drained
3–4	Tbls wine vinegar or more to taste	*36	large pitted black olives
⅓	cup olive oil	¼	cup minced parsley

Wash and dry tomatoes. Slice into ¼" circles. Slice onions into thin circles. Alternate tomato and onion slices in the center of a large round platter. Sprinkle them with vinegar, olive oil, and salt and pepper. Place a circle of drained sardines on top of the tomatoes. Surround tomatoes with black olives. Sprinkle sardines and tomatoes with parsley. Chill for 1 hour and serve.

*If you wish, use so-called "Greek" black olives.

Rumanian woman teaching embroidery to a child

Vegetables . . . .

LENTEN EGGPLANT

serves 4–5

2 large eggplants, washed	2 large tomatoes, finely chopped
½ cup vegetable oil, or more as needed	Salt and pepper to taste
2 Tbls salt	1 Tbls flour
1 large onion, minced	3 Tbls minced parsley
6 scallions, minced	24 Greek olives or black olives from a
2 Tbls minced dill	can

Cut eggplant into small cubes, place the cubes on a platter, and sprinkle them with 2 tablespoons of salt. Let stand for 15 minutes. Then blot with paper towels, squeezing out as much juice as possible. In a large skillet, heat oil and add eggplant, onion, scallions, dill, tomatoes, and salt and pepper to taste. Reduce heat, cover, and cook, stirring often, for 10–15 minutes. If necessary, add a little water, about 2–3 tablespoons. When vegetables are tender, sprinkle them with flour and parsley and cook for an additional 5 minutes, stirring occasionally. Add the olives just to heat them through. Serve hot or cold.

ZUCCHINI PURÉE

serves 6

6 medium zucchini	2 Tbls butter
2 cups water	4 Tbls breadcrumbs
1 tsp salt	3 Tbls butter
1 large onion, minced	

Wash zucchini but do not peel them. Cut in ½" slices and cook in salted water until tender. Drain well and mash them with a fork. In a skillet brown onion in 2 tablespoons butter. Add zucchini and cook, stirring until well blended. Put the mixture into a shallow baking dish. Sprinkle with breadcrumbs, dot with 3 tablespoons butter and brown under the broiler.

CORN CUSTARDS WITH FRIED TOMATOES

serves 6

1	cup corn kernels	2	cups light cream
4	beaten eggs	6	ripe tomatoes
1	Tbls onion, minced	3	Tbls butter
½	tsp salt		Salt and pepper to taste
	Dash of cayenne pepper	2	Tbls white wine

Preheat oven to 350°. Combine corn, beaten eggs, minced onion, salt, and cayenne pepper. Scald cream and add it slowly. Pour mixture into a well-buttered baking dish. Place dish into a shallow pan of hot water in a preheated 350° oven. Bake for 35 minutes or until custard is set.

While the custard is baking, slice off tops and bottoms of tomatoes. Then cut each tomato into two thick slices. Fry in butter for 4–5 minutes. Season with salt and pepper. When tomatoes are dark brown on both sides, place them on a heated platter. Add 2 tablespoons wine to the pan where the tomatoes were cooking. Simmer and stir until reduced to a glaze. The glaze should be thick, but easily spreadable. Pour the glaze over the tomatoes. Serve the tomatoes with corn custard.

Pelicans in the Danube delta

CREAMED BROCCOLI WITH CHEESE
serves 4–5

2   pounds fresh broccoli
2   Tbls butter
    Salt to taste

Wash and trim broccoli and slice into 1 inch lengths. Cook in rapidly boiling salted water until still crisp. About 4 minutes. Drain well. Butter a baking dish well and place the broccoli into the dish.

Sauce

6   Tbls oil
6   Tbls flour
3   cups hot milk
1   cup grated cheddar cheese

1   cup grated Parmesan cheese
    Salt and white pepper to taste
3   Tbls butter

In a sauce pan, beat oil, flour, and hot milk with a whip until very smooth. It should be the consistency of thick cream. Cook over a low fire until slightly thickened. Add cheddar cheese, ¾ cup Parmesan cheese, salt, and pepper. Mix well and pour over the broccoli. Sprinkle with the remaining Parmesan. Dot with butter. Bake in a 350 ° oven for about 15 minutes, or until golden brown.

EGGPLANT WITH CREAM
serves 5–6

2   medium eggplants, peeled
    Salt to taste
⅓   cup butter
½   pound mushrooms, sliced

⅓   cup beef broth
    Salt and pepper to taste
1   cup whipping cream
¼   cup chopped parsley

Slice eggplant into ¼-inch thick, 3-inch long sticks. Place eggplant sticks on paper towels, sprinkle liberally with salt, and cover them with another paper towel. Let stand for 30 minutes. Gently squeeze out the excess moisture. In a skillet, melt butter and simmer eggplant and mushrooms for 10 minutes. Add broth and simmer until eggplant is tender, about 15 minutes. Sprinkle with salt and pepper. Add cream and heat, but do not boil. Garnish with parsley before serving.

FISH ROULADE
serves 6

6	filets of sole	1	cup shredded crabmeat (use lump crabmeat or Alaskan king crab)
	Salt and pepper	½	cup fine bread crumbs
2	Tbls lemon juice	½	tsp salt
2	onions, finely chopped	¼	tsp pepper
3	Tbls butter or margarine	2	Tbls finely chopped parsley
10	medium mushrooms, finely chopped		

Sprinkle fish with salt, pepper, and lemon juice and set aside. Sauté onions in butter until just transparent. Do not brown. Add mushrooms and cook until tender. Add crabmeat, bread crumbs, salt, pepper, and parsley. Bring to a boil and set aside to cool slightly. Place about 2–3 tablespoons of crab mixture onto each sole filet, roll up each filet, and place seam side down into a well-buttered baking dish.

Sauce

4	Tbls butter or margarine	¼	tsp basil
3	Tbls flour	½	cup pale dry sherry
½	cup chicken broth	2	tsp prepared mustard
⅔	cup light cream	1	cup finely ground Swiss cheese
½	tsp salt	½	tsp paprika
½	tsp pepper		

In a saucepan, melt butter, add flour, and bring to a boil. Add broth and cream. Bring to a boil again. Add seasonings, sherry, and mustard. Fold in one-half of the Swiss cheese. Pour over the fish. Bake for 30–35 minutes in a 375° oven. Sprinkle with the remaining Swiss cheese and the paprika. Bake for another 10 minutes, or until the fish is tender and flakes easily with a fork.

TROUT ON A GRILL
serves 6

6	small trout, cleaned, but with heads and tails left on	½	tsp sage
½	cup melted butter		Salt and pepper to taste
½	tsp oregano	4	Tbls fresh lemon juice
½	tsp basil		Lemon slices to garnish

Wash the trout and pat dry. Mix melted butter with oregano, basil, and sage, and sprinkle with salt and pepper. Place a grill into a baking pan. Brush trout on all sides with herb butter and place onto the grill. Preheat the broiler for 5 minutes and place baking pan about 6 inches from the heat. Broil trout about 6–8 minutes on one side. Turn, brush with remaining butter, then broil for 6–8 minutes on the other side, or until the fish flakes easily. Pour lemon juice over the fish and serve garnished with lemon slices.

STUFFED BAKED YELLOWTAIL OR RED SNAPPER
serves 6

3–4	pounds yellowtail or red snapper (a whole, cleaned fish with the backbone removed)	¼	tsp white pepper
		½	tsp Italian seasoning
		2	Tbls melted butter
	Salt to taste	1	small pickle, sliced
⅓	cup lemon juice	⅓	cup bread crumbs
1	pound sole filet, cut into pieces	2	Tbls finely grated Parmesan cheese
2	egg whites	½	cup melted butter for basting
½	tsp salt		

Preheat oven to 350°. Use a whole fish, with head and tail intact. Have the butcher remove the insides and the backbone. Rub inside and out with a little salt and lemon juice.

Now, prepare stuffing: Put sole filet and all other ingredients except the 4 tablespoons of butter into a blender and purée until very smooth. Stuff the fish with the mixture. Place stuffed fish in a baking dish and bake at 350° for 45 minutes, or until the fish flakes easily when tested with a fork. Baste with melted butter.

RUMANIAN CHICKEN
serves 6

1	3-pound chicken, cut up		Salt and pepper to taste
	Salt and pepper to taste	1 ½	cups water
3	Tbls butter	1 ⅓	cups sour cream
3	Tbls flour	1	Tbls lemon juice
3	Tbls minced parsley	5	sprigs parsley
2	Tbls poppy seeds		

Clean chicken pieces and pat them dry with a paper towel.
Sprinkle with salt, and pepper. Sauté chicken pieces in butter in
a large skillet. When chicken is brown on all sides, remove it to
a platter and set aside. Stir flour into the skillet drippings, scraping
the sides and bottom. Add parsley, poppy seeds, salt, pepper, and
water and bring to a boil. Add chicken, cover, and simmer until
tender, about 50–60 minutes. Remove chicken to a heated platter.
In a bowl beat sour cream with the pan juices until the mixture
is smooth. Bring the mixture just to the boiling point. Remove
skillet from heat. Stir in lemon juice. Pour the sauce over the
chicken. Garnish with parsley.

Intricate woodcarving from Rumanian Danube region

CHICKEN WITH GARLIC SAUCE
serves 6

3 boned chicken breasts
   Salt and pepper to taste
1 cup flour

2 Tbls butter
2 Tbls oil

Remove skin from breasts. Cut each breast into 4 pieces. Flatten each piece with a mallet. Sprinkle with salt and pepper. Dip them into flour. In a skillet, heat butter and oil. Brown the chicken pieces on both sides, reduce heat, and cook until tender. Set aside.

Sauce

3 Tbls fresh chopped basil
   or 1 Tbl dry basil soaked in 2 Tbls
   white wine
4 cloves garlic

5 Tbls oil
4 Tbls tomato paste
⅛ tsp black pepper
   Salt to taste

In a bowl, combine fresh chopped basil or the dry basil soaked in wine and drained with garlic which has been pressed through a garlic press. Add oil, beating steadily with a whisk. Add tomato paste and black pepper. Beat the mixture until it is very smooth. Add a little salt to taste.

2 Tbls oil
½ pound small button mushrooms
   Pinch of salt

12 slices French bread
3   Tbls butter

In a skillet, heat oil and add mushrooms which have been washed and dried. Cook the mushrooms quickly, browning them slightly on both sides. Sprinkle with a pinch of salt and add the sauce. Simmer, stirring constantly, for 3 minutes.

Pour sauce over the chicken. Heat but do not boil. Sauté 12 thin slices of French bread in butter. Drain them on absorbent paper. Place chicken with the sauce onto a heated platter and surround it with the French bread.

DUCKLING JUBILEE
serves 6–8

1 **4–5 pound duck**	3 **carrots, sliced**
Salt and pepper to taste	3 **stalks celery, sliced**
½ **cup chopped parsley**	1 **onion, sliced**

Preheat oven to 450°. Clean duck. Sprinkle with salt and pepper. Place vegetables into the cavity of the duck. Secure the cavity with 2 small skewers. Bake for ½ hour: then prick the skin with a fork. Reduce heat to 350° and bake the duck until it is tender. Cut duck in half or in quarters and discard the vegetables.

Apricot Sauce

1 **16-ounce can sliced apricots (in heavy syrup)**	½ **tsp apricot flavoring or almond extract**
½ **cup sugar**	3–4 **Tbls brandy or apricot brandy**
½ **cup apricot preserves**	6 **ounces dried apricots**
1 **Tbls Dijon mustard**	1 **cup sugar**
1 **Tbls lemon juice**	⅔ **cup sweet sherry**
1 **grated lemon rind**	½ **cup water**
½ **cup orange juice**	1 **cup heavy cream**
1 **tsp grated orange peel**	½ **cup honey**
¼ **tsp each of nutmeg, allspice, ginger, coriander, finely ground white pepper**	4–5 **Tbls brandy or apricot brandy**

In a blender, combine canned apricots, sugar, and apricot preserves and blend until smooth. Pour into a saucepan and add mustard, lemon juice, lemon rind, orange juice, orange peel, seasonings, flavoring, and brandy. Bring to a boil and set aside. In another saucepan, combine dried apricots, sugar, sherry, and water. Simmer for 30–45 minutes, until very soft. Cool slightly, place into a blender, and add cream and honey. Blend until smooth. Add the mixture to the blended canned apricot mixture. Pour into a saucepan, stir well, and bring to the boiling point. Add brandy, stir, and keep warm until serving. Or, if you have prepared the sauce ahead, heat it before serving. If sauce thickens too much, add more sherry or cream before heating. Serve sauce with the duck.

CHICKEN GIVECH
serves 4–5

4 Tbls margarine or vegetable shortening	6 Tbls tomato paste Salt and pepper to taste
1 large mild onion, thinly sliced	¼ tsp oregano
2 washed cloves of garlic	¼ tsp basil
2 sweet red peppers, thinly sliced (green peppers may be used)	¼ tsp rosemary
4 celery stalks, sliced	½ cup dry white wine
1 chicken, cut into serving pieces	2 zucchini, thinly sliced
	½ pound sliced mushrooms

Melt margarine in a large pot and add onion, garlic, pepper, and celery. Cook, stirring frequently, for 5 minutes. Add chicken and stir well. Cook for 15 minutes. Add tomato paste, seasonings, and wine. Cook for 35–40 minutes. Add zucchini and cook for 5 minutes or until tender. Add mushrooms and cook 5 minutes longer, or until tender. Serve with rice.

Rumanian windmill tavern near Danube delta. Photo courtesy James McAnally, Graphic House, Inc., New York

ARNAUT HASH
serves 6

1	large onion, diced	2	cloves minced garlic
4	Tbls butter or margarine	½	tsp oregano
2	green peppers, diced	½	tsp marjoram
1	Tbls paprika	1	12-ounce jar or can of tomato sauce
1½	pounds ground beef	2	cups cooked kidney beans
	Salt and pepper to taste		

Sauté onion in butter or margarine with green peppers until just limp. Add paprika and meat. Cook, stirring constantly, until all red color disappears from the meat. Add seasonings, tomato sauce, and beans. Simmer for 5–7 minutes.
Serve with Pita bread or Italian bread.

LAMB MARINATED IN VINEGAR
serves 6

5	cups red wine	15	peppercorns
2½	cups vinegar		Salt to taste
3	medium onions, chopped	3	pounds boned leg of lamb
2	carrots, chopped		Salt to taste
2	stalks of celery, sliced	½	cup vegetable oil
3	Tbls mint leaves		

In a deep glass bowl, combine wine, vinegar, onions, carrots, celery, mint, peppercorns, and salt. Add meat to marinade. Be sure that the meat is completely covered by the marinade. Seal bowl with lid or foil and refrigerate for 24 to 36 hours. Remove meat and reserve 1½ cups of marinade. Pat meat dry and sprinkle it with salt. Heat oil in a large skillet and sauté meat. Add reserved marinade, cover the skillet, and simmer meat for 2 hours, or until tender.
Serve lamb with dumplings and the sauce from the skillet.

VEAL SCALOPPINE WITH MUSHROOM PURÉE
serves 6

2 pounds very thin veal cutlets	¼ cup sherry
Salt and pepper	½ cup chicken stock
1½ cups flour	16-ounce can imported sliced chan-
1 Tbls paprika	terelles or cepes (optional)
5 Tbls butter	

Cut veal cutlets into small pieces and pound very thin. Sprinkle with salt and pepper. Combine flour and paprika. Coat meat with flour and brown meat on both sides in a large skillet in butter. Add sherry and chicken stock to the veal. Cover and simmer for 10 minutes. Remove the meat to a warm platter. Open the can of chanterelles, drain, and add them to the pan. Heat thoroughly and spread over the meat. Pour the purée over the mushrooms and meat and serve immediately.

Purée (for béchamel sauce, see page 74)

3 Tbls butter	¼ tsp marjoram
3 Tbls flour	Pinch of nutmeg
2 cups light cream	Salt and finely ground white pepper
3 cups chopped raw mushrooms	to taste
2 Tbls dried mushroom powder	3 egg yolks
3 Tbls dry sherry	

In an enameled saucepan, melt butter, add flour, and cook for 2 minutes, stirring constantly. Add cream and cook, stirring constantly, until slightly thickened. In a blender, start blending raw mushrooms with the béchamel sauce. Blend about 1 cup of mushrooms and ½ cup of sauce at a time. Pour the mixture back into the saucepan. Add dried mushroom powder, dry sherry, marjoram, a pinch of nutmeg, and salt and finely ground white pepper to taste. Cook, stirring constantly, for 2–3 minutes. Remove from heat. Add egg yolks, beating well after each addition. Continue cooking on low heat, stirring constantly, for another 2–3 minutes. If the sauce thickens too much, add a little more cream and stir well. Heat, but do not boil. Pour over the veal and sliced mushrooms.

MEAT ON SKEWERS
serves 6

½	cup red wine	12–16	cherry tomatoes
	Juice of 1 lemon	12–16	chunks of green pepper
1	onion, chopped	12–16	chunks of onion
¼	cup olive oil	12–16	whole small mushroom caps
½	tsp salt	2	Tbls chopped fresh onion
⅛	tsp pepper		Parsley
½	tsp sage		
½	tsp rosemary		
3	pounds boneless lean lamb (leg or shoulder meat), cut in 2 inch cubes		

Combine red wine with the juice of 1 lemon. Mix with chopped onion, oil, salt, pepper, sage, and rosemary. Place the cubed lamb in a bowl and pour the marinade over lamb cubes. Stir gently to coat meat with the marinade. Cover and refrigerate for several hours or overnight. Drain the lamb cubes and string them on metal skewers, alternating with tomatoes, green peppers, mushrooms, and onions. Barbecue lamb and vegetables over hot coals, about 6–7 minutes on each side, turning once. Or grill them under a broiler in the oven. Arrange lamb and vegetables on a serving platter and sprinkle with 2 tablespoons of chopped fresh onion. Garnish with parsley. Serve with rice.

VITEL CU CIUPERCI
Veal with Mushrooms
serves 6

1¼	pounds mushrooms	2	tsp flour
3	Tbls butter		Salt and pepper to taste
2½	pounds veal, cut into 1–1½-inch cubes	⅓	cup beef broth
		⅔	cup sour cream
2	medium onions, chopped	¼	cup chopped parsley

Wipe mushrooms off with a damp cloth. Leave small ones whole. Cut large mushrooms in half. In a large skillet, melt butter and brown veal cubes and mushrooms. Add onions and cook for 10 minutes. Sprinkle with flour and salt and pepper, add broth, cover the skillet, and simmer for 45–50 minutes, or until the veal is tender. Add sour cream and bring to a boil. Garnish with parsley.

MITITEI
Barbecued Meat Fingers
serves 6

2 ½ pounds ground beef	Salt and pepper to taste
¼ pound ground suet	2 minced cloves garlic
½ tsp cayenne pepper or hot pepper flakes	⅛ tsp baking soda
	⅓ cup beef broth

In a blender or a food processor, combine meat with suet and grind until mixture is very fine in texture. Add seasonings and baking soda and mix thoroughly. With lightly greased hands, knead the meat mixture, adding bouillon slowly, until mixture adheres together. Take small pieces of the mixture and shape into 3-inch long, ½-inch wide fingers. Place them under a broiler, approximately 5 inches from the heat source, or use a charcoal grill. Brown for 7 minutes on each side.

Typical village house in Rumania (very similar to Hungary)

CHIFTELUTE DE CARNE CARTOFI
Ground Meat and Potatoes
serves 6

3 Tbls vegetable oil or shortening	1 Tbls minced parsley
2 medium onions, diced	8 raw potatoes, peeled and grated
¾ pound ground beef	Salt and pepper to taste
2 lightly beaten eggs	¾ cup vegetable oil
2 Tbls flour	

In a skillet, heat 3 tablespoons oil and sauté onion and meat until slightly browned. Set aside. In a bowl, thoroughly combine eggs, flour, parsley, and potatoes. Add the meat-onion mixture. Sprinkle with salt and pepper. Mix with your hands and form into golf-sized balls. Heat oil in a skillet and brown the meat balls on all sides. Serve with a green salad. To serve as a appetizer or as hors d'oeuvres, make very small balls and serve them on toothpicks.

. . . .*Side Dishes*

RICE, RUMANIAN STYLE
serves 7–8

½ cup olive oil	¼ tsp ground coriander
4 thin slices of ham, diced	½ tsp ground fennel
4 strips of bacon, diced	1 tsp salt
2 onions, chopped	½ cup tomato sauce
2 green peppers, chopped	1 package frozen peas
2 ½ cups rice	1 jar pimientoes, diced and heated
4 cups chicken broth, boiling	

In a large saucepan, heat oil and add ham, bacon, onions, and peppers. Cook, stirring occasionally, until onions are transparent and peppers are just tender. With a slotted spoon, remove vegetables and meat from the skillet onto another dish and set aside. Place rice into saucepan and sauté for 5 minutes. Add boiling broth, coriander, fennel seed, salt, and tomato sauce. Stir once or twice. Cover and cook for 20–25 minutes on a low heat until the liquid has been absorbed. Add peas and cook for another 5–7 minutes, until the peas are tender. Add ham, bacon, onions, peppers, and pimientoes. Toss together and serve.

NOODLES WITH GARLIC SAUCE
serves 6

1	**pound medium egg noddles**
5	**Tbls olive oil**
6	**mashed garlic cloves (less if desired)**
3	**Tbls minced parsley**

1   **tsp minced fresh basil (or ½ tsp dry basil)**
Coarsely ground black pepper

A few minutes before the noodles are cooked, heat oil with mashed garlic in a small saucepan over low heat. Do not allow the garlic to brown. When oil is hot add parsley and basil. Mix well. Take off heat. Drain noodles. Place into a heated serving dish; add garlic sauce and toss well. Sprinkle with black pepper and serve immediately.

Variation

Use 6 ripe tomatoes. Drop tomatoes into boiling water. Remove immediately and peel off the skin. Slice tomatoes in half and gently squeeze out the seeds. Chop tomatoes, place them into a skillet and cook, stirring frequently until purée-like—for about 10 minutes. Add salt to taste. Add oil and garlic mixture. Mix well and serve over noodles or any of your favorite pasta.

WHEAT AND CORNMEAL BREAD
makes 2 loaves

1 ½   **packages granulated yeast**
⅓   **cup lukewarm water**
1   **Tbls sugar**
2   **cups lukewarm water**

3   **Tbls melted shortening**
2   **tsp salt**
4 ½–5   **cups all purpose unbleached flour**
1   **cup yellow cornmeal**

Preheat oven to 350°. Butter well and sprinkle with cornmeal 2 9-inch cake pans. In a large bowl combine yeast, ⅓ cup lukewarm water and sugar. Let stand for 5 minutes. Add 2 cups water, shortening, salt, and 2 cups flour. Beat with a wooden spoon for 30 seconds. Mix remaining flour with cornmeal and add to the yeast mixture one cup at a time, beating well after each addition. Knead with your hands for 3–4 minutes or with a bread hook for 1–2 minutes. Turn the dough out onto a floured board and knead until smooth and elastic. If dough feels sticky, add additional flour, ½ cup at a time. Form into a ball. Place dough into a well-greased bowl, brush top of dough with additional shortening, cover bowl, and let dough rise in a warm place for about 1 ½ hours or until doubled in bulk. Punch down the dough and form into 2 round loaves. Place loaves into the cake pans. Cover and let rise again in a warm place for 1 hour. With a very sharp knife cut a cross on top of each loaf and sprinkle lightly with cornmeal. Bake in a preheated 350° oven for about 50–55 minutes or until well browned and the bottoms sound hollow when tapped. Cool in cake pans for 10 minutes, then on a cake rack.

Basket of Rumanian pottery

Desserts . . . .

SOUR CREAM CAKE
serves 8

4	egg yolks	½	tsp salt
4	Tbls melted unsalted butter	4	tsp baking powder
⅓	cup granulated sugar	4	egg whites
1	tsp vanilla extract	2	Tbls butter
2	Tbls chopped, blanched, roasted almonds	⅓–½	cup corn flake crumbs
2	Tbls raisins	2	cups sour cream
½	cup plus 1 Tbl unsifted all-purpose flour	1	cup chopped walnuts
		¾	cup maraschino cherries
		1	cup powdered sugar

Preheat oven to 375°. Beat egg yolks until thickened, add melted butter and sugar, and beat for at least 2 minutes with a whisk or electric beater. Add vanilla, almonds, raisins, flour, salt, and baking powder. Blend thoroughly. Beat egg whites until stiff and add them to the batter. Fold in the whites lightly but thoroughly. Grease well and dust with corn flake crumbs a 6" × 10" round mold with a fluted bottom. Or use an 8-inch round cake pan with a removable bottom and sides. Pour batter into the baking pan and bake in a 375° preheated oven for about 30 minutes. Allow to cool. In a bowl, mix together sour cream, walnuts, cherries, and powdered sugar. Do not beat. Blend quickly. With a sharp knife, slice through the center of the cake, cutting it in half. Using three-quarters of the filling, spread it over the bottom half. Place the other half over filling and then use the remaining filling to ice the top of the cake. Place cake in the refrigerator for 1 hour before serving or serve immediately.

The cake may be made ahead of time and frozen. Defrost before filling. The cake may be served without filling as a coffee cake. Sprinkle the cake with ½ cup powdered vanilla sugar (see recipe on page 37).

BOW TIES
serves about 18–22

2 eggs	1 Tbls rum or brandy
3 egg yolks	1 cup plus 2 Tbls sifted flour
2 Tbls sugar	Oil or vegetable shortening for frying
1 Tbls rich cream	Confectioners' sugar
½ tsp salt	

Beat eggs and egg yolks together until very light. Beat in sugar, cream, salt, and liquor. Stir in flour. This dough should be soft. Knead dough on a floured board until smooth. Cover dough and let it stand for 10 minutes. Roll the dough out until it is very thin, about ⅛ inch. Use a small amount of dough at a time and keep the rest covered, because it dries fast. Cut the rolled-out dough into long strips about 1 ½ inches wide, using a scalloped edge cutter, if you have one. Then cut each strip into 2 ½–3-inch pieces. Slit each piece in the center and pull one end through the slit to form a loose loop. Or just twist the strip in the center. Keep shaped dough covered until ready to fry. Fry the bows, a few at a time, in deep fat (375°F) until slightly browned. Drain them on paper towels. Sprinkle with confectioners' sugar.

HONEY CONFECTION
makes 16–18 squares

4 eggs	3 cups sifted flour
1 tsp salt	1 cup honey
1 Tbls cream	¾ cup sugar
1 Tbls vanilla	

Beat eggs well and add salt, cream, and vanilla. Add flour and knead dough until very smooth The dough should be very stiff. Cover and let stand for 20 minutes. Roll dough between your hands into long ropes about ¼-inch thick. Cut the ropes into small balls. Fry in deep fat (354° on a candy thermometer) until golden brown. Drain them on paper towels and place them in a bowl. Heat honey and sugar together, stirring constantly, until sugar is liquified and honey is clear. Pour honey over the balls and mix well. Pack balls firmly into a buttered pan and let them cool. Place the pan into hot water for a few minutes and then invert the pan. Cut the confection into bars or squares.

LEMON POUND CAKE
serves 8–10

½ pound sweet butter
2 cups granulated sugar
2 cups sifted all-purpose flour (measure before sifting)
2 Tbls brandy

1 Tbls grated lemon rind
3 Tbls lemon juice
6 large eggs
3 tsp baking powder

Preheat oven to 375°. Grease well and dust with flour a 8–9-inch fluted tube pan (Bundt pan). The butter and eggs should be at room temperature.

In a large bowl, cream butter until very fluffy, add sugar, and cream the ingredients together for at least 3 minutes. Add flour and blend well. Add brandy, lemon rind and lemon juice and blend well. Add eggs one at a time, beating well after each addition. Add baking powder and beat for 30 seconds with a wooden spoon. Bake in a preheated 375° oven for 35 minutes. Reduce heat to 350° and bake for an additional 15 minutes, or until a cake tester comes out clean. Cool in the pan for 15–20 minutes, loosen with a knife around the edges and center, and invert the cake onto a platter. Dust with powdered sugar and more grated lemon rind. If you wish, you may add ½ cup of chopped walnuts, ⅔ cup of seedless white raisins, or ½ cup of toasted, slivered, blanched almonds to the batter. You may also bake this cake in 2 loaf pans.

Lemon Glaze Frosting

In the top of a double boiler, combine 1 cup powdered sugar and the juice of one lemon. Cook over gently boiling water, stirring constantly, until the mixture has the consistency of thick cream— about 12 minutes. Spread the glaze immediately over the cake.

VEONA'S HONEY CHEESE
serves 6–8

1 pound softened cream cheese	¼ cup sour cream
½ cup soft, creamy cheddar cheese	3 drops Tabasco sauce
⅓ cup crumbled bleu cheese	Salt to taste
6 Tbls honey	¼ cup ruby port

Blend cream cheese, cheddar cheese, bleu cheese, and honey together. Beat the mixture with an electric hand beater until very smooth. Add sour cream, Tabasco sauce, salt, and ruby port and beat thoroughly again. Refrigerate for at least 2 hours. Serve in a glazed pottery dish or a crock, with crackers.

SMALL PANCAKES
makes about 16–18 pancakes

4 eggs	Pinch of salt
¼ cup milk	¾ cup sifted flour
¾ cup sour cream	4 Tbls honey

In a blender, beat eggs with milk, sour cream, and salt. Add flour and honey, Beat well, until very smooth. Set aside for 15 minutes. Bake in very well-greased 5-inch crêpe pans. Pour about 2–3 tablespoons of batter into the pans and tilt and turn to spread evenly. Brown pancakes on both sides. Stack, with wax paper between the pancakes, or spread side by side on a large platter.

Filling

3 apples, peeled and minced	½ cup sweet butter
6 Tbls sugar	½ cup honey
½ tsp cinnamon	

Preheat oven to 375°. In a bowl, mix peeled and minced apples with sugar and cinnamon. In a separate bowl, beat sweet butter together with honey. Set aside. Fill each pancake with 1–2 tablespoons of the apple mixture. Roll pancakes cigar fashion and place them into a buttered oven-proof dish. Spread 1 tablespoon of honey-butter over each pancake, sprinkle with cinnamon, and bake in a 375° preheated oven for 20 minutes. Serve immediately with additional honey-butter on the side.

APPLE MOUSSE
serves 6

⅔	cup currants	3	egg yolks
1	cup red port	¼	cup sugar
5	Delicious apples	1	tsp vanilla
1	cup water	⅛	tsp each of nutmeg and cinnamon
1	cup sugar	3	sprigs of grapes
	Pinch of salt	2	egg whites, lightly beaten
2	Tbls cornstarch	1	cup fine granulated sugar
½	cup red port		

Soak currants in 1 cup of red port for 1 hour. Drain. Peel, core, and quarter the apples. Place apples into a saucepan and add water, 1 cup of sugar, and salt. Cook until very, very, tender. Cool. Press the apples through a sieve or purée them in a blender. Pour apple purée into an enameled saucepan. In a small bowl, mix cornstarch with ½ cup of red port. Add to apples. Cook on low heat, stirring constantly, for about 10 minutes. Cool. Beat egg yolks with ¼ cup of sugar and vanilla until light in color and thick. Whisk yolks into the apple purée. Add nutmeg and cinnamon and continue beating until the mixture is very smooth. Fold in the currants. Spoon into serving dishes and decorate with frosted grapes. To frost, dip grapes into egg whites and roll in granulated sugar. Let dry on paper towels. Chill the mousse for 2–3 hours before serving.

CHAPTER

BULGARIA:
The Enigmatic Balkan Land

NEAR the small border town of Giurgiu, the Danube once again becomes a natural dividing line between two countries—Rumania and Bulgaria. Then 290 miles further east at Silistra, it lazily turns north to traverse Rumania on the last leg of its long journey.

Bulgaria, which stretches south and east from the Danube, is a colorful patchwork of wild mountains, green forests, cool waters, orchards, and some of the best vegetable-growing land in the world. The untamed Balkan mountain range curves away from the Danube to the Black Sea encircling the fertile lowlands of Moesia and Thrace. This enigmatic land is a treasure trove of legends, traditions, and customs—a marvelous blend of the ancient and the modern.

The banks of the Danube are dotted with small fishing villages and towns, where dripping fish nets hang loosely on the age-darkened fences. Small white-washed houses stand amidst colorful gardens, and each day during the warm months women and young girls climb down to the water's edge carrying reed baskets filled with laundry, which they carefully place in the shallow waters of the Danube. They rub the homespun garments and linens with handmade yellowish cakes of soap, and then pound the clothes vigorously on the rocks, as their ancestors have done since time immemorial. Later they hang the wet clothing on heavy ropes strung between trees, on fences, and on bushes to dry in the sun.

Every small village has an onion-domed chapel, some of which are so old that the wooden walls have been bleached by the ages. But on the inside the icons and wall paintings are still kept up, and their bright hues light up the interiors of the chapels.

Bulgaria has been a state since 681 A.D. when a proto-Bulgarian tribe, which migrated from Central Asia, united with Slavs who lived on the Balkan soil. They were ruled by Byzantium for several centuries, and then, like most of the Balkans, were swallowed up by the Ottoman Empire in the 14th century.

Today Bulgaria is a blend of Slav, Greek, and Russian lifestyles and culture, strongly accented by Turkish influence. It has retained the soulful part-Ottoman, part-Western character and a bond with their Eastern Orthodox persuasion. It has some of the oldest and most beautiful Eastern Orthodox churches and monasteries outside of Russia. All over the country, the golden, onion-shaped domes of the churches and monasteries are etched against the blue sky. Inside these are treasure troves of mosaics, wall frescoes, and icons, which seem to glow in the defused candlelight.

Their alphabet is still cyrillic, and their songs, music, dances and legends are reminiscent of old Russia. Their rulers were called *Voevodas* or *Boyars*, and their kings, *Tsars*. It is a country which has been living in the past. The present has been dormant for a long time and is just starting to awaken and reach for the new world.

The capital city of Sofia is verdant with sprawling trees and wide avenues which are liberally dotted with colorful fruit and vegetable stands that create colorful mosaics against the background of gray, somewhat neglected, buildings.

There are a few restaurants in the city which are quite good, featuring an array of interesting Bulgarian dishes. The vegetable dishes are about the tastiest, because for centuries the Bulgarians were regarded as great horticulturists; they grew some of the best vegetables in Europe.

Bulgaria is the undisputed center of yogurt production and yogurt here is served and eaten as a side dish with practically every meal. Yogurt and *kaimak* (the baked sour milk) are sold in huge wooden tubs along with the ewe cheese which is supposed to be the finest in the Balkans.

The longevity of the Bulgarians is legendary, and they claim that it is not accident that there are so many centenarians living in the country. The heritage of generations of strong, healthy

Beautiful Bulgarian artwork, the Tetraevangelia, showing Ivan Alexander and family

people, an active life among high mountain peaks, a semi-vegetarian diet, and the abundance of yogurt seems to be a contributing factor to the vitality and longevity of the people.

Bulgaria is also a land of artists, poets, and craftsmen. In villages and small towns, artisans labor over intricate silver and gold filigree pieces of jewelry, goblets, and ornaments in medieval settings. Talented hands create beautiful wood carvings, unusual pottery, and colorful fabrics and embroideries.

But there is nothing in the world that can match the beauty of the Valley of Roses. Here nature has created a magic world of brilliant hues and fragrance. This enchanting valley is encircled by forbidding, snow-capped mountains which shield the rose fields from the harsh northern winters.

In spring and summer the entire valley is ablaze with a myriad of roses. Dark-eyed, lithe girls in lovely native costumes gently pick the flowers and place them into baskets to be taken to processing plants where rose attar, the precious essence, is extracted from the delicate petals.

Like the art and architecture of the country, Bulgarian cuisine also reflects many different influences. There are hamlets where the fare is vegetarian and dairy. In other parts the gastronomy is still Turkish or Greek and some dishes are still prepared in the Russian or central Asian way. Others are a pleasant mixture of all the influences or resemble the cooking of Yugoslavia and Rumania. The Bulgarian women set the pace of the native cookery. They have molded and shaped the Bulgarian diet which evolved after the end of the Turkish occupation.

Bulgarian cooking is seasonal, using available ingredients to their full potential. There are many stews and hearty soups using all parts of lambs or poultry and much grilled meats, vegetables, and cheese pastries. The desserts consist mainly of sweetmeats in rich sugar or honey syrup, puddings, and compotes made of dried fruit.

Like all the people who live along or near the Danube, the Bulgarians have a long-standing love affair with the river, which gives them fertile lands, nourishment, and an aquatic highway.

SHOPSKA SALATA
Salad Appetizer
serves 6

4 green bell peppers	½ tsp salt
4 ripe tomatoes, diced	¼ tsp pepper
2 cucumbers, diced	½ cup olive oil
1 large onion sliced into paper-thin circles	4 Tbls minced parsley
	1 cup grated Feta cheese
¼ cup wine vinegar	6 small hot peppers (chili or jalapeno)

Roast peppers in a baking pan in a 400° oven for about 6–8 minutes, or until the skins start turning brown. Peel off the skin. Seed the pepper and dice. Place into a bowl. Add diced tomatoes and cucumbers. Place onion slices between 2 sheets of wax paper and hit with a mallet slightly to mash the onion. Add to the other vegetables. In a small bowl mix together vinegar, salt, pepper, and olive oil. Pour dressing over vegetables and toss lightly. Chill for 1 hour. Add more salt, pepper, or vinegar to taste.
Place onto 6 chilled salad plates. Sprinkle with parsley and with grated Feta cheese. Stick a hot pepper in the center of each salad.

KASKAVAL PANE
Fried Cheese
serves 5–6

1 lb Kaskaval (Caciocavallo cheese) or Provolone	3 eggs well beaten with 2 Tbls water
	1 cup flavored breadcrumbs
½ cup light cream	1–2 cups vegetable oil for frying
1 cup flour	

Use Kaskaval or Provolone cheese. Slice into 1½" squares, ½" thick. Brush thoroughly with breadcrumbs. Heat oil in a skillet until a haze appears. Fry the cheese until golden brown on both sides. Serve immediately.

FISH ROE PASTE

2 fresh carp roe (or roe of any other fresh-water fish)
½ cup milk
4 Tbls lemon juice
1 small onion, minced

3 Tbls water
1 tsp paprika
   Salt and pepper to taste
3–4 Tbls olive oil

Place fish roe into milk. Soak for 10–15 minutes. Remove roe and peel off the skin. Discard milk. Place roe, lemon juice, onion, water, and paprika in a blender and blend for 3–4 seconds. Add salt and pepper to taste. Keeping the blender on lowest speed, add oil, one teaspoon at a time, blending for 2–3 seconds after each addition. You should have a thick paste. Add more salt and pepper to taste, and if you wish a tarter taste, more lemon juice.

Soups . . . .

BULGARIAN LAMB SOUP
serves 6–7

8 cups water
1 Tbls salt
1 pound lean lamb, cut into ½-inch cubes
4 medium tomatoes, finely chopped
3 green peppers, finely chopped
2 large onions, finely chopped

3 Tbls butter
2 Tbls flour
3 Tbls yogurt
3 Tbls lemon juice
1 tsp grated lemon rind
2 Tbls dill, minced

In a large soup pot bring water with salt to a boil; add lamb cubes and simmer for 35 minutes. Skim off the foam. Add tomatoes, peppers, and onions. In a small saucepan melt butter; add flour and, stirring constantly, cook until it is golden brown. Add 2 cups of soup to butter mixture, beating steadily, and pour into the soup. Stir, and simmer for about 10 minutes. Beat yogurt, lemon juice, rind, and dill together until smooth. Add this to the soup. Heat, but do not boil. Add more salt if needed. Serve immediately, sprinkled with additional dill if desired.

SOUR LAMB SOUP
serves 6

1	pound lean lamb, cut into 1″ cubes	¼	cup long grain rice
3	Tbls oil		Salt to taste
1	large onion, diced	½	cup water
2	tsp paprika	2	Tbls flour
8	cups water	2	eggs
3	sprigs parsley, 4 scallions, 4 sprigs dill, tied together with a string	2–3	Tbls or more vinegar or lemon juice to taste
3	stalks celery, sliced thin	3	Tbls minced parsley
2	carrots, peeled and sliced thin		

In a soup pot brown lamb cubes in hot oil for about 5–6 minutes. Add onion and continue cooking, stirring often, until onion turns golden. Add paprika, stir well, and add water. Cook for 10 minutes. Then add the tied-up greens, celery, carrots, rice and salt. Cook uncovered over low heat, until the meat is very tender, for about 30–40 minutes. Beat water and flour together until smooth, add 1 cup of hot soup and mix well. Add to the soup. Bring to a boil and simmer for a few minutes, stirring occasionally. Beat eggs and add to the hot soup, stirring well. Add vinegar or lemon juice to taste. Do not boil any further. Serve sprinkled generously with parsley.

VEGETABLE AND CHEESE SOUP
serves 6–7

3	medium potatoes, peeled and diced	2	Tbls flour
2	carrots, peeled and diced	1	cup milk
8	cups water		Salt and pepper to taste
1	pound string beans, sliced	1	cup yogurt
2	cups shredded cabbage	1½	cups grated Swiss or Fontina cheese
2	green peppers, diced	4	Tbls chopped parsley
4	Tbls olive oil (or you may use butter or margarine)		

Place potatoes and carrots into a large soup pot. Add water and cook for 10 minutes. Add string beans, cabbage, and pepper. Cook for about 10–15 minutes or until the vegetables are tender. In a saucepan heat oil or butter, and add flour, stirring continuously until the flour is golden brown. In a bowl mix milk with 1 cup of hot soup. Add to the flour and oil mixture, beating steadily. Cook on low heat, stirring continuously, until mixture thickens. Add to the soup. Add salt and pepper to taste. Cook for a few minutes until slightly thickened. In the same bowl beat yogurt and 2 cups of soup with a whisk until smooth. Add to the soup and stir. Heat, but do not boil. Serve sprinkled with cheese and parsley.

Square in Sophya

POTATO SALAD
serves 6

7 medium boiled potatoes, peeled and thinly sliced	Salt and pepper to taste
5 Tbls wine vinegar	2 large onions, sliced into thin strips
1 tsp dry mustard	1 tsp salt
5 Tbls olive oil	2 bell peppers, sliced into very thin strips
3 Tbls lemon juice	
3 Tbls parsley, minced	18–20 black pitted olives or black "Greek" olives
3 Tbls scallions, minced	
2 Tbls dill, minced	

Place warm sliced potatoes into a bowl. Mix vinegar and mustard until well blended and pour over the potatoes. Cover and set aside. In a small bowl, whisk together olive oil, lemon juice, parsley, scallions, dill, salt, and pepper. Pour over the potatoes. Toss and set aside. Place sliced onions in a napkin, sprinkle with salt, and crush with a mallet or a rolling pin. Hold the napkin with the onion inside under cold running water. Then squeeze dry and add to the potatoes. Add green peppers. Toss well. Serve decorated with black olives.

WILTED SPINACH SALAD
serves 6

2½ lbs fresh spinach leaves	3 hard boiled eggs, coarsely chopped
6 cups water	12 pitted black olives, coarsely chopped
2 tsp salt	Salt and pepper to taste
½ cup olive oil	
4 Tbls lemon juice	

Remove stems from spinach leaves and wash the leaves thoroughly. Bring water and salt to a boil. Drop in the spinach leaves. Bring to a boil again. Drain immediately and place into a large bowl with ice water. Leave in ice water for 5 minutes. Drain the leaves in a colander. Then wrap into a kitchen towel and refrigerate. Mix olive oil and lemon juice. Place spinach into a salad bowl and pour oil mixture over the spinach. Add chopped eggs. Toss lightly. Add salt and pepper and garnish with chopped olives.

ZUCCHINI SALAD
serves 6

6 medium zucchini	4 Tbls lemon juice
2 Tbls minced parsley	⅓ cup olive oil
2 Tbls minced dill	3 cloves garlic
½ tsp tarragon	2 cups water
Salt to taste	2 Tbls chopped scallions ⎫
⅛ tsp red pepper flakes or more to taste	Lemon juice to taste ⎬ garnish
2 bay leaves	Thin lemon slices ⎭

Trim and wash the zucchini. Slice into ¼" slices. Place zucchini and all other ingredients into a saucepan. Bring to a boil, reduce heat and simmer for 5–6 minutes. Cool in the cooking liquid and adjust seasoning by adding more salt and pepper. Chill and serve with some of the liquid and garnished with scallions, lemon juice, and lemon slices.

Vegetables . . . .

MUSHROOMS WITH RIPE OLIVES
serves 6

1 pound mushrooms, sliced	2 Tbls white wine
2 cloves garlic, mashed	Juice of 1 lemon
¼ cup olive oil	3 Tbls parsley, chopped
1 cup pitted, sliced black olives	2 Tbls scallions, minced
½ cup tomato purée	

Wash, dry, and slice mushrooms and cook with garlic in ¼ cup olive oil for 2–3 minutes. Add olives, tomato purée, and wine. When heated through, add lemon juice, chopped parsley, and scallions.

EGGPLANT CASSEROLE
serves 6

3 medium eggplants, sliced into ¾-inch slices	Salt and pepper to taste
2 Tbls salt	½ tsp oregano
2 cups olive oil	2 cups Ricotta cheese (low fat)
4 garlic cloves, mashed	6 large thinly sliced tomatoes
	⅓ cup grated Parmesan cheese

Wash eggplants and slice. Sprinkle eggplant slices with salt and let stand for 15 minutes. Blot with paper towels. Fry eggplant slices in oil until golden brown on both sides; blot on paper towels. Place a layer of eggplants in the bottom of a baking pan. Sprinkle with mashed garlic, salt, pepper, and oregano. Spread half of Ricotta cheese over the eggplant. Place a layer of tomato slices over the cheese. Sprinkle with salt, pepper and oregano. Then add another layer of eggplant, cheese, and tomatoes. Sprinkle each layer with seasonings. Top with grated Parmesan cheese and bake in a 350° oven for 45–50 minutes. Serve immediately.

SPINACH ZAGORA STYLE
serves 6

2 Tbls butter	1 cup walnuts, coarsely chopped
3 10-ounce pkgs frozen chopped spinach, thawed and very well drained	3 Tbls freshly grated Parmesan cheese
2 cloves garlic, minced	1 Tbls onion, minced
1½ cups sour cream	Salt and pepper to taste

Preheat oven to 350°. Butter a 1½-quart baking dish. Combine all ingredients in a bowl. Mix well. Pour into the baking dish and bake for 30 minutes. Serve immediately.

THREADED MUSHROOMS
serves 6

36 medium mushroom caps	1 Tbls fresh basil, minced (or 1 tsp dry
Salt to taste	basil)
3 Tbls lemon juice	¼ tsp black pepper
1 cup olive oil	½ cup brandy
3 cloves garlic, minced	

Wipe mushroom caps clean with a damp cloth. Thread 6 mushrooms onto a skewer leaving about ¼" space between them. Sprinkle with salt and lemon juice. In a bowl mix oil, garlic, basil, and black pepper and beat with a whisk. Brush mushrooms generously with oil all over. Put a grill into a baking pan and place mushrooms on the grill.

Broil about 6" away from heat for 12 minutes, turning often. Baste once with oil.

Place mushrooms onto a serving platter. Heat brandy in a ladle or a small pot until just lukewarm, ignite, and pour over the mushrooms.

Bulgarian youngsters in national costumes

BRAISED LEEK WITH RICE
serves 6

5 Tbls butter	1 ½ cups chicken broth
1 large onion, diced	1 tsp paprika
6 whole leeks, cut into 1" slices, washed well and drained	Salt and pepper to taste
½ cup long grain rice	3 Tbls dill, minced

In a skillet heat butter, add onion, and sauté until just transparent. Add the leeks and cook until barely tender. Add rice and cook with onions and leeks, stirring gently for 5–6 minutes. Add chicken broth, paprika, salt, and pepper. Bring to a boil, reduce heat, cover, and simmer for about 20 minutes or until rice is tender and broth has cooked down. Sprinkle with dill and serve.

LAYERED GREEN BEANS
serves 6

2 pounds green beans, cleaned but left whole	¼ cup water
2 large onions, sliced into thin strips	½ cup milk
2 bell peppers, minced	½ cup yogurt
4 cloves garlic, mashed	3 Tbls dill
1 cup coarsely chopped walnuts	2 tomatoes, sliced thin
Salt and pepper to taste	2 Tbls oil
¼ cup oil	Salt to taste

Place half the beans in a thin layer into a well-greased baking dish. In a bowl toss together onions, peppers, garlic, walnuts, and salt and pepper to taste. Place half the vegetable mixture over beans. Spread another layer of beans over the vegetables and then another layer of vegetable mixture. In a bowl beat together oil, water, milk, yogurt, and dill. Pour over beans and vegetables. Spread tomatoes over vegetables. Sprinkle with 2 tablespoons of oil and salt. Bake in a 350° oven for 35 minutes.

Fish . . . .

SHRIMP SOPHYA
serves 6

2	quarts water	1	tsp dry mustard
½	tsp thyme	¼	tsp black pepper
½	tsp basil	2	Tbls capers
42–48	large shrimp, shelled and deveined	2	cups mayonnaise
3	hard-cooked egg yolks	1	large onion, sliced into very thin circles
3	Tbls white wine vinegar	½	cup whipped cream
2	Tbls sugar or more to taste	½	cup sour cream, whisked smooth

In a large pot, bring water to a boil; add thyme and basil. Drop the shrimp in the pot. Bring to a boil again; reduce heat and simmer for 5 minutes or until shrimp are pink. Drain and cool completely. Press egg yolks through a sieve into a large bowl. Add vinegar, sugar, mustard, and pepper. Blend well. Add capers, mayonnaise, onion, and shrimp. Blend well again. Fold in whipped cream and sour cream. Taste for seasoning. The taste should be sweet and sour, and you may wish to add more pepper and a pinch of salt.

ROLLED FLOUNDER FILETS
serves 6

5	Tbls olive oil	4–5	Tbls flour
12	thin flounder filets	1	tsp paprika
	Salt and pepper to taste	2	cups prepared tomato sauce
12	bay leaves	½	cup parsley, minced

Oil a baking dish well with 3 tablespoons oil. Sprinkle filets with salt and pepper. Place a bay leaf on each filet and roll up filets around the bay leaves. Mix flour and paprika. Sprinkle the filets with flour. Place filets into the baking dish and pour tomato sauce over them. Sprinkle with the remaining oil and bake in a 350° oven for 35 minutes. Serve immediately, sprinkled with parsley.

FISH KEBABS
serves 6

3 pounds halibut or scrod	3 green peppers
1 tsp paprika	2 large onions
4 Tbls lemon juice	⅓ cup olive oil
3 Tbls olive oil	Juice of 1 lemon
Salt and pepper to taste	Salt and pepper to taste
8 bay leaves	½ cup minced parsley
4 tomatoes	

Preheat the broiler or have coals ready in a barbecue unit. Cut fish into 1 ½" cubes. Place into a shallow dish. In a bowl combine paprika, lemon juice, oil, salt, pepper, and crumpled bay leaves. Pour mixture over the fish and turn the cubes several times. Refrigerate for 2–3 hours. Cut tomatoes, pepper, and onions into 1 ½" slices. Thread fish, alternating it with the vegetables, onto 6 skewers. Place onto a grill in a baking pan and broil 4–5" away from the flames for about 5 minutes on each side. Turn once, or grill over coals on a barbecue unit.

While fish is broiling, in a bowl beat together oil, lemon juice, salt, and pepper with a whisk or electric beater until smooth and thickened. Add parsley. Serve sauce with the fish.

BAKED FISH WITH VEGETABLES
serves 6–8

¼ cup vegetable oil	½ cup parsley, chopped
3 onions, sliced into ½" slices	*6 fish filets, cut into 2" pieces
3 bell peppers, sliced into ½" slices	Salt and pepper to taste
3 tomatoes, diced	2–3 Tbls oil
Salt and pepper to taste	

In a skillet heat oil and add onions and peppers. Cook until just tender. Add tomatoes, salt and pepper, and parsley. Stir gently and cook for 5 minutes. Sprinkle fish with salt and pepper. Add to vegetables. Stir. Oil a large piece of double foil well. Place vegetables and fish mixture into the foil. Seal well, place foil package onto a cookie sheet, and bake in a 375° oven for 25 minutes.

*Use scrod, red snapper, white fish filets, or any other fish you like.

FISH AND SAUERKRAUT

serves 6

1	onion, diced	*6	fish filets cut into 2–3″ pieces
½	cup bacon drippings		Salt to taste
2½	lbs fresh sauerkraut	1	tsp paprika
1	apple, peeled and diced		

Grease a baking dish well. Set aside. In a skillet sauté onion in bacon drippings until golden brown. Drain sauerkraut, reserve some of the drained liquid, and wash in cold water if a milder taste is desired. Toss with the browned onions and the apple. Add ½ cup of reserved liquid or water. Sprinkle fish filets with salt and paprika and add to the sauerkraut. Toss gently together. Place all the ingredients into the baking dish. Cover and bake in 375° oven for 30 minutes. Serve immediately.

*Use scrod, white fish, snapper, or any other fish filets.

Strong Eastern influences in these costumes is seen in headgear and embroidery

CHICKEN, VARNA STYLE
serves 7–8

2 frying chickens, cut up into serving pieces	3 Tbls butter
Salt and pepper to taste	3 Tbls vegetable oil
¼ tsp thyme	4 cloves of garlic, crushed
	2 onions, finely chopped

Sauce

1 6-ounce can tomato paste	1–2 Tbls sugar or more to taste
½ cup dry sherry	1 tsp prepared mild mustard
Salt and pepper to taste	1 cup whole canned tomatoes well-drained and chopped
⅛ tsp basil	½ pound fresh mushrooms, sliced
⅛ tsp thyme	
1–2 Tbls wine vinegar or more to taste	

Sprinkle the chicken with salt, pepper, and thyme. In a large skillet heat butter, oil, and chicken and cook until the chicken is golden brown on both sides. Add crushed garlic and cook for 2–3 minutes longer. Remove chicken from the skillet and place into a buttered baking pan.

In the same skillet where chicken was cooking sauté the onions until just golden brown; set aside.

Sauce

In a bowl blend tomato paste, sherry, seasonings, vinegar, sugar, and mustard well. Taste for seasoning; add more salt, sugar, or vinegar if desired. Add this to the onions in the skillet and simmer for 3–4 minutes, stirring constantly. Add chopped tomatoes and cook, stirring frequently, until a smooth paste is formed. Add sliced mushrooms and spread over chicken. Cover baking dish with foil and bake in a 350° oven for 45 minutes to 1 hour. Serve sprinkled with parsley in a ring of white rice.

DUCK WITH VEGETABLES
serves 4–6

2 ducks, cut into serving pieces	Salt to taste
⅓ cup shortening or lard	6 ripe tomatoes, diced
Salt and pepper to taste	½ cup red wine
3 large onions, diced	½ cup chicken broth
1 Tbls paprika	2 Tbls scallions, minced
1 Tbls flour	2 Tbls parsley, minced
5 Italian (pale green) peppers diced	

Defrost ducks in refrigerator (if frozen) and cut into serving pieces. In a large skillet heat shortening or lard. Fry duck in fat, turning often until crisp on all sides. Remove ducks from skillet and set aside. Sprinkle with salt and pepper. In the same skillet cook onions until pale golden. Add paprika and flour and stir well. Add peppers and cook for 5 minutes, stirring well. Sprinkle with salt. Place duck pieces into the skillet with onions and peppers. Add diced tomatoes, wine, and chicken broth. Cover and simmer for 20–25 minutes or until duck is very tender. Adjust seasoning. Serve sprinkled with scallions and parsley.

BAKED CAPON WITH BEANS
serves 5–6

1 10-ounce package red kidney beans	¼ tsp sage
	¼ tsp rosemary
1 capon, cut into serving pieces	Pinch of nutmeg
Salt and pepper to taste	1 cup sour cream
12–16 slices bacon	1 Tbls paprika
3 large onions, cut into thin circles	Pinch each of black pepper, sage, rosemary
1 cup dry sherry	
½ tsp salt	¼ tsp salt
¼ tsp black pepper	

Cook beans as directed on the package the day before and reserve. Preheat oven to 350°. Have the butcher cut the capon into serving pieces. Cut off as much fat as possible. Wash the pieces and pat dry. Sprinkle the pieces with salt and pepper and set aside. Line a large baking dish with the bacon slices.

Cut onions into very thin circles and place half the onions over the bacon. Spread beans over onions, then remaining onions over beans. Mix sherry with ½ teaspoon salt, ¼ teaspoon black pepper, sage, rosemary, and nutmeg. Pour the mixture over onions and beans.

Mix sour cream with paprika, black pepper, sage, rosemary, and ¼ teaspoon salt. Coat the capon pieces with the sour cream mixture and place with the skin side up on top of the onion layer. Cover baking pan with foil. Bake in a 350° oven for 1½ hours. Uncover and bake for ½ hour or until the capon pieces are brown. If the beans look a little dry while baking, pour a little water over the beans, about 2–3 tablespoons at a time. Turn the capon pieces and bake until browned on the underside. Turn again skin side up and bake for an additional 10–15 minutes until skin is crisp again.

POTTED CHICKEN
serves 6

2	broiling chickens, cut into serving pieces	1	cup hot chicken broth
6	medium tomatoes, chopped fine	2	bay leaves
3	cloves garlic, mashed		Salt to taste
2	large onions, diced	2	tsp paprika
½	cup bacon drippings	12	peppercorns
		½	cup parsley, finely chopped

Place chicken, tomatoes, and garlic into a pot. Cover and cook over low heat for 15 minutes, stirring often. Add onions, bacon drippings, chicken broth, bay leaves, salt, paprika, and peppercorns. Stir well. Cover tightly and cook over low heat, stirring occasionally until the chicken is very tender, for about 1 hour. Add parsley and more salt if needed. Cook for 5 minutes longer.

STUFFED ZUCCHINI
serves 4–5

8	zucchini (squash), as large as possible	2	tsp salt
2–3	quarts water	4	Tbls lemon juice

Wash zucchini and cut crosswise. With a grapefruit knife or melon baller, scoop out the inside. Do not break the vegetable while taking out the inside. In a large kettle, bring water to boil; add salt and lemon. Drop zucchini in the water. Blanch for 2–3 minutes. Remove from water and cool.

Stuffing

2	cups cooked lamb, finely chopped or ground	2	Tbls sauteed onion, minced
1	cup cooked rice	1	Tbls parsley, minced
3	Tbls melted butter	2	eggs
½	cup breadcrumbs	*2	cups béchamel sauce with salt, pepper and nutmeg added
½	cup milk	1	cup tomato sauce, plain
¼	tsp pepper	1	cup crumbled Feta cheese
½	tsp salt		

Combine meat with rice, butter, breadcrumbs, milk, pepper, salt, onion, parsley, and eggs. Blend until smooth. Stuff the zucchini with the mixture. Place in a baking dish side by side. Pour the béchamel sauce over the zucchini, then tomato sauce over the béchamel. Bake in a preheated oven for 25 minutes at 350°. Just before serving, sprinkle with Feta cheese.

*Béchamel (Basic White Sauce)

2 Tbls butter
2 Tbls unbleached flour
2 cups light cream
  Salt and pepper to taste

Melt butter and add the flour, stirring constantly with a wooden spoon. When butter and flour bubble up, add cream, stirring constantly. Bring to a boil, again stirring constantly. Cook for about 3 minutes on low heat until sauce thickens. Add salt and pepper.

LAMB IN PASTRY
serves 6

1 leg of lamb, about 3–4 lbs, boned	1½ tsp salt
2 cloves garlic, mashed	4 Tbls lemon juice
3 Tbls butter, softened	1 egg, plus 2 Tbls milk, beaten
½ tsp thyme	together
½ tsp oregano	1 recipe for Pastry (below)
½ tsp basil	

Have the butcher bone the leg of lamb and tie it for roasting. Make 20–25 small incisions in the lamb. Mix together garlic, butter, thyme, oregano, and basil. Refrigerate until hardened. Place a small piece of very hard butter into each incisions. Place in a roasting pan. Rub with salt and lemon juice and roast in a 375° oven for 45–55 minutes or longer to desired doneness. Cool completely.
Roll out the pastry to about ½-inch thick. Envelop the leg of lamb in the paste and seal well. Make fancy cut outs with cookie cutters. Brush with egg and decorate the leg of lamb with them. Brush again with egg and milk. Bake in 350° oven until the pastry is golden brown.

Pastry

4 cups sifted all-purpose flour
1 pound unsalted butter
½–¾ cup ice water

Place flour and unsalted butter on a cutting board. Butter must be very cold, but not frozen. Do not handle; just chop. When it resembles a coarse meal, add ice water a little at a time. Continue chopping until the dough starts sticking together. Press gently into a ball, then flatten, fold over and chop a few times. Repeat this twice more. Form into a ball. Wrap into wax paper and refrigerate for at least 4 hours.

ROLLED STEAK
serves 6

6 3 × 6-inch very thin-sliced beef	Salt and pepper to taste
⅓ cup oil	1 beaten egg
3 Tbls peppercorns	3 Tbls oil
3 Tbls whole coriander	1 cup dry red wine
1 large onion, sliced	1 cup tomato sauce
⅔ cup dry red wine	

Have the butcher cut the beef slices. Pound meat with a mallet until paper-thin. Brush meat generously with oil on both sides. Place onto foil side by side. Sprinkle generously with peppercorns and whole coriander, and hit with the mallet again once or twice to push peppercorns and coriander into the meat. Spread onion over meat. Pour ⅔ cup dry red wine over meat; seal in foil, and refrigerate for 36 hours. Remove from foil and discard onion, peppercorn, and coriander. Sprinkle with salt and pepper to taste. Place about 1–2 tablespoons of filling on the edge of each strip of meat, roll up tightly, and secure with a toothpick. Dip the open ends into beaten egg and sauté the rollades in oil until browned on all sides. Pour 1 cup red wine over the meat and simmer for ½ hour. Add tomato sauce and simmer for 15–20 minutes or until the meat is very tender.

Filling

⅔ cup ham, minced	½ cup green pepper, minced
½ cup breadcrumbs	⅓ cup red wine
3 scallions, minced	⅛ tsp allspice
½ cup parsley, minced	Salt and pepper to taste
1 egg	

Combine all ingredients in a bowl and blend thoroughly.

LAMB WITH CARROTS
serves 6

2 pounds cubed shoulder of lamb	1¾ cups water or more as needed
Salt and pepper to taste	2 garlic cloves, mashed
1 large onion, thinly sliced	2½ Tbls flour
½ cup butter	6–8 sliced carrots

Salt meat to taste and sprinkle with pepper. Sauté onion in butter in a large skillet. Add meat cubes and brown. Pour in ¾ cup of water, add garlic, cover and simmer for 2 hours or until meat is tender. Add water as needed. Remove meat cubes and place them in a dish. Add flour to the pan drippings and stir until brown. Add 1 cup water, bring to a boil. Add carrots and simmer for 15 to 20 minutes or until carrots are tender.

Another part of the Tetraevangelia (see page 275)

LAMB MEATBALLS WITH CHEESE
serves 6

1 ½ lbs ground lamb (beef may be substituted)
1   cup grated Kaskaval or Provolone cheese

Salt and pepper to taste
1   egg
½   cup cold water
4   Tbls oil

In a bowl combine all the ingredients except the 4 tablespoons oil. Mix and knead until very well blended and smooth. Refrigerate for 2 hours. With damp hands roll into golfball sizes and then flatten them to 1″ thickness. In a large skillet heat the oil and brown the meatballs on both sides. Reduce heat, cover pan, .and cook until cooked through and cheese is melted.

MOUNTAINIERS KEBAB
serves 6

1 ½ pounds lamb, coarsely ground or chopped
2   large onions, finely chopped
2   tsp fresh mint, chopped (or 1 tsp crumbled dry mint)
2   cloves garlic, mashed

1   cup white wine
2   Tbls tomato paste
    Salt and pepper to taste
4   Tbls butter
¼   cup parsley, minced

Have the butcher grind the lamb through a large blade. Or chop with a cleaver into tiny cubes. Place meat into a bowl. Add onions, mint, garlic, and wine mixed with tomato paste. Cover and let stand at room temperature for 2 hours. Add salt and pepper. Melt butter in a skillet and add meat with the marinade. Cover and cook slowly, stirring occasionally until meat is tender and the mixture has thickened. Add more salt and pepper if needed. Serve with minced parsley, and if desired, a bowl of yogurt on the side.

CABBAGE AND PORK
serves 6

½ cup bacon drippings
1 ½ lbs lean pork, cut into 1" cubes
1 large white cabbage, cored and chopped
  Salt and pepper to taste
3 cloves garlic, mashed

½–1 small chili or jalapeno pepper, minced
½ cup water
4 tomatoes, sliced into ¼" slices
  Salt and pepper

In a large skillet heat ¼ cup of bacon drippings. Brown the pork cubes for about 5 minutes, then add cabbage and salt and pepper. Cover and simmer for about 15 minutes, stirring occasionally. Add garlic, hot pepper and water. Mix and bring to boil once. Place mixture into a well-greased deep baking dish with a cover. Place tomato slices on top. Pour remaining ¼ cup bacon drippings over the tomato slices. Sprinkle with a little salt and pepper. Bake covered in 350° oven for 1 hour. Serve with a salad and a bowl of yogurt on the side.

. . . . *Side Dishes*

POTATO ESCALLOPE
serves 4

2 Tbls butter or margarine
1 onion, sliced
1 clove garlic, minced
1 tsp salt
½ tsp basil
½ tsp oregano

⅛ tsp pepper
1 can (1 pound) tomatoes, chopped
3 medium Idaho potatoes, pared and thinly sliced
½ cup grated Parmesan cheese

Melt butter in a large skillet. Add onion and garlic, and cook until tender, but not brown. Add salt, basil, oregano, pepper, and tomatoes. Add potatoes, mixing gently until potatoes are coated with seasonings and tomatoes. Place into a greased baking dish. Sprinkle with Parmesan cheese. Bake in 350° oven for 50 minutes, or until potatoes are tender when pierced with a fork.

RICE WITH VERMICELLI
serves 6

1 cup long grain rice	1 medium onion, minced
3 cups hot water	2½ cups chicken broth
½ tsp salt	¼ tsp pepper
1 cup vermicelli, broken into 1"	1 tsp paprika
pieces	½ cup scallions, minced
8 Tbls butter	½ cup parsley, minced

Place rice into a bowl, add hot water and salt. Stir. Cover bowl and set aside until completely cool. In a large ovenproof saucepan* or a pot with a cover sauté the vermicelli in 3 tablespoons butter until golden brown. In a skillet sauté onion in 2 tablespoons butter until golden. Add onions to the vermicelli then add chicken broth and the remaining 3 tablespoons butter, pepper, and paprika. Bring to a boil, then add rice, stir, and bring to boil again. Reduce heat to low, cover saucepan, and simmer for 20–25 minutes or until all broth has been absorbed. Remove from heat, add the scallions, and mix gently. Place a damp napkin on top of rice. Cover and place saucepan into a 150° oven for 1 hour. Serve mounded on a platter and generously sprinkled with parsley.

KACAMAK
Cornmeal
serves 6

4 cups water	3 cups yellow cornmeal
4 Tbls butter	4 Tbls Feta or Brindza cheese, grated
Salt to taste	½ cup butter (optional)

In a saucepan bring water with butter and salt to boil. Slowly add cornmeal, stirring continuously. Cook on low heat, stirring frequently until very stiff. Mix in the grated cheese. Butter an 8–9" pie pan well. Spread the corn mixture evenly in the pan and pat down with the back of a silver spoon. If the spoon sticks, dip in cold water. Serve sliced in wedges with vegetables, fish, or meat, or slice into squares and brown on all sides in butter. Serve as a side dish, or try the plain or fried cornmeal in a bowl topped with yogurt or sour cream.

*See Raisin Pilaf recipe on page 299 for description of ovenproof saucepan or pot.

RAISIN PILAF
serves 8

2 cups long grain rice	1 tsp paprika
4 cups boiling water	2-3 Tbls soft butter
1 tsp salt	3 cups water
½ cup butter	½ cup sugar
3½ cups chicken broth	2½-3 cups seedless grapes
¼ tsp black pepper	2-3 Tbls toasted white sesame seeds

Place rice in a bowl and add boiling water and 1 teaspoon salt. Stir well, cover, and let stand until completely cooled. Drain through a sieve and set aside. In a large oven-proof saucepan* or a pot with a cover, combine butter, chicken broth, pepper, and paprika. Bring to a boil and boil until butter is melted. Add rice to the boiling broth. Stir once, bring to boil again, reduce heat to a minimum, cover saucepan and cook for 10 minutes. Then reduce heat and simmer the rice for an additional 15 minutes or until all liquid has been absorbed. Remove pan from heat. Place a barely damp napkin over the rice. Cover tightly and place into a 150° oven for 1 hour. Grease a 10-inch ring mold well with the soft butter. Fill with hot rice and pack down the rice firmly. Set aside. In a saucepan bring water and sugar to a boil, add grapes, and bring to boil again. Drain immediately. Unmold the rice onto a round platter and fill the center with the hot grapes. Sprinkle with toasted sesame seeds.

*Oven-proof saucepan should have metal handle(s) and a completely metal lid.

Bulgarian gypsy musicians in a tavern

PUMPKIN PANCAKES
about 6 pancakes

May be served plain with turkey or ham

4 eggs
1 cup light cream
2 Tbls butter
⅛ tsp salt
4 Tbls sugar
1 cup flour
2 tsp baking powder

1 cup pumpkin purée (use ½ can of a 16-ounce pumpkin pie filling) or cook and purée fresh pumpkin to make 1 cup
⅛ tsp nutmeg
⅛ tsp cinnamon
Butter for frying

Place all ingredients into a blender and blend at medium speed until very smooth. Let stand for ½ hour before baking. In a large skillet melt about 3 tablespoons butter and pour batter into the skillet, making 2½–3″ pancakes. Fry on both sides until browned. Serve plain or dusted with powdered sugar or your favorite syrup.

NEW POTATOES IN MILK
serves 6

2 pounds small new potatoes
2 cups milk or more as needed
2 well-beaten eggs
2 Tbls lemon juice

Salt and pepper to taste
4 Tbls melted butter
½ tsp paprika

Peel the potatoes and cook them in milk with salt to taste. Add more milk if the milk cooks out and potatoes seem dry. When potatoes are tender, mix eggs with lemon juice and pepper and add this to potatoes. Simmer for a few minutes. Add butter and sprinkle with paprika.

CHERRY PUDDING

serves 6

2 large cans dark pitted cherries in heavy syrup	3 Tbls comstarch
	⅓ cup water
3 Tbls cherry preserves	1 cup sweet whipped cream
¼ cup cherry wine	

Drain cherries; *reserve juice*. Pour the juice into a saucepan, and add cherry preserves and cherry wine. Bring to a boil. Add cherries. Mix cornstarch and water and add to the cherry mixture. Simmer until thickened. Pour into a glass dish or any other serving dish, and refrigerate. Serve topped with whipped cream or serve with milk.

You may use raspberries, blueberries, blackberries or any other berries for this recipe instead of cherries. Sieve berries first. Use the sieved pulp, eliminate the cherry wine and add ¼ cup sugar per 1 cup of pulp. Proceed as above.

If you wish to make a mold, add 1 envelope of plain gelatin softened in ¼ cup cold water to the hot pudding. Mix well, and pour into a mold. To unmold, invert onto a platter and hold a hot towel over the mold, shake from side to side, and slide off the mold. Serve with whipped cream or milk.

Street in Sophya with ancient mosque and minaret

SPONGE CAKE WITH APPLE SAUCE
serves 8

6 eggs
¾ cup granulated sugar
1 tsp lemon juice

Butter well and sprinkle with flour two 9" spring form pans. Preheat oven to 350°. Use a glass double boiler; if you don't have a glass one use a glass bowl. Place top of double boiler or bowl over simmering water. Break the eggs into it, add sugar, and beat with a whisk until the eggs feel hot to the touch. Do not let the water boil or the eggs will cook. Remove from heat and pour into another glass bowl and beat with an electric beater for 5 minutes or until the eggs have tripled in bulk and form soft peaks. Add lemon and beat for another minute. Add a little sifted flour and a little liquid clarified butter and fold in gently. Continue adding flour and butter and folding in. Gently work in flour—no flour should be visible. Pour the batter into the two pans. Bake the cakes for 30–35 minutes or until a cake tester comes out clean. Do not overbake. Cool on a rack and unmold.

Use one cake for the apple topping. Or if you wish, double the apple recipe and use both cakes. You can also freeze the other cake and use it later. If you wish, use for other purposes as an excellent sponge base.

Topping

8 large baking apples, cored
½ cup ruby port or any other sweet wine
2 cups powdered sugar
1 tsp grated lemon rind
2 tsp lemon juice or more to taste
2 egg whites
3 Tbls maraschino cherry syrup
   Maraschino cherries for decoration

Slice the cake into 8 slices. Place each slice onto a dessert dish and set aside.

Place the apples into a baking dish. Pour port into each cored apple. Bake in a 350° oven for 25–35 minutes or until the apples are very tender. Cool apples and with a spoon scrape out the pulp into a bowl. Add 1 ½ cups sugar, lemon rind, and lemon juice and beat with a whisk. Beat 2 egg whites until foamy, add ½ cup sugar, and beat until very stiff. Fold into the apple purée and beat with a whisk. Add maraschino syrup and mix well. Pour over the cake slices. Decorate with maraschino cherries and refrigerate for 2–3 hours before serving.

Note: Sweet dark cherry syrup, raspberry, or boysenberry syrup may be used instead of maraschino cherry syrup. For decorations, use any glacéed or canned fruit. If some of the apple purée is left over, serve in small cups with one of the syrups.

FARINA HALVA

serves 6

1 ½	cups sugar	½	cup melted butter
1	cup water	1 ¼	cups regular (not quick) farina
1 ½	cups milk	¾	cup pine nuts (pignolias)
1 ½	tsp cinnamon	2–3	cups yogurt

In a saucepan combine sugar, water and milk. Simmer over low heat, stirring constantly for about 10–12 minutes or until thickened. Add 1 teaspoon cinnamon. Set aside. In a saucepan melt the butter, add farina, and ¼ cup pine nuts. Cook, stirring constantly over low heat, until farina and pine nuts are golden brown. It will take about 15–20 minutes. Be careful not to burn nuts or farina. Reheat the milk mixture, but do not boil. Pour the hot mixture into the saucepan with farina, stirring constantly. Cook over low heat, stirring occasionally, until all the syrup has been absorbed. Place a damp napkin over the farina. Cover tightly and let stand on a shut-off stove burner for 40 minutes. Meanwhile brown the remaining ¼ cup pine nuts in a 350° oven until light brown.

Stir the farina mixture lightly. Mound onto a serving platter. Sprinkle with the remaining ½ teaspoon cinnamon and ¼ cup toasted pine nuts. Serve warm or chilled with a bowl of yogurt on the side.

CREAM PUDDING
serves 6

½ cup cornstarch
½ cup cold milk
3 cups light cream
¾ cup sugar
⅛ tsp salt

*3–4 Tbls rose water
½ tsp cinnamon
½ cup pistachio nuts, coarsely ground

Mix cornstarch with cold milk. In a stainless steel or enameled saucepan bring cream and sugar to a boil, stirring continuously. Add salt. Add the cornstarch mixture, stirring quickly into the cream. Simmer, stirring constantly, until thick and glossy. Pour the rose water into a serving dish and swish around a few times so that the dish is well coated. Invert for a few minutes over paper towel or plate and let the excess run out. Pour in the cream pudding. Sprinkle with cinnamon and chill for 2–3 hours. Serve sprinkled with pistachio nuts. If desired, pour some raspberry or strawberry syrup over the pudding.

BOYAR CHEESE CREME
serves 6

16 -ounce package of cream cheese, softened at room temperature
⅔ cup sour cream
3 egg yolks
1 cup powdered vanilla sugar (see page 37)

3 egg whites
*2–3 Tbls rose water
1 cup fresh pink rose petals if available or
1 cup strawberries or a melba sauce

With an electric beater, beat cream cheese until very fluffy. Add sour cream and add egg yolks one at a time, beating well after each addition. Add ½ cup vanilla sugar. Beat well. Beat egg whites until frothy; add remaining ½ cup of sugar and beat until very stiff. Fold into the cheese cream. Pour rose water into a serving bowl and swish it around. Invert for a few seconds over paper towels. Spoon the cream into the bowl. If available decorate with carefully washed pink rose petals, or with strawberries or serve with melba sauce.

*Rose water is available in some gourmet stores and in Greek and Middle Eastern stores.

BAKED PEACHES
serves 6

2	Tbls butter, softened
12	medium ripe peaches
24	cloves
1½	cups sugar
½	cup brandy or more as needed

| 2 | cups lightly sweetened whipped cream |
| ½ | cup coarsely crushed pistachio nuts or toasted almonds |

Preheat oven to 350°. Butter a baking pan well. Wash and dry the peaches. Cut each peach in half and remove the stones. Stick a clove into each peach half. Sprinkle about ½–¾ cup sugar into the baking pan. Place peaches skin down into the baking pan. Sprinkle with the remaining sugar. Bake in a preheated 350° oven for 30 minutes. Sprinkle with ¼ cup brandy and bake 15 minutes longer. Pour the remaining brandy over peaches, basting frequently with the pan juices. Bake for an additional 30–40 minutes or until peaches are very tender. If the pan juices cook down too much or caramelize, add more brandy and a little water. You should have about ½–⅔ cup pan juices. Place peaches onto a serving platter, pour pan juices over them, cool them, and refrigerate for 2 hours. Serve with whipped cream and crushed nuts on the side. Serve as desert or with meat or fowl.

CHAPTER  8

Christmas Along the Danube

O many people who now live in Eastern Europe, for years Christmas was just a fond memory. To most children in that part of the world, it was a wondrous story told by the glow of a fire or a few candles by a grandma or grandpa who still cherished the old traditions and were sentimental—often reverent—about recollections of the loveliness of holidays past.

In the last few years, however, in Hungary, Czechoslovakia, Yugoslavia, Rumania, and even in Bulgaria, Christmas is once again being celebrated in a manner reminiscent of years gone by. The day may be January 1st, but ancient, traditional customs of Christmas once again permeate the scene, from the tree itself to the lovely homemade decorations and holiday sweets which adorn

307

its deep green branches. Christmas sweets, small toys, and gingermen are the results of generations of inventive genius, and it takes the total effort of the entire household to prepare, bake, and wrap the multitude of homemade delicacies which are then hung on the tree.

The Christmas or New Year's celebration—by whichever name one wishes to call it—is still a festival for children and a time when a delightful combination of warmth and family togetherness spins a shimmering cocoon around innocence. In Eastern Europe, Christmas gifts are now brought to children by a little Christmas angel, which may well be closer to them in both size and spirit than the fat, bearded man who "ho-ho's" his way down the American chimney.

At Christmas time in Hungary, mothers and grandmothers begin long before the festive day to prepare and hoard precious Christmas delicacies. And there are still bakers who refuse to give up magnificent medieval forms for ginger cookies, honey cakes, and breads! They spread the thick dough into the antique carved wooden molds so that it retains the imprint of the design during baking.

Still today, the Christmas tree, besides all the glitter and color, is also bedecked with ropes of popcorn. Popped corn is strung on long threads to make this adornment.

In Hungary the Christmas Eve feast may consist of goose baked to a lovely crispness, with a huge goose liver poached in wine, and apples stuffed with nuts; or perhaps a fish paprikash with potato purée, and a large basket of glazed fruits and oranges. Another holiday dinner may begin with a special turkey giblet ragout soup, followed by a tender she-turkey, which has been fattened on walnuts, and is served with chestnut dressing surrounded by plums stuffed with almonds simmered in red wine. In Hungary, the branch cake, which for years was a bridal gift, is now one of the things to make and give for Christmas. *Dióspatkó* and *Makospatko* are the pride of each housewife. These are walnut- and poppyseed-filled, horseshoe-shaped, yeast dough "strudels."

Because Yugoslavia is such a melange of nationalities, religious traditions, and customs, Christmas celebration varies according to regions. On the Mediterranean coastline, the Yugoslavian Christmas echoes the country's seafaring past and, as in Greece, St. Basil brings the Christmas toys and is said to make his round in a boat! Anchors, boats, and letters of the alphabet are formed into Christmas ornaments, and there are flaming torches—similar to Tiki lights—which are placed in front of houses to guide St. Basil with his bounty.

Throughout the country, a favorite Christmas bread is a fragrant, anise-flavored loaf with a coin baked inside. Legend has it that whoever gets the coin will have good luck all year long. The Christmas honey nut bread is filled with raisins, figs and walnuts and glazed with honey, but Christmas entrées vary from province to province and it may be a fat turkey, huge carp, goose, duck, whole suckling pig or goat cooked on a spit which is served for the festive holiday dinner.

The Christmas tree in Rumania is symbolic of friendship and togetherness, and is always laden with homemade decorations—free-hand paper cutouts, baked angels, toadstools, snowflakes, and delicate jugs made from eggshells.

Christmas in Rumania (especially in the Transylvanian hills) has retained much of its storybook fascination, and on Christmas Eve when the first star appears, the family gathers for the feast. On the farms, sheaves of grain are tied with colored ribbons and placed in the corners of the humble abodes. A thin layer of hay is sometimes placed under the festive tablecloth in memory of the Child in the manger. This particular custom may have travelled down from Poland along the Carpathian crescent.

The Bulgarians, who drew most of their customs from their Russian mentors, still celebrate Christmas in a truly Slavic manner, even today when the religion has been officially abolished. The day of Christ's birth is observed according to the Georgian calendar—13 days later than the Roman calendar date of December 25th. Especially in the country, "Father Winter," dressed in a red suit and sporting a white beard, comes on Christmas Eve to bring good children presents and also the Christmas tree. The festive meal may be quite meager, but there is always the *kutya*—honey and cooked wheat porridge with poppyseeds and nuts, and *mdovnik*, a lovely honey confection.

In Czechoslovakia, mothers and children labor for months creating whimsical figurines—horsedrawn carriages and other items taken from country life—to decorate the tree. Gingerbread figures, Christmas tree cakes made of marzipan, and *kolachki* (featherlight buns) are also among the traditional decorations.

Czechoslovakia, Hungary, and Austria have overlapping and

intertwined customs and cuisine, and Czechoslovakian Christmas dishes are reminiscent of Austria and other neighboring countries. Roast goose stuffed with sauerkraut and surrounded by *houskove knedliky* (bread dumplings) is often part of the traditional Christmas feast, or an especially festive ham may be served at Yuletide. Boiled beef (*hovezy maso*) with delicious apple-horseradish is also a favorite. Dumplings are a holdiay and year-round mainstay, and the truly inventive housewife prepares dumplings of every size and shape during the Christmas season. Hearty soups and marvelously succulent sausages are also part of the celebration.

But nowhere is Christmas more reverent and celebrated with more joy than in Austria and Germany. St. Nicholas comes early on Advent night of December 6th to bring good children sweets, oranges, and small toys. He travels with *Knecht Ruprecht* in Germany and *Krampus*, a kind of benign Beelzebub, in Austria. These villainous fellows scare the children who have been bad and stop St. Nicholas from placing goodies into their shoes, which the children customarily place onto window sills on the night of Advent. People dress up for the occasion and roam the streets attired as the legendary Bishop of Bari—St. Nicholas, or the *Krampus* and his disciples. They stop in neighbors' houses, in friendly stores, and while the parents place gifts into the shoes on the window sills, the crafty fellows down a few jiggers of schnapps and move on to continue their fun mission.

Christmas tradition actually originated in Germany and the stately fir tree *Tannenbaum* became the symbol of the holy days. *Knecht Ruprecht*, the mythical Teutonic being who is St. Nick, Father Winter, and *Krampus* all in one, roams the earth during Advent, and during Christmas in some parts of Germany. But most often *Kristkindle*, baby Jesus, is the one children wait for on Christmas Eve to bring joy and gifts, which are placed under an elaborately decorated Christmas tree. Mothers, grandmothers, and aunts labor long hours beginning with the start of Advent to create a beautifully decorated tree and the most scrumptious delicacies for a truly joyous holiday filled with warmth, good spirit, and love.

In the Black Forest, Christmas is especially lovely when the trees are covered with powdery, glistening snow, which creates a fairytale-like setting. It is a family holiday when all gather around the fire. Adults drink *Gluhwein* or *Krambambuli* while children eagerly open their presents. There is singing and joy and crass commercialism is left out in the cold.

The German Christmas fare is substantial and hearty. There are huge hams, fat geese, elaborate puddings, and other sweets.

In Austria, as in Germany, the holiday labor of love begins on December 6th and from that day forward there is a palatable feeling of joy and happiness in the air. Christmas carols and carolers are everywhere. After all, it was a humble Austrian village priest who composed the poignant immortal carol, "Silent Night, Holy Night."

The Christmas feast in Austria is as elaborate as circumstances permit. Stuffed goose, ducks, whole suckling pig, fragrant chicken soup, and mounds of heavenly sweets are all part of the feast.

In Salzburg the gingerbread and candle makers have been using the same beautifully-carved molds since the early sixteenth century. These are cherished by adults and children alike. In Austria, roccoco and Biedermeier influence is still strong and the tree decorations and foods reflect these elaborate "chi-chi" periods. It is a family holiday but also a time for visiting, for merry-making and caroling, all to the accompaniment of the most beautiful Christmas music on earth.

Germany · · · · · · · · · · · · · · · ·

BLACK FOREST HAM
serves 8–10

4–5 pounds fully cooked boned ham (if you wish, buy smoked ham and cook it yourself—follow the directions on the package)	3–4 Tbls Cointreau or brandy
½ cup honey	½ tsp allspice
	¼ tsp powdered cloves
	1 tsp dry mustard
	1 Tbls orange rind

Preheat oven to 400°. Place ham on a double sheet of foil. If desired, cut off all the excess fat first. Brush ham on all sides with honey, Cointreau, and seasonings. Seal foil, place the wrapped ham into a baking pan, and bake for 45 minutes in a preheated 400° oven. Open foil and baste ham with the liquid that has formed around it. Bake for another 10 minutes, basting 3–4 times. Pack the dressing on top of the ham and place the pan on the lowest rack in the oven. Turn the oven to broil and broil until slightly browned and bubbly, about 10 minutes. Baste topping a few times with the liquid that has formed around the ham. Cool the ham completely before serving.

If you are cooking your own ham, remove as much fat as possible and cook thoroughly in water before baking. If you wish, have the butcher bone the ham for you, but this is not necessary.

Ham Topping

2 cups walnuts	½ tsp ginger
¼ cup honey	½ tsp allspice
1 cup brown sugar	¼ tsp cloves
½ cup candied orange peel	¼ tsp salt
½ cup orange marmalade or preserves	½ tsp white pepper
4 tsp prepared mustard	3 Tbls Cointreau or brandy
1 tsp dry mustard	

In a bowl, combine all ingredients and blend well. Place on top of the ham.

CARP WITH BLACK SAUCE
serves 6

A Christmas Eve dinner, traditionally served with favorite dumplings

4–5	pounds dressed whole carp		½	bay leaf
	Salt to taste		⅛	tsp thyme
1	cup vinegar		½	tsp lemon peel, grated
1 ½	cups thinly sliced parsnips		1 ¼	cup red wine
1 ½	cups thinly sliced carrots		3 ½	Tbls vinegar
1	large onion		2–4	Tbls water
⅓	cup butter		3	Tbls black currant jam
⅔	cup grated gingerbread		⅔	cup coarsely crushed blanched almonds
⅔	cup grated day-old rye bread			Juice of ½ lemon
7	peppercorns			
½	tsp allspice			

Wash carp and rinse in vinegar. Cut carp into serving size portions, season with salt, and set aside. In a large skillet, sauté parsnips, carrots, and onions in butter. Add gingerbread, rye bread, and seasonings. Pour in wine and vinegar and stir. If mixture is too thick, add water. Simmer for 10 minutes. Add the carp and simmer for 20 minutes. Remove fish to a hot platter. Strain the contents of the skillet and add currant jam, almonds, raisins, and lemon juice. Simmer 5–10 minutes and then add carp. Serve immediately or refrigerate and warm up for the following day. The flavor of the carp and its sauce improves when the fish is allowed to marinate overnight in the refrigerator.

CHRISTMAS CHOCOLATE LOG
serves 10–12

4	egg yolks	1	Tbls sugar
1	cup sugar	3	teaspoons powdered vanilla sugar
1	tsp lemon juice		(see recipe on page 37)
½	tsp grated lemon rind	3	teaspoons Cointreau
1	cup sifted flour	10	ounces semisweet chocolate
¼	teaspoon baking powder	1	cup heavy whipping cream
4	egg whites	½	cup candied orange peel, minced
⅛	teaspoon cream of tartar		Red and green candied cherries

Preheat oven to 375°. Butter a 10″ × 16″ jelly roll pan lined with greased wax paper. Beat egg yolks with sugar until thick and lemon colored. Add lemon juice and lemon rind. Sift flour and baking powder together, add to the egg mixture, and blend well. Set aside. Beat egg whites with the pinch of cream of tartar until soft peaks appear. Add 1 tablespoon of sugar and beat until stiff, but not dry. Do not overbeat. Fold egg whites into the egg yolk mixture. Spread the batter evenly in the prepared pan and bake for 10–12 minutes, until golden brown.

Spread out a sheet of wax paper a little larger than the cake and dust it with powdered sugar. Invert cake onto wax paper and peel off the wax paper. Sprinkle with Cointreau. Roll jelly roll fashion into wax paper and then into a towel. Cool for at least 1 hour.

Melt chocolate in the heavy cream, stirring constantly, until well blended and very creamy. Set aside until cooled completely. Unroll cake and spread the inside evenly with half of the cream. Reserve 1 tablespoon of candied orange peel and sprinkle the rest over the cream. Roll up the cake like a jelly roll (do not roll with the paper). Place onto a serving platter and spread the remaining cream over the cake. If desired, score lengthwise with a fork to simulate the bark of a tree. Decorate with the remaining orange peel and red and green cherries. Refrigerate overnight before serving.

THE VERY FANCY GINGERBREAD CAKE
serves 8–10

Butter two 8-inch loaf pans and sprinkle them generously with
flour. Invert and tap sharply on the edge of the sink to get rid of
excess flour. Set aside.

½ pound sweet butter	2⅔ cups all-purpose flour
2 cups dark brown sugar	1 cup sour cream
2 whole eggs	½ cup orange juice
2 egg yolks	4 tsp baking powder
⅔ cup honey	1 cup currants
¼ cup brandy	1 cup blanched, slivered, toasted
2 tsp ginger	almonds
1 tsp cinnamon	4 cups sweetened whipped cream
¼ tsp nutmeg	Grated orange rind
¼ tsp cloves	Grated chocolate

Preheat oven to 350°. Cream butter with an electric egg beater
until very fluffy. Add sugar and beat again until smooth. Add eggs
and yolks one at a time, beating well after each addition. Add
honey, brandy, and all the spices and blend. Add 1 cup of flour and
sour cream and blend. Add orange juice, the remaining flour, and
baking powder and beat for at least 1 minute. Add currants and
almonds and mix well. Bake in a 350° oven for 1 hour to 1 hour
and 15 minutes, or until a cake tester comes out clean. Cool the
cake in the pans for 15 minutes, unmold them onto a rack, and
cool completely.

Slice each cake lengthwise into two sections. Spread about ⅓ cup
of cream on the bottom piece. Cover with the top piece and frost
completely with whipped cream. Grate some orange rind and
chocolate over the whipped cream. Repeat the same procedure
with the second cake. You may also leave it plain and dust it with
powdered sugar and decorate it with red and green candied
cherries.

GOOSE WITH FRUIT STUFFING
serves 5–6

1	frozen goose, about 10–12 pounds	1	tsp cinnamon
1	12-ounce package mixed dried fruit, about 1½–2 cups	½	tsp nutmeg
1	cup orange liqueur or brandy	¼	tsp allspice
1	cup orange juice	⅛	tsp mace
½	cup light brown sugar	2	eggs, well beaten
12	slices white bread	1	cup brandy
½	tsp ginger		Salt and pepper

Preheat oven to 400°. Defrost frozen goose for 48 hours or longer in the refrigerator until completely defrosted. Remove giblets and cut off as much fat as possible from the inside and all over the goose. Wash goose, pat dry with paper towels, and set aside. Chop dried fruit and place in a bowl. Mix orange liqueur and orange juice with light brown sugar in a saucepan. Stir well. Bring to a boil, remove from heat immediately and pour over the fruit. Cover bowl with foil and let steep for 1 hour.

Cut off crust and cut bread into small cubes. Spread on a cookie sheet and toast in 400° oven, stirring cubes occasionally until golden brown on all sides. Place bread cubes into a large bowl. Add ginger, cinnamon, nutmeg, allspice, mace, and steeped fruit. Toss lightly. Add the beaten eggs and ½ cup brandy. Toss until all bread cubes are moistened. Stuff the neck cavity with the mixture, fold over the skin and secure skin with a skewer. Stuff the body cavity and cover opening with a piece of foil or close up with skewers. Sprinkle goose with salt and pepper all over. Place the goose on a rack in a shallow pan. Place into a preheated 400° oven and roast for ½ hour. Prick skin all over with a fork. Reduce heat to 350°. Insert meat thermometer into the thickest part of the breast without touching the breast bone. About every 20 minutes, pour fat out of the baking pan. Baste the goose frequently with the remaining ½ cup of brandy. Bake for 2½–3 hours or until thermometer reaches 185°. Let cool for 15 minutes, place onto a heated platter, and carve at the table.

MÁKOS ÉS DIÓS KALACS
Poppy Seed and Walnut Strudel
serves up to 24

Strudel Dough

3	envelopes granulated yeast		Grated rind of 1 lemon	
½	cup lukewarm water	3	Tbls heavy dark rum or 1 tsp rum	
½	cup sugar		extract	
1	cup milk	5	egg yolks	
12	Tbls unsalted butter	3	whole eggs	
1 ½	tsp salt	2	egg yolks, well beaten with	Egg
5–6	cups all-purpose flour	3	Tbls heavy cream	wash

Preheat oven to 350°. In a small bowl, combine yeast, ½ cup lukewarm water, and ¼ cup sugar. Mix lightly and set aside for about 5 minutes. Scald milk with butter, ¼ cup sugar, and salt. Stir until butter is melted. Cool slightly and pour into a large bowl. Add 2 cups flour, yeast, lemon rind, and rum. Beat with a wooden spoon for 2 minutes, or for 30 seconds if you are using a mixer. Add egg yolks, whole eggs, and the remaining flour. Beat until a smooth dough is formed. You may need only 5 or 5 ½ cups of flour.

Turn dough out onto a well-floured board and knead for about 5–7 minutes, or beat for 4 minutes if you are using an electric beater with a hook. While kneading the dough, you may have to add small amounts of flour if the dough feels sticky. The dough should be very smooth and elastic, with blisters on the surface. Shape the dough into a ball and place into a very large well-buttered bowl. Turn dough once to coat it with butter, cover the bowl, and let dough rise in a warm place for about 1½ hours, or until doubled in bulk. Punch down the dough and knead it lightly for another 2 minutes. Divide dough in 2 parts. Roll out one part and fill it with walnut filling; then roll out second part and fill it with poppyseed filling. Roll the dough out on a floured board to about ¼-inch thickness. Spread the filling over the dough, leaving a 2-inch border free of filling. Roll up jelly roll fashion and seal the ends and along the seam. Turn seam down, form into a horseshoe, and press the ends securely together. Butter a jelly roll   *317* pan well and sprinkle it with flour. Slide the horseshoe-shaped strudel off the board onto the jelly roll pan. Let rise, covered, until doubled in bulk. Brush with egg wash and bake in a preheated 350° oven for 50–55 minutes, or until golden brown.

Walnut Filling

2	cups ground walnuts	½	cup heavy cream
½	cup sugar	¼	cup dark rum
½	cup apricot preserves	½	cup raisins

In a saucepan, combine walnuts, sugar, apricot preserves, and cream and cook for 5 minutes, stirring constantly. Combine rum and raisins. Let stand for 10 minutes; add to the nut mixture. Cool the mixture completely.

Poppy Seed Filling

Poppy seeds should be ground in a poppy seed grinder or bought from someone who has a grinder. However, poppy seeds from a jar work well in this recipe.

1	jar "Baker" poppy seed filling	¼	cup dark rum
½	cup apricot preserves	½	cup crushed walnuts
½	cup raisins		

Combine the prepared poppy seed filling with apricots. Soak raisins in rum for a few minutes and add to the poppy seeds with the walnuts. Use the same way as the nut filling.

OR

½	pound ground poppy seeds (see directions on page 188)	½	cup chopped raisins
			Grated rind of 1 lemon
¼	cup melted butter	¼	tsp cinnamon
½	cup honey	¼	tsp nutmeg
½	cup heavy whipping cream	½	cup chopped walnuts

Combine all ingredients in a bowl and mix well. Use as directed.

THE CAKE TREE

This unusual tree and cake combination originated in Transylvania as a bridal cake tree, but later it was adopted throughout Hungary and made in a smaller version for Christmas. To make this tree, pick out a branch with an interesting shape, one that will fit into the oven later. The most important thing is the central post, which should have as many branches growing upward as possible.

The bark is taken off, and then the tree is sanded with sandpaper until it is completely smooth. Then the dough is made and cut into strips, which are wrapped around the post and around all the branches. Several layers may be wrapped onto the tree, but this is optional. After the tree has been baked, it is adorned with all kinds of edible cookies, gingerbread, and honey cakes, as well as with ribbons and with fruit made of marzipan. The main stem is placed into a pot filled with clay or earth. The children break off branches, nibble on the cake coating, and devour the edible decorations.

Dough for an 18–24-inch tree with about 6 branches

3 cups all-purpose unbleached flour	2 tsp double-acting baking powder	
6 egg yolks	1 or 2 egg whites, slightly beaten	
3 Tbls sugar	Powdered vanilla sugar for dusting	
2 Tbls dark rum or ½ tsp rum extract	(see recipe on page 37)	
2 Tbls sour cream	2–3 egg yolks beaten with	Egg
½ tsp salt	2–3 Tbls heavy cream	Wash

Preheat oven to 350°. Place flour into a large bowl. Make a well in the center. Place egg yolks and sugar into the well and, with your fingers, knead them into the dough. Add rum, sour cream, salt, and baking powder. Knead the dough in the bowl, adding a bit more flour or sour cream if needed. Turn out onto a floured board and knead until the dough is very thick and smooth, about 6–7 minutes. Place dough under an inverted bowl and let it rest for 20 minutes. On a lightly floured board, roll the dough into a thin sheet about ¼ inch thick. Cut into long strips, each about 2 inches wide. Start wrapping the tree at the bottom of the stem, working your way up and overlapping the strips, pressing them together so that they adhere to each other. To make the strips adhere better, use a bit of egg white when pinching two strips together. When winding the strips around the branches, set the bottom of the tree into the pot to hold it upright or have someone hold it upright while you are winding on the strips. Wrap each branch completely into the dough, sealing the ends. You may wish to wrap it twice or even three times, depending on how much dough you have.

Place 1-inch thick rolled strips of foil at each end of a cookie sheet and on both sides to prop up the tree so it does not touch the baking sheet. Brush the tree on all sides with the egg wash and bake it in a preheated 350° oven until it is golden brown on all sides. Turn the tree over once so that the underside browns evenly. Depending on the size of the tree and on how many strips you have wound around the tree, baking time varies from 25–45 minutes.

When it is golden brown all over, remove the tree from the oven. Cool it and place it into the pot, with the stem anchored securely. Place artificial snow or cotton around the base. Place the pot onto newspapers and, if you wish to have a snowy effect on the branches of the "cake tree," brush them lightly with the slightly whipped egg whites and, using a flour sifter, dust them with vanilla sugar. However you may leave the branches nice and brown and shiny. The branches may be broken off and the cake coating nibbled off each branch. *Make certain that children do not eat the wood.*

After the tree has been baked and powdered with sugar, decorate it with the edible ornaments.

If you wish, you may preserve the tree: Cool it and let it dry for a few days. Coat the cake with several layers of clear varnish or spray with polyurethane. Let it dry completely between applications and apply several coats; this way the tree will keep for a few years. DO NOT EAT IT ONCE IT HAS BEEN VARNISHED!

CHRISTMAS CHEESE BALL
serves 10–12

2 8-ounce package cream cheese, softened	3–4 Tbls minced scallion or chives
⅔ cup crumbled bleu cheese	1 Tbls Worcestershire sauce
1 Tbls caraway seeds	3 Tbls port wine (straw-colored)
½ tsp garlic powder	2 cups minced parsley
	1 large (7oz.) jar pimientoes

Blend cheeses, caraway seed, garlic powder, minced scallion, chives, Worcestershire sauce, and wine together. Roll into a ball. Then roll the ball into minced parsley, covering it completely. Using your cookie cutters or small decorative cutouts, cut out different shapes from pimientos and place on top of the ball. Place the ball on a platter, preferably a wooden one. Put pearl onions and stuffed olives on toothpicks and stick the toothpicks in a circle into the cheese ball.

Serve the cheese ball with assorted crackers.

. . . . .Austria

ADVENT PRETZEL
serves up to 24

For the Pretzel:

1 cup milk	Grated rind of 1 lemon
½ cup sugar	1 tsp ground cardamom
1 tsp salt	3¼ cups all-purpose flour
4 Tbls unsalted butter or margarine	4 Tbls cornstarch
2 packages granulated yeast	½ pound unsalted butter or margarine
½ cup warm water	1 egg, well beaten
3 egg yolks	¼ cup sugar
1 egg white	

Filling for 2 pretzels:

2 cans almond paste	1½ cups sugar
1 egg white	1 tsp almond extract
2 cups blanched, toasted, and coarsely chopped almonds	

Crumble almond paste into a bowl, add egg white, and mix until smooth. Add the rest of the ingredients and mix well.

Making up the dough

In a saucepan, scald milk and add sugar, salt, and 4 tbls of butter or margarine. Stir until butter is dissolved. Set aside. In a small bowl, mix yeast and warm water together and stir until dissolved.

Set aside for 5 minutes. Pour milk into a large bowl and add the yeast. Beat egg yolks and egg white and add to the yeast mixture. Add lemon rind, cardamom, and 1 ½ cups of flour. Beat for 1 minute with a wooden spoon. Add the rest of the flour and the cornstarch. Mix well, but do not beat. Refrigerate for 2 hours.

With a wooden spoon, cream the ½ pound of butter or margarine. Place onto wax paper and flatten to form a 6" × 8" rectangle. Cover with wax paper and refrigerate for 2 hours.

Roll out the dough into a 12" × 16" rectangle. Place the butter in the center of the dough rectangle. Fold long ends of the rectangle over the butter, one side over the other. Square off the open ends. Turn the dough toward yourself with one of the open ends facing you. Pat down very gently with a rolling pin to flatten down the dough into another oblong. Fold into thirds; refrigerate for ½ hour. Roll out gently and fold into thirds; roll and fold again. Chill for ½ hour, roll and fold twice again and chill 2 hours or overnight.

Cut dough in half. Roll out into a 10" × 16" rectangle about ¼-inch thick. Spread half the filling over the rolled-out dough. Roll up jelly roll fashion and seal well. Taper the 2 ends and bring them into the center of the circle to form a pretzel. Butter 2 cookie sheets well and sprinkle them with flour. Place pretzel on one of the sheets. Refrigerate for 1 hour. Make up the second half of the dough and refrigerate. Brush with beaten egg and sprinkle with sugar. Bake in a preheated 375° oven for 15 minutes, reduce heat to 350°, and bake 15 minutes longer.

Note: You may make one very large pretzel, or you may use one-half of the dough for 1 pretzel. Make up ½ of the filling and if you wish, form a circle instead of a pretzel. With a sharp knife, cut 1 inch deep cuts, 2 inches apart on the outside, and bake as before.

Using the second half of the dough to make pastry

Cut the chilled dough and roll it into 3" × 5" rectangles and cut each rectangle into 3 strips. Braid the strips. Brush them with beaten egg and sprinkle them with sugar and crushed nuts. Chill and bake 20 minutes in a 350° oven. Cut the dough into squares about 4" × 4". Brush squares with beaten egg and sprinkle them with sugar and crushed nuts or with sugar and currants. Cut with a knife 1" deep, 2" apart. Then twist the square into odd shapes. Bake as directed.

You may fill the squares with preserves, thick vanilla cream, or almond paste. Bring the corners together and seal, exposing some of the filling.

LEBKUCHEN
The Austrian Gingerbread
serves 8–10

This recipe is from the Weber House of Candlemakers and Gingerbread Bakers, established in Salzburg, Austria in 1583. Austrian candlemakers also bake gingerbread. This traditional recipe includes honey, enabling Austrians to use all the products of the honeybee. Gingerbread is the traditional Austrian Christmas cookie.

The Gingerbread

⅔	cup honey	1	tsp cinnamon
¾	cup sugar	1	tsp baking powder
1	Tbls cooking oil	2	cups all-purpose unbleached flour
2	Tbls water	1½	tsp cocoa
1	egg yolk	1½	cups ground almonds
1½	tsp powdered ginger	¼	cups currants
1	tsp lemon peel	½	cups slivered, blanched, toasted
1	tsp orange peel		almonds
¼	tsp ground cloves		

Preheat oven to 350°. Grease a cookie sheet and sprinkle with flour. In a saucepan slowly heat together honey, sugar, oil, and water. Blend until smooth and let cool. Add egg yolk, ginger, and all other seasonings. Sift the flour with cocoa and baking powder, and add to the honey mixture. Now add the ground almonds, currants, and slivered almonds. Mix well with your hands until the dough is smooth. Roll out to ¼" thick on a well-floured board. Trim to fit the cookie sheet and bake whole on the cookie sheet. Or cut out into different cookie shapes. Bake exactly 10 minutes—do not overbake. Cool before icing. Cut the single baked sheet into squares or any shapes you desire.

Icing

1 egg white
⅔ cups powdered sugar
¼ tsp lemon juice

Beat egg, sugar, and lemon juice until thick. Spread on the cookies and decorate them with nuts, raisins, or glazed fruit.
This gingerbread will keep for as long as 3 months. Place it in a tightly sealed container. Put a few small apples into the container with the gingerbread; the apples keep the gingerbread fresh.

CROWN ROAST OF PORK
serves 6–8

1 14–16 chop crown roast of pork
Salt and pepper to taste

Have the butcher make up the crown roast for you and have it tied securely with a string. Sprinkle with salt and pepper on the inside and outside. Place into a large baking pan, rib ends up. Place a meat thermometer into the thickest portion of a chop, without touching the bones. Cover each protruding 1–2" of the ribs with foil to prevent too much browning. Place the stuffing into the hollow of the roast, mounding it slightly. Cover the stuffing with foil and roast in a 350° oven for about 2 hours or until roast is very brown and the thermometer reaches 185°. Remove thermometer and foil covers before serving. If you wish, place kumquats onto each rib or place multicolored frills over the ribs.

Note: Paper frills are available in gourmet stores and some butcher shops.

Chestnut Stuffing

1 large onion, minced
3 Tbls butter
2 stalks celery, minced
8 strips of bacon, diced
3 cups prepared bread stuffing
2 15-ounce cans of whole chestnuts or
1 ½ pounds fresh chestnuts, cooked
1 tsp salt

½ tsp poultry seasoning
¼ tsp white pepper
¼ tsp thyme
¼ tsp basil
2 eggs, well beaten
1 cup chicken broth or less
¼ cup melted butter mixed with ½ cup dry sherry

Saute onions and celery in butter until both are just limp. Cook bacon in a separate skillet until golden brown. Drain off half the fat. Add breadstuffing, chestnuts, onion mixture, and seasonings. Toss together and add eggs and chicken broth. Add just enough to moisten the stuffing. Stuff the roast and bake as directed. If you have stuffing left over, when the roast has been baking for about 1 ½ hours, drain off some of the fat from the pan and place the stuffing made into patties around the roast, sprinkle with the butter and sherry mixture, and bake along with the roast. Serve the roast with the chestnuts and prunes.

CHESTNUTS AND PRUNES
serves 6

*1 recipe of buttered chesnuts	¼ tsp salt
1 12-ounce package pitted prunes	⅛ tsp white pepper
1 cup ruby port	⅛ tsp cinnamon

Prepare the buttered chestnuts and set aside. Place prunes into a saucepan. Add port, salt and pepper, and cinnamon. Cook over low heat until very tender, about 8–10 minutes. Combine prunes with the chestnuts in a skillet. Mix gently together, simmer for 3 minutes (just to heat).

*Buttered Chestnuts

serves 6

1½ pounds cooked chestnuts or 1 15-ounce can of whole chestnuts, drained	½ cup butter or margarine Salt and pepper to taste ⅛ tsp ground fennel seeds

Boil the chestnuts as directed. Melt butter in a large skillet. Add cooked or canned chestnuts and the seasonings, stir to coat the chestnuts with butter, and simmer for just a few minutes until chestnuts are heated thoroughly. Use for stuffings and also as an accompaniment for duck, goose, or turkey.

How to cook chestnuts

Make a slit on the flat side of each chestnut and pour about ½ inch oil into a large skillet to accommodate all your chestnuts. Place chestnuts into the skillet and turn several times to coat with oil. Heat and cook over moderate heat for about 10–15 minutes, stirring occasionally. Remove from pan onto absorbent paper towel. Cool for a few minutes and remove the shells and inner skins with a sharp knife. Finish cooking in water or milk for about 25–30 minutes or until tender. Cook 10–15 minutes for chestnut purée.

To make chestnut purée

Boil chestnuts as directed, in water or milk, until very tender. Drain chestnuts and press them through a very fine sieve. Flavor the purée as desired.

Note: For chestnut purée used in souffles and other desserts, boil chestnuts in milk with a vanilla bean until very tender. Be careful that the milk does not scorch.

If fresh chestnuts are not available, most gourmet stores and Italian grocery stores have canned whole chestnuts packed in water as well as canned chestnut purée. The canned chestnuts and the purée may be used very successfully instead of fresh home-cooked chestnuts. (These should not be confused with Chinese water chestnuts).

Czechoslovakia . . . .

VANOCKA
Czechoslovakian Christmas Braid
serves 12–14

2 packages granulated yeast	⅛ tsp cardamom
½ cup lukewarm water	⅛ tsp crushed anise seeds
1 Tbls sugar	1 cup raisins soaked in
1 cup milk, scalded	½ cup rum
¾ cup sugar	½ cup coarsely chopped blanched almonds
1 tsp salt	
¼ pound unsalted butter	2 well-beaten egg yolks
3 well-beaten egg yolks	1 Tbls milk
4½–5 cups all-purpose flour	½ cup sliced blanched almonds
1 tsp grated lemon rind	Granulated sugar

In a small bowl, combine yeast, lukewarm water, and sugar. Stir well and set aside. Add sugar, salt, and butter to the scalded milk. Stir until the butter is melted. Pour milk mixture into a large bowl and add egg yolks, eggs, yeast, and 2 cups of flour. Beat with a wooden spoon for 1–2 minutes or for 30 seconds with an electric beater. Add lemon rind, cardamom, anise seed, and remaining flour to make a fairly stiff dough. Knead for 2–3 minutes in the bowl by hand or for 1 minute with an electric beater, until the dough is stiff and leaves the sides of the bowl. Turn out onto a floured board and knead for at least 7 minutes. You may have to add a bit more flour to the dough if it is sticky. Knead dough until it is smooth and elastic and blisters appear. Place into a clean, large well-buttered bowl, cover, and let rise in a warm place for 1–1½ hours, or until doubled in bulk. Drain raisins, place with crushed almonds into a plastic bag, and add ½ cup of flour. Shake well. Add to the dough and knead well until raisins and almonds are well distributed. Divide dough into 6 parts. Three parts should be larger and three smaller. Roll the larger three parts into three long ropes. Pinch the first three ropes together and braid them. Then roll the smaller three parts into ropes and braid them together. Brush the larger braid with beaten egg yolk and milk. Place the smaller braid on top and press down firmly. Place into a well-buttered jelly roll pan. Cover and let rise for about 35 minutes. Preheat oven to 350°. Brush with beaten egg yolks and milk and sprinkle with sliced almonds. Bake in a preheated 350° oven for 1 hour to 1 hour and 15 minutes, or until a cake tester comes out clean and the braid is golden brown. Remove braid from oven and immediately sprinkle it with sugar. Cool completely, cover, and let stand overnight before slicing.

CORNISH GAME HENS WITH RICE STUFFING
serves 6–8

6 cornish game hens or very small frying chickens	¼ tsp pepper
Salt and pepper to taste	¼ tsp ground nutmeg
2 cups long grain rice	¼ tsp sage
⅔ cup red burgundy wine	¼ tsp mace
2 tsp sugar	1 cup toasted almonds, slivered and blanched
1 tsp salt	¼ cup melted butter

Wash hens, pat dry with paper towels, and sprinkle with salt and pepper on the inside and outside. Set aside. Cook rice as directed on the package. The rice should be fluffy and well cooked. Add the burgundy, sugar, salt, and all other seasonings. Mix well. Add almonds and toss lightly. Stuff hens with the mixture. Cover the openings with a piece of foil. Place into a well-buttered baking pan. Brush hens with melted butter and cover pan with foil. Bake in a 375° oven for 35 minutes, uncover the pan, brush hens with the wine sauce and bake for 1 hour longer, basting occasionally with the wine sauce. Remove foil and serve with a salad, glazed chestnuts and cranberries.

Wine Sauce

½ cup red burgundy wine
4 Tbls butter or margarine
2 tsp lemon juice
2 Tbls dark brown sugar

In a small saucepan combine burgundy, melted butter, lemon juice, and brown sugar. Stir until well blended and sugar has melted. Baste the hens with the sauce after 35 minutes of baking.

Note: If some stuffing is left over, place around the hens in the baking pan during the last 15–20 minutes of baking.

HOLIDAY SAVORIES
serves 6

¼	pound salt pork, cut into ¼" cubes	½	tsp mace
3¼	cups water	½	tsp sage
2½	pounds lean pork, cut into 1" cubes	1	tsp salt
2	bay leaves	¼	tsp pepper
1	small onion, peeled but left whole and stuck with 2 cloves	½	cup bacon drippings

Soak salt pork cubes in 2 cups water for 2–3 hours. Drain and pat dry. Place pork and salt pork into a pot, and add the remaining 1¼ cups water, bay leaves, onion, and seasonings. Bring to a boil, reduce heat, and cook over low heat, stirring frequently, until water has evaporated and the meat is very tender—about 2½–3 hours. Remove bay leaves and onion. Cool slightly. While meat is still warm place onto a cutting board and mince with a cleaver or a large knife. Add more salt or pepper to taste. Place the minced meat into 2–3 small bowls and pack down firmly. Pour bacon fat on the meat and refrigerate. Before serving take out of the refrigerator and let stand for about ½–¾ hour. Serve with thinly sliced pumpernickel or rye bread.

HOLIDAY BEAN POT
serves 8–10

6	Tbls bacon drippings	½	cup wine vinegar, or less to taste
3	large onions, diced	3	Tbls brown sugar
2	tsp paprika	1	cup water
8	cups cooked Great Northern Beans	½	tsp salt
12	crumpled bay leaves	¼	tsp pepper

Butter a 2½ quart clay pot well and sprinkle generously with seasoned bread crumbs. In a large skillet sauté onions in the bacon drippings until limp and transparent. Add paprika and stir well. Divide beans into 4 parts and onions into 3 parts. Place a layer of beans into the pot, then a layer of sautéed onions. Sprinkle with some of the crumpled bay leaves.

Mix vinegar, sugar, water, salt, and pepper together. Pour a little over the layers of beans and onions. Reserve some liquid for the top layer. Keep layering beans, onions, and bay leaves, finishing with the beans. Pour remaining liquid over the beans. Cover pot with foil, then seal into a double sheet of foil. Bake in a 325° oven for 3 hours. Serve hot with meat or poultry, or as a main dish with a green salad.

ROASTED SUCKLING PIG
serves 10–12

8–10	pound dressed suckling pig		1	large onion, thinly sliced
3–4	quarts boiling water		2	carrots, sliced
1	Tbls salt		2	celery stalks, sliced
1	tsp pepper		½	cup dry sherry
	Stuffing (see recipe below)		½	cup Slivovitz (plum brandy)
¼	pound soft unsalted butter			
16-ounce	jar purple plums in heavy syrup			
16-ounce	jar spiced apple rings			for garnish

Preheat oven to 450°. Place cleaned and dressed suckling pig into a large, deep pan. Pour boiling water over it. (Be careful not to scald yourself!) Remove pig from water and place onto a thick layer of paper towels. Drain well and pat dry on the inside and the outside. Sprinkle all over with salt and pepper. Stuff the cavity, and using skewers and string, lace the opening together. Brush the entire surface of the pig generously with soft butter. Stretch the forefeet forward and the hind feet backward and tie the feet together with a string. Insert a small apple or potato into the mouth. Cover the ears and tail with foil. Place the onion, carrots, and celery into the bottom of a large pan. Pour sherry over the vegetables. Place pig onto the vegetables and bake in 450° oven for 20 minutes. Reduce heat to 325°. Insert a meat thermometer into the thickest part of the thigh and bake until the thermometer reaches 185°, or about 30 minutes per pound. Baste often with Slivovitz and the pan drippings. Serve whole on a large platter with a raw apple in the mouth and surrounded by hot purple plums and spiced apple rings.

Stuffing

1 large onion, finely chopped	½ tsp basil
½ cup butter	1 Tbls dill, minced
5 cups seasoned crouton bread stuffing	2 large apples, grated
Salt and pepper to taste	½ cup Slivovitz
½ tsp sage	2 eggs well beaten

In a large skillet sauté the onion in butter until pale golden. Place bread stuffing into a large bowl, add the sautéed onion and all other ingredients and toss together lightly. Use as directed.

POTICA
Christmas Nut Roll
makes 2 nut rolls

1 package granulated yeast plus 1 teaspoon	½ cup sugar
	⅓ cup unsalted butter
½ cup lukewarm water	1 tsp salt
4 ½ cups all-purpose unbleached flour	2 eggs plus 1 yolk
1 cup milk	2 yolks beaten with 1 Tbls cream

Preheat oven to 350° before baking. Butter a jelly roll pan well and sprinkle generously with flour. In a small bowl combine yeast with lukewarm water. Stir and set aside for 3–4 minutes. In a large bowl or the bowl of a stand-up beater combine 2 cups flour and the yeast. In a saucepan heat together milk, sugar, butter, and salt, stirring constantly until lukewarm and the butter has melted. Add to the flour and yeast mixture. Beat at low speed for about 1 ½ minutes. Add eggs and the yolk and the remaining flour. Knead with a bread hook, scraping down the sides of the bowl from time to time with a spatula, for about 2–3 minutes or until the dough leaves the sides of the bowl. Turn the dough onto a lightly floured board; knead for about 3 minutes until dough is smooth and elastic. Place into a well-buttered bowl. Turn the dough over once in the bowl. Cover and let rise in a warm place (about 80°—something like the top of a cooled stove), for about 1 hour or until doubled in bulk.
Divide the dough into two parts. On a floured surface roll out each piece of dough into a 15" × 23" rectangle. Spread each rectangle with half of the walnut filling and roll up into a loose roll. Pinch the ends together and seal along the seams. Twist each

roll into a horseshoe shape and place in the jelly roll pan. Cover and let rise for 40–45 minutes. Bake in a preheated 350° oven for 20 minutes. Brush with the beaten yolks and bake for 20 minutes longer. Cool for 15 minutes and frost with the sugar icing. Sprinkle generously with coarsely chopped walnuts.

Filling

½ cup honey
1 cup light brown sugar
6 Tbls unsalted butter
½ cup light cream
½ tsp cinnamon

3 ½ cups ground walnuts
½ cup chopped white raisins
2 eggs, well-beaten
1 tsp orange rind, grated
1 tsp lemon rind, grated

In a saucepan combine honey, sugar, butter, and cream. Bring to a boil, reduce heat, and stirring continuously, simmer for 2–3 minutes. Add cinnamon, walnuts, and raisins; mix well. Cool to lukewarm. Add the beaten eggs and orange and lemon rinds and blend well. Cool completely before using. Divide in two parts for the two rolls.

Icing

2 cups powdered vanilla sugar (see page 37)
½ tsp cinnamon

¼–⅓ cup milk
1 cup coarsely chopped walnuts

Mix sugar and cinnamon with just enough milk to make a thick but spreadable paste. Frost the two rolls with the sugar icing and sprinkle with chopped walnuts.

ROASTED BELL PEPPERS

serves 8–10

3 green bell peppers
3 red bell peppers
   Salt and finely ground white pepper
   to taste

⅔ cup olive oil
*3 cloves crushed garlic

Preheat oven to 375°. Wash peppers and pat dry with paper towel. Place upright onto a jelly roll pan. Bake in preheated 375° oven for about 25–30 minutes, or until the peppers just begin to brown. Remove from oven, cool slightly, and peel off the skin with a sharp knife while still warm. Cut peppers in half, remove seeds, and slice into ¼″ long strips. Sprinkle the strips with salt and white pepper to taste. While peppers are baking, combine olive oil and crushed garlic and set aside. Place the pepper strips (alternating green and red) into a salad bowl and strain olive oil through a fine strainer over the peppers. Refrigerate overnight. Let stand for 1 hour at room temperature before serving.

*To crush garlic

Peel off skin, place garlic cloves onto a cutting board, place a metal spatula onto a clove and hit spatula with heel of your hand, crushing the garlic.

ALMOND AND PIGNOLI (PINENUT) MACAROONS

makes about 2–2 ½ dozen

2 egg whites
⅛ tsp cream of tartar
⅔ cup powdered sugar
⅓ cup granulated sugar
¼ tsp almond extract

1 ½ cups finely ground, blanched toasted almonds
2 cups pine nuts, slightly toasted
½ cup or more granulated sugar

Preheat oven to 350°. Beat egg whites with a pinch of cream of tartar in a very clean bowl* with an electric beater until foamy.

*Use glass or stainless steel bowl.

333

Add sugar a few tablespoons at a time, beating well after each addition. Then add almond extract and beat until egg whites are very stiff. Gently fold in almonds. Sprinkle the pine nuts onto wax paper then drop the egg white–almond mixture by a teaspoon onto the pine nuts. Sprinkle tops of the meringues with the remaining pine nuts and granulated sugar. Butter a cookie sheet and sprinkle with flour. Scoop up each meringue with a metal spatula and gently transfer onto the cookie sheet. Bake in a preheated 350° oven for 15 minutes or until golden brown. Cool then store in an air-tight container. For a gift, place into a glass jar with a tight cover.

SATOU DE SMEURA
Raspberry Chateaux
serves 6

6 egg yolks
⅔ cup sugar
Grated rind of 1 large lemon

*½ cup raspberry juice
1 cup sweet white wine (Muscatel or white port)

Place the yolks and sugar into top of a glass double boiler. Set over barely simmering water. Beat with an electric hand beater or rotary beater until the eggs begin to thicken—about 10 minutes. Add lemon rind and continue beating at low speed for an additional 5–7 minutes or until the mixture is very thick. Do not let the water boil and beat steadily at the same speed.

*To make raspberry juice

Press 1 cup fresh or defrosted raspberries through a fine sieve. Measure out ½ cup and set aside. In a small saucepan bring white wine to a boil. Pour in a steady stream into the yolk mixture. Continue beating for about 5 minutes. Place top of double boiler on direct medium heat and beat for about 5–6 minutes, without letting the mixture boil, until it is very thick. Heat the raspberry syrup and quickly fold into the egg mixture, beating once, just to create a red swirl. Pour into 6 serving dishes and serve with lady fingers or vanilla cookies.

QUAIL WITH CURRANT RICE

serves 6

This is a festive recipe served during holidays, especially for Christmas and New Year.

6 dressed quail, weighing about ¾–1 pound each	1 large onion, minced
2 tsp salt	2 cups long grain rice
¼ tsp finely ground white pepper	4 cups water
2 tsp fresh minced basil or 1 tsp dry basil	1 cup currants soaked in
2 cloves garlic, mashed	1 cup sweet red wine (Marsala or Madeira)
¾ cup unsalted clarified butter (see page 37)	½ cup toasted pine nuts

Wash and dry the quail. Sprinkle on inside and outside with 1 teaspoon salt, white pepper, and basil. Rub the birds on the inside with garlic. In a large, heavy pot heat 5 tablespoons butter. Brown quail, 2–3 at a time, turning them often with tongs, until the birds are evenly brown on all sides. Remove from pot onto a heated platter and keep warm in a 150° oven. Add the remaining butter and onion to the pot where quail were browned. Sauté onion, stirring often until pale golden in color. Add rice and cook for about 3–4 minutes, stirring continuously, until rice begins to turn yellow. Add water and the remaining teaspoon of salt. Bring to a boil, reduce heat, stir once, cover, and cook over low heat for about 10 minutes. While rice is simmering soak currants in wine and add to the rice. Mix well. Place quail on top of the rice, cover pot, and place into a 375° oven. Bake for about 30–35 minutes or until all liquid has been absorbed by the rice and the birds are tender. To test for doneness, pierce the thigh of one bird with a sharp knife. If the juice is pale yellow in color, the birds are done. Place quail onto a large heated platter. Cover to keep warm. Fluff up the rice and bake for an additional 5–7 minutes. Surround quail with the rice and sprinkle rice with toasted pine nuts. Serve immediately.

HOLIDAY SWEETS
makes about 12–14 pieces

5 cups macaroon cookie crumbs
1 cup seedless raspberry preserves
½ cup dark, pungent rum

⅔ cup candied orange peel, minced
1 cup coarsely ground roasted pistachio nuts

In a bowl combine 4 cups macaroon crumbs, preserves, rum, and orange peel. Knead into a smooth paste. Add more crumbs if the mixture seems to be too damp and sticky. Spread the remaining crumbs on wax paper and shape the mixture into a 2-inch thick roll. Cut into 2-inch long pieces. Roll each piece into the pistachio nuts and place on a serving plate.

FISH STUFFED WITH NUTS
serves 6

1 cup roasted and coarsely ground hazelnuts
1 cup cooked rice
½ cup olive oil
1 medium onion, finely chopped
½ minced jalapeno or chili pepper
  Salt to taste
2 Tbls lemon juice

1 3–3 ½ pound bass, carp, scrod, or pike, cleaned but with head and tail left on
¼ tsp salt
¼ tsp basil
¼ tsp rosemary
¼ cup lemon juice

In a bowl combine hazelnuts and rice. Set aside. In a skillet sauté onion and pepper in 3 tablespoons oil until pale golden. Cool. Add salt to taste and lemon juice. Mix onions with the nuts and rice. Wash fish and pat dry with paper towels. Sprinkle inside with salt, basil, and rosemary. Stuff fish with the nut mixture and close opening with skewers. Pour 2 tablespoons oil into a long baking dish large enough for the fish. Place fish into the baking pan. Pour the remaining oil over the fish and bake in a 350° oven for 30 minutes. Pour lemon juice over the fish and bake for an additional 10–15 minutes or until fish flakes easily. Serve on a heated platter with the pan juices and white rice.

Wines Along the Danube

TIMES ALONG THE DANUBE

By the time of its Golden Age, Greece had introduced commercially organized wine-making to its northern neighbors. Thracia—now a part of Bulgaria—became so well-versed in this field that Homer celebrated its wine in the *Iliad*. But Grecian viticulture was not confined only to the Balkan region; it diffused sporadically to reach as far north as Austria (Carnunum).

Only with the rise of the Roman Empire, however, were the arts of viticulture and wine-making systematically cultivated in all of the Danubian countries. For wherever the Romans spread their civilizing influence, they also thoroughly taught their knowledge of vines and wines—a fact attested by numerous artifacts. The Wine Museum at Speyer (Germany), for example, displays a local golden wine made over 1600 years ago.

This wine would not be acceptable by modern standards, even in a slightly less aged form, but the Romans laid the foundations of the arts associated with wine that wine-growers and makers along the Danube practice and try to improve to this day.

VINES ALONG THE DANUBE

In deference to the sheer variety of vines cultivated in Danubian countries, this section examines only the truly ubiquitous vines of the region.

White
MUSCAT OTTONEL
This resilient vine bears medium-sized grapes whose ripe flavor and aroma carry through to its finished wines. The dessert wines it makes—sweet, light, and scented—are particularly popular.

RHINERIESLING

This Germanic vine buds and ripens late (early November), needing every hour of sunshine during the growing season. It grows best in native conditions on the Rhine and Moselle, where it makes some of the finest white wines in the world. Though prolific in other regions, the resulting wines tend to be a little "flabby": dull and unbalanced in acidity.

SILVANER

This early ripening vine is popular due to its easy growth and disease resistance. Though it is losing ground to new varieties, it makes light, pleasant, and refreshing wines.

WÄLSCHRIESLING

This French vine is more extensively planted in central Europe than *Rhineriesling*, whose flavor and balance it shares. Though it does not reach the same heights attained by its German cousin, its wines are nonetheless excellent.

Red

KADARKA

Named after the ancient Albanian town of Skardarka, where it is supposed to have originated, this vine is the characteristic red-grape vine of the Danubian countries. It grows best in the former Yugoslavia and Hungary, however, where it is one of the varieties that produces the legendary Bull's Blood of Eger. Generally *Kadarka* grapes produce deep-colored, full-bodied, and tannic wines.

PINOT NOIR (SPÄTBURGUNDER in Germany)

This classic French noble vine of fragile grapes is planted extensively in almost every Danubian country, though not always producing wines with the unmistakable Pinot subtle bouquet and flavor. German Pinot Noirs, for example, have traditionally been mediocre; however, recent breakthroughs—lower yields, higher must weight and tannin levels— have allowed the production of some truly fine red wines.

WINES ALONG THE DANUBE

Producing approximately 37 million hectoliters per year, the Danubian countries enjoy a wealth of unique and attractive wines—a wealth that far exceeds the constraints of this chapter. Recommendations are therefore based not only on the quality and variety of the wines, but also on their availability as exports.

Germany (96,000 hectares)
German viticulture occurs in thirteen legislated regions, the most famous of which are Baden, Franken, Rheingau, Rheinhessen, and Pfalz. White wines represent eighty-seven percent of wine production, twenty-one percent of which is Rhineriesling.

KLINGELBERGER (Dry, White)
A Riesling from the Ortenau district of Baden, this wine is a powerful variation on the traditional Riesling. It is spicy and full-flavored with a highly refined, flowery bouquet.

MARKGRÄFLER NOBLING (Dry, White)
The Nobling, a cross between Silvaner and Gutedel, is a recent variety of the Staatliches Weinbau. Grown almost exclusively in Markgräfer vineyards, it makes fruity and complex wine of a sprightly acidity and a delicate, fragrant bouquet.

FRANKENER SILVANER (Dry, White)
The Silvaner is often used as a workhorse for dull products, but finds its greatest expression in Franken, where it makes distinctly dry wines with a smoky aroma. These wines can be reminiscent of fine Chablis, or even opulent with exotic fruit notes.

Austria (47,000 hectares)
There are four wine-growing regions: Lower Austria, Burgenland, Styria, and Vienna. White wines account for eighty-nine percent of the country's production, one-quarter of which stems from Grüner Veltliner. These wines almost exclusively contain between 11.5 and 12.5 percent alcohol.

GUMPOLDSKIRCHEN (Sweetish, White)
If not the finest Austria has to offer, this wine is at least the most recognizable. Made from Spätrot and Rotgipfler grapes, it is fresh and full-flavored (fruity); and though alcoholically strong, it maintains a refreshingly balanced acidity.

WACHAU GRÜNER VELTLINER (*Dry, White*)
This light-bodied wine distinguishes itself with a delicate but pronounced flavor and aroma, as well as with the small quantity of carbon dioxide it contains. Though not in the category of a sparkling wine, it nonetheless causes a faint prickle on the tongue. Like most Austrian wines, it is best when consumed young.

The Czech Republic (15,070 hectares)
Its vineyards are strictly limited to the areas of Melnik (Bohemia) and Moravia, which make only a limited quantity of wine (less than one million hl.) annually. The Republic thus imports the vast majority of its wine. Though its exports are difficult to find, the best from Moravia—fresh and fruity varietal wines—are worth searching out.

MORAVIAN RED, HUSTPEA-HODONIN REGION (Dry, Pink-Red, 11%)
Sharply tart with a racy edge, this light-bodied wine makes an immediate impression on the palate—especially complemented by a citrus and berry bouquet, laced with an herbal accent.

Slovakia (30,600 hectares)
Though slightly more prolific than its neighbor, Slovakia still imports far more wine than it exports. Its native wine production is concentrated around the towns of Modra & Pezinok, and consists of mostly white wines. One interesting exception is the 'Tokaji' district on the border of Hungary, which makes red wines in that tradition.

HUBERT (*Dry, White*)
Since 1825 this sparkling wine has been made at Seved from local vines. Light and effervescent, it distinguishes itself with its balanced, full flavor.

Hungary (200,000 hectares)
Hungarian wines have been renowned for their excellence for centuries. The country's viticulture occurs in fourteen wine-making districts, the most substantial being Eger, Szekszárd, Tokaj-Hegyala, Badascony, and Matraaljai. In contrast to Upper Danubian countries, Hungary's red wines account for thirty percent of its total production.

EGRI BIKAVÉR (*Dry, Dark Red*)
More commonly known as "Bull's Blood," this tangy wine is known

the world over for its full flavor and robustness. It originates from the Eger region and consists of Kekfrankos grapes mixed with Cabernet, Blue Portuguese, and Merlot.

The legend of Bull's Blood dates from 1552, when the fortress of Eger, defended by István Dobó and his men, was besieged by the overwhelming forces of the Turkish Army under Ali Pasha. The legend holds that the Hungarian men, having been served the wine by their women, gained strength from it and rushed out to do battle. The Ali Pasha, seeing their beards soaked in red, believed them to have drunk bull's blood. He subsequently withdrew, and the fortress of Egri remained unconquered.

SZEKSZÁRDI BIKAVÉR (Sweet, Red)
One of the most famous wines from the Szekszárd region, it is made from Kekfrankos, Kadarka, and Cabernet grapes. This deep, full-bodied wine possesses a spicy and pleasant fragrance.

TOKAJI ASZÚ ESSENCIA (Sweet, White)
This rich, full-bodied wine is the hallmark white wine of the Tokaj region. Sweet with a dry finish and blessed with an incomparable aroma, it is known as "Vinum Regnum, Rex Vinorum" ("The Wine of Kings, the King of Wines")—an appellate given, perhaps, in light of Russian Tsars who employed Cossacks to ensure the safe arrival of the wine to the cellars of Saint Petersburg.

The Former Republic of Yugoslavia (280,000 hectares total)
Given the amount of destruction in the region in the last decade, it is almost impossible to give accurate estimates regarding its wine industry. Tentatively speaking, its annual wine production averages 6.3 million hectoliters with four times as much white wine produced as red.

Croatia (65,000 hectares)
Croatia's viticulture is comprised of eleven regions, the most prolific being Plesivica, Istra, Dalmatinska Zagora, and Moslavina. Due to its higher median temperature, thirty-two percent of its total wine production is red (with one percent rose).

PLAVAC (Sweet, Dark Red)
This strong, full wine is made of Dingač and Postup, both late-picked, sun-dried grapes from Dalmatinska Zagora.

POŠIP (Dry, White)
Smooth with a high extract, this aromatic wine is produced from Pošip grapes (Furmint) with Marastina and lesser amounts of other local varieties.

Macedonia (32,000 Hectares)
Betraying the viticultural influence of the Greeks, Macedonia's most important production occurs on the border of Greece, in the valley of the Vardar River. Though two-thirds of its harvest consists of table grapes, there are some quality Macedonian wines to be found.

KRATOŠIJA (Dry, Dark-Red)
Possessing a distinctive taste and aroma, this wine is made from native Vranac & Kratošija. Its smooth, full body is best tasted immediately.

Serbia (97,000 hectares)
The wine-growing areas of Serbia are Smederevo (on the outskirts of Belgrade), Župa, and Timok. Approximately seventy percent of its wine is of the white variety.

VLASOTINAČKA PLEMENKA (Dry, White)
The native vines, Prokupac and Plovdina, combine to make this pleasant, fragrant wine. Traditionally, it is "much appreciated by those who suffer from hyper-acidity."

ŽUPSKA RUŽICA (Dry, Rose, 13%)
This light-bodied wine, made from Prokupac grapes, boasts a full flavor and a rich, fragrant bouquet.

Slovenia (23, 000 hectares)
The country's wine regions are the Drava banks, Slava banks, Primorsko-Kras, and Slovenian Istria.

CVIČEK (*Sweet, Ruby*)
Made from Zamenta crnina, Rot Portugieser, and Modra Frankinja grapes, this light wine possesses a low alcohol content. It is a regional specialty, matured in the cellars of the former Cisternian monastery at Kostajevica and in the castle at Breziče.

LJOTMER WÄLSCHRIESLING (*Dry, White*)
This light, well-balanced wine has been world-renowned since the days of the Hapsburg Empire (then Luttenberger).

Vojvodina (25,000 hectares)
This small republic possesses three wine-districts: Fruska Gora, Suboticka Pescara, and Banat.

BERMET (Sweet, Red)
Made since the 18th century, *Bermet* is a light, aromatic, and full-flavored type of fortified Vermouth. It is based on Gamay and Pinot Noir flavored with wormwood, sugar, and Fruškogorski Biser, and makes a perfect aperitif.

BANATASKI RIZLING (Dry, White)
Produced from Rheinriesling, this well-balanced, fruity wine holds its own with Ljotmer, to which it is very similar.

Romania (300,000 hectares)
Romanian vineyards fall into eight regions, the most prolific of which are Dragasani and Arges, Transylvania, Cotnari, and Dobrudja.

GRASĂ DE COTNARI (Sweetish, White)
The best Romanian white wine, *Grasă* pleases with a deep flavor and aroma. Made in the Tokaji-style, this wine is a blend of Grasă, Fetească, and Frîncuşă (each 30%) rounded off with Tamiioasa (10%).

PERLA (Semi-sweet, White)
A pleasant wine that fulfills the Romanian claim that it combines the "aroma of Muscat, the acidity of (Waelsch) Riesling, and the finesse of Fetească." A blend of the aforementioned grapes, it is a regional specialty of Transylvania.

Bulgaria (224,000 hectares)
This Balkan country boasts four regions—Shuren, Suhindol, Haskovo, and Sungulare Valley—which produce primarily dry, red wine.

MAVROOD (Dry, Red, 13%)
Made exclusively in the Assenovgrad region, this deep-colored wine recommends itself with a rich bouquet and dense, tannic taste. It is a

"controliran" wine—a label the Bulgarian government confers on only the country's finest wines.

SUNGULARE MUSKAT (Dry, White, 11.5%)

This light and fruity wine is a four-to-one mixture: four parts large, white "Bulgar" grapes and one part aromatic, green "Egyptian Muscat' grapes. It is also an exclusive "controliran" label.

TRAKIYA (Dry, Red, 12%)

Made from Cabernet Sauvignon grapes, it is a full-bodied, full bouquet wine. It is imported in the USA by Monsieur Henri Wines, Ltd. (White Plains, NY).

Index

351

352

356

Veal, *(cont.)*
 Roast, Karlsbad, 128
 Roast Rack, with Tarragon Butter
  Imperial, 84
 Rolls, 229
 Salad, 115
 Sauerkraut Stew, 124
 Scallopine with Mushroom Purée, 262
 Shish Kebab, 225
 Stuffed Breast, 26–27
 Stuffed Breast, with Buttered Chestnuts,
  85–86
 Stuffed Breast, Viennese, 88
 Viennese Stuffed Breast, 88
 Yugoslavian Meat Pie, 228
Vegetable(s):
 Baked Fish with, 287
 Cheese Soup, 280
 Chicken with, 222
 Fish and, 219
 Lamb Chop and Vegetable Casserole,
  230–31
 Mixed, 217
 Noodles with, 232
 Pancake, 134
 Ulm Style, 18
 See also specific vegetables
Venison, 51
Veona's Honey Cheese, 271
Vermicelli:
 Rice with, 298
 See also Noodles
Very Fancy Ginger Cake, 315
Viennese cuisine, 51–55
Viennese Stuffed Breast of Veal, 88
Vinaigrette Sauce, 79

Walnut(s):
 Arnaut Candy, 235
 Christmas Nut Roll, 331–32

Crêpes a la Budapest, 200
Custard Cake, 236–37
Filling, I, 141
Filling, II, 141
Hungarian Nut Cake, 192–93
Layered Green Beans, 285
Lemon-Nut Crescent, 238
Noodle Pudding with Cherries and
 Nuts, 135–36
Nut Squares, 137–38
Spinach Zagora Style, 283
Strudel, 317–18
Torte, 95–96
Vár Nut Torte, 201
Watercress:
 Potatoes with, 89
Weisswurst, 33
Westphalian Ham Cornucopias, 57
Wheat and Cornmeal Bread, 266–67
Weiner Schnitzel, 51, 87
Wilted Spinach Salad, 281
Wine:
 Sauce, 328
 Soup, 65

Yellowtail:
 Stuffed Baked, 256
Young Lamb Boiled in Milk, 230
Yugoslavian Chicken, 221
Yugoslavian cuisine, 204–06
Yugoslavian Meat Pie, 228

Zucchini:
 Hongroise, 166
 Lamb Soup with, 214
 Noodles with Vegetables, 232
 Purée, 252
 Salads, 250, 282
 Stuffed, 292–93

Other cookbooks of interest from Hippocrene . . .

Taste of Romania, Expanded Edition
Nicolae Klepper
Now updated with a chapter of Romanian-Jewish Recipes!
"A brilliant cultural and culinary history . . . a collection of recipes to be treasured, tested and enjoyed."
—George Lang, owner of Café des Artistes
" . . . dishes like creamy cauliflower soup, sour cream-enriched *mamaliga* (the Romanian polenta), lamb stewed in sauerkraut juice and scallions, and *mititei* (exactly like the ones I tasted so long ago in Bucharest) are simple and appealing ... . Klepper paints a pretty picture of his native country's culinary possibilities."
—Colman Andrews, *Saveur* magazine
A real taste of both Old World and modern Romanian culture. More than 140 recipes, including the specialty dishes of Romania's top chefs, are intermingled with fables, poetry, photos and illustrations in this comprehensive and well-organized guide to Romanian cuisine.
335 pages • 6 x 9 • photos/illustrations • 0-7818-0766-2 • $24.95hc • (462)

Traditional Bulgarian Cooking
Atanas Slavov
This collection of over 125 authentic recipes, the first comprehensive Bulgarian cookbook published in English, spans the range of home cooking: including many stews and hearty soups using lamb or poultry and grilled meats, vegetables and cheese pastries; desserts of sweetmeats rich in sugar and honey, puddings, and dried fruit compotes.
200 pages • 5½ x 8½ • 0-7818-0581-3 • $22.50hc • (681)

The Art of Hungarian Cooking, Revised edition
Paul Pogany Bennett and Velma R. Clark
Whether you crave Chicken Paprika or Apple Strudel, these 222 authentic Hungarian recipes include a vast array of national favorites, from appetizers through desserts. Now updated with a concise guide to Hungarian wines!
225 pages • 5½ x 8½ • 18 b/w drawings • 0-7818-0586-4 • $11.95pb • (686)

Best of Austrian Cuisine
Elisabeth Mayer-Browne
Nearly 200 recipes from Austria's rich cuisine: roasted meats in cream sauces, hearty soups and stews, tasty dumplings, and, of course, the pastries and cakes that remain Vienna's trademark.
224 pages • 5 x 8½ • 0-7818-0526-0 • $11.95pb • (633)

All prices subject to change without prior notice. **To purchase Hippocrene Books** contact your local bookstore, call (718) 454-2366, or write to: HIPPOCRENE BOOKS, 171 Madison Avenue, New York, NY 10016. Please enclose check or money order, adding $5.00 shipping (UPS) for the first book and $.50 for each additional book.